COMPLEMENTATION: ITS MEA

TYPOLOGICAL STUDIES IN LANGUAGE (TSL)

A companion series to the journal "STUDIES IN LANGUAGE"

Honorary Editor: Joseph H. Greenberg
General Editor: T. Givón

Editorial Board:

Volumes in this series will be functionally and typologically oriented, covering specific topics in language by collecting together data from a wide variety of languages and language typologies. The orientation of the volumes will be substantive rather than formal, with the aim of investigating universals of human language via as broadly defined a data base as possible, leaning toward cross-linguistic, diachronic, developmental and live-discourse data. The series is, in spirit as well as in fact, a continuation of the tradition initiated by C. Li *(Word Order and Word Order Change, Subject and Topic, Mechanisms for Syntactic Change)* and continued by T. Givón *(Discourse and Syntax)* and P. Hopper *(Tense and Aspect: Between Semantics and Pragmatics)*.

Volume 10

Evelyn N. Ransom

*Complementation:
Its Meanings and Forms*

COMPLEMENTATION:
ITS MEANINGS AND FORMS

EVELYN N. RANSOM
Eastern Illinois University

JOHN BENJAMINS PUBLISHING COMPANY
Amsterdam/Philadelphia

1986

Library of Congress Cataloging in Publication Data

Ransom, Evelyn N.
  Complementation: its meanings and forms.

(Typological studies in language, ISSN 0167-7373; v. 10)
Bibliography: p.
1. Modality (Linguistics) 2. Grammar, Comparative and general -- Verb phrase. I. Title.
II. Series.
P299.M6R36   1986   415   86-3554
ISBN 90-272-2880-9 (hb.)/90-272-2879-5 (pb.) (European; alk. paper)
ISBN 0-915027-87-9 (hb.)/0-915027-88-7 (pb.) (U.S.; alk. paper)

To my father,
who taught me to enjoy language
and my mother,
who taught me to enjoy

TABLE OF CONTENTS

LIST OF TABLES

Tables

PREFACE

This book is a stage in the evolution of a theory of modality meanings and forms. It covers only complements, but I am already working to extend the analysis to all sentence types (Ransom 1981 and Ransom 1984 in preparation).

There are two questions that this book addresses. Can one find a small, finite set of meanings which systematically underlies the enormous variety of meanings found in complements? And can one make any predictions from this set of meanings about the variety of forms they take? The answer to both questions is yes.

In the fifteen years that this book has been evolving, many people affected its shape. For the early stages, Jerry Morgan, Georgia Green, Howard Maclay, and Kris Lehman offered helpful suggestions about my dissertation, on which this book is based. I am indebted to the works of Lees, Rosenbaum, Ross, R. Lakoff, G. Lakoff, Sadock, Newmeyer, Bresnan, the Kiparskys, Karttunen, Horn, Givón, Hooper, and Thompson for their ideas about complementation, meanings, and forms. For the later stages, I owe much to T. Givón, Sandy Thompson, Joan Bybee, Haj Ross, and Bernard Comrie for their insights into language and their much needed encouragement. I am thankful to all those whose conversations and questions prodded me on, especially to Alice Davison for her suggestions and for playing the devil's advocate. Also, my thanks go to my native consultants for their contributions of data and insights. Eastern Illinois University generously provided me with sabbatical time to prepare this book and a faculty research grant, which made some of the data collection possible. Finally, I want to thank Jeannie Difanis for typing and support, Sue Ann Kendall for her invaluable assistance in editing, and Harriet Gabriel for helping me let go.

CHAPTER I

An Introduction to Complement Meanings and Forms

> ...language-makers, that is ordinary speakers, are not very accurate thinkers. But neither are they devoid of a certain natural logic, and however blurred the outlines may sometimes be, the main general classifications expressed by grammatical forms will always be found to have some logical foundation. (Jespersen 1965: 81)

Complement constructions are as intricate and varied as the patterns on a Persian tapestry, as can be seen from the following examples:

(1)   a.   Marina regrets that she won the game
          b.   It is likely that Marina won the game
          c.   Marina seems to have won the game
          d.   Marti believes Marina to have won the game
          e.   Marti wonders whether Marina won the game
          f.   Marti predicts that Marina will win the game
          g.   Marina wants to win the game
          h.   Marti saw Marina win the game
          i.   Marti told Marina to win the game
          j.   Marina managed to win the game
          k.   It was important for Marina to win the game
          l.   The game was easy for Marina to win
          m. Marina wondered whether to win the game

These examples show a multiplicity of meanings and forms which raise the following questions: Is there a logical foundation underlying these variations as Jespersen suggested? Can one reduce the multiplicity of meanings to a small, finite set of meanings? Can one show a relationship between these meanings and the many forms they take?

In trying to answer these questions, this study will focus on certain types of meanings and forms, while excluding others. First of all, we will look at a type of sentence embedded as a noun phrase subject or object, one which linguists have called by various names: noun clauses, noun complements, predicate complements, and sentential complements.[1] We will not look at simple sentences, adjective clauses, or adverb clauses because, although their meanings and forms are similar, they do not provide the full array found in complement constructions (cf. Ransom 1981 and 1984). We will also not look at any types of sentences embedded as noun phrases but not functioning as subjects or objects, though these too appear to have similar meanings and forms.[2]

While the full gamut of complement forms will be acknowledged, including complementizers, modals, mood, tense, word order, grammatical relations, and the suprasegmentals of pitch, stress, and juncture, we will look primarily at complementizers because they represent a fuller display of meanings and because in most cases they interact in more predictable ways with the meanings analyzed. We will focus on finite and infinitive complementizers rather than gerunds and nominalizations. Although they all seem to represent a similar array of meanings, finite and infinitive complementizers tend to be predictable on the basis of certain meanings while gerunds and nominalizations are not. All truncated infinitives with missing subjects will be assumed to be derived from full sentences, since the motivation for having VP complements in deep structure is eliminated when the majority of these constructions can be predicted on general principles.

The meaning distinctions that contribute to complement meaning will be recognized as the same old elephant that we have been blindly fumbling with since Aristotle: meaning distinctions related to sentence types such as declaratives, interrogatives, and imperatives; speech act types such as statements, predictions, questions, commands, promises; epistemic and deontic modal notions like knowledge, obligation, permission, ability; logical modal notions like truth, necessity, possibility, probability; the negation of all these; and semantic notions like permanent states, changeable states, events, intentional and unintentional acts; and time reference notions like speech time, before speech time, and after speech time. All of these meaning distinctions will be shown to play a part in complement meaning.

In analyzing complement meaning, we will distinguish between *propositional content*, *propositional modality*, and *discourse function*. The term *propositional content* will be used to refer to the lexical and morphological meanings of a sentence, including time reference,[3] and those grammatical meanings that include the notions "subject", "predicate", "object", etc. The term *propositional modality* will be used to refer to certain meanings that represent attitudes about the propositional content. The term *discourse function* will be used to refer to the conventional uses that a sentence can have, its illocutionary forces (cf. Searle 1970 and 1979).

We will look at the literal meanings of a sentence, both simple and complex, as a combination of the meanings of the propositional content (PC), the propositional modalities (PM), and the disourse functions (DF) of the sentence as a whole:

Simple Sentence Meaning = [DF + PM + PC]
Complex Complement Sentence Meaning =
[DF + PM + PC [PM + PC]]

This modular approach allows one to identify similarities and differences in meaning and form that could not previously be compared.

While propositional content and propositional modalities will be treated as belonging to the realm of semantics, discourse functions will be treated as belonging to the realm of pragmatics. It is assumed that a semantic theory of the literal meanings of sentences must be coupled with a pragmatic theory of illocutionary forces or speech acts. Although the present analysis focuses primarily on the literal or semantic aspect of sentence meaning and the ways that it interacts with syntactic forms, some attention is also given to the semantic composition of certain illocutionary forces or speech acts and the ways that these pragmatic meanings affect syntactic forms.

A serious problem in the study of semantics has been the verification of meanings. Many philosophers and linguists believe that the meanings of a proposition can be verified only by establishing a set of logical entailments based on truth values, that is, based on the correspondence between the meaning of the proposition and the real world ('The snow is blue' is true just in case the snow is blue). One of the problems that they have come up against is that propositions involving questions, imperatives, and performatives do not have truth values in the same way as assertions. This is also the case with certain complement meanings.

In order to account for the full range of meanings found in language, one needs to distinguish between the subject matter of logic, which is the relation between language and the real world, and the subject matter of linguistics, which is the relation between language and the users of language. Consequently, the present analysis uses the generally accepted practices of generative transformational linguists in verifying the meanings of a proposition by native speaker judgments about what is acceptable or not, what contradictory or semantically incompatible, what is similar in meaning and what different. Based on these judgments, one can begin to delineate the semantic or pragmatic, rather than logical, entailments of the proposition, that is, how native speakers interpret the proposition, rather than how it relates to the real world.

In this study, we will examine certain complement meanings and the ways that they correlate with certain types of forms. Although English is the primary language of investigation, examples are taken from other languages to show that these modality meanings and their systematic relationship with forms are important candidates for language universals.

Although this analysis is rooted in the concepts of standard generative transformational theory, it has of necessity evolved new concepts, many of which deviate from those held in current favor. In this chapter, in order to prepare for these new concepts, we will trace their development and show why some of the old concepts had to be abandoned.

The Information Modalities

In the late sixties and early seventies, when I was working on complement constructions for my dissertation, I had been impressed with Rosenbaum's (1967) syntactic analysis of complementizer placement rules and the rules used to account for the many variations in word order and grammatical relations. His analysis aroused optimism that one could find order in the way these syntactic forms related to meaning, suggesting that Jespersen was right that a logical foundation could be found.

In pursuing the meaning restrictions on certain types of complements, I first observed that some complements can take stative or nonstative predicates, while others require nonstative:

(2)   a.   Sherry happened to be 21 years old
      b.   Sherry happened to play chess well

(3)   a.   *Sherry managed to be 21 years old
      b.   Sherry managed to play chess well

Although *happen* can take either the stative *be 21 years old* or the nonstative *play chess well*, the verb *manage* can only take the nonstative.

The criteria that G. Lakoff (1970) gave for distinguishing nonstative predicates included the possibility of the predicate taking the progressive aspect and the possibility of the predicate being used as a command. Although all nonstative predicates can be used with a progressive, it became clear that not all nonstative predicates can be used as a command:

(4)   a.   Joe is playing chess well
      b.   Joe is being taken by surprise
      c.   Joe is losing his sense of balance

(5)   a.   Joe, play chess well!
      b.   *Joe, be taken by surprise!
      c.   *Joe, lose your sense of balance

Furthermore, some complements require nonstative predicates with no restriction on their type, while others require only those nonstative predicates that can be used as commands:

(6)   a.   *Sherry watched Joe being 21 years old
      b.   Sherry watched Joe play chess
      c.   Sherry watched Joe being taken by surprise
      d.   Sherry watched Joe lose his sense of balance

(7)   a.   *Sherry forced Joe to be 21 years old
      b.   Sherry forced Joe to play chess
      c.   *Sherry forced Joe to be taken by surprise
      d.   *Sherry forced Joe lose his sense of balance

The complements of *watch* and *force* can only have nonstative predicates, but while the complement of *watch* can have any type of nonstative predicate, that of *force* has to be the type that can be used as a command. Thus two types of nonstative predicates have to be distinguished: one type that involves events or acts of any kind, which I call the *Occurrence* type, and one that involves acts that are controllable by voluntary means, which I have called the *Action* type.[4] The complements which allow both stative and nonstative predicates, I call the *Truth* type.

One last set of restrictions was noted. Some complements require their predicates to have a future time reference and thus to be interpreted as undergoing a change. Consequently these predicates are more likely to be temporary states, events, or acts, but not permanent states, since they usually cannot be interpreted as undergoing change:

(8)   a.   *Sherry predicted that Joe would be an Aries soon
      b.   Sherry predicted that Joe would be taken by surprise
      c.   Sherry predicted that Joe would lose his sense of balance
      e.   Sherry predicted that Joe would play chess well

This type of complement I call the *Future Truth* type.

Thus, on the basis of restrictions on the complement predicate, four types of complements can be distinguished: *Truth*, *Future Truth*, *Occurrence*, and *Action*. Certain of these four types have further restrictions on their propositional content: restrictions on the identity of the complement subject and on the time reference of the complement. There are also restrictions on the types of complement forms. In English, one can predict a finite *that* or *whether* complement with Truth types and an infinitive or *whether to* with Action types. In Basque, one can predict *-elako*, *-ela*, or *-en* for Truth complements, and these contrast with *-teko* in certain Action complements. These restrictions on meaning and form will be discussed in more detail in the next chapter.

In trying to understand the nature of the meaning differences among these four types of complements, I realized that it is not a matter of differences in propositional content, since the same content can be used in all four:

(9) a. TRUTH
         Hal says that Ben plays chess tomorrow
     b. FUTURE TRUTH
         Hal predicts that Ben plays chess tomorrow
     c. OCCURRENCE
         Hal will watch Ben play chess tomorrow
     d. ACTION
         Hal pressured Ben to play chess tomorrow

(10) a. TRUTH
         Ben decided that he'd play chess tomorrow
     b. ACTION
         Ben decided to play chess tomorrow

In each of these sentences, the propositional content of the complement is about Ben's playing chess tomorrow. In (9), the higher predicates differ, but in (10), they are the same, so that the propositional content of both the higher and the lower clause is the same. The differences in the meanings of the complements result not from differences in the propositional content of either the complement or the higher sentence, but rather from differences in the modality meanings of the complement. These modality meanings impose a certain interpretation on the propositional content: the same propositional content could be interpreted as information about the truth of the proposition that someone plays chess tomorrow, or as information about someone performing the act of playing chess tomorrow.

Thus the four meaning types represent types of information: information involving knowledge of the world (the truth or future truth of a proposition or occurrence of an event) or behavior in the world (the performance of an act). These four types of modality meanings, I call the *Information Modalities*.[5] They will be discussed in Chapter II.

The Evaluation Modalities

In the late sixties and early seventies, some important differences in meaning were being observed and related to differences in form. Lees (1960) had noted a distinction between *factive* and *action* nominals. The Kiparskys (1970) had identified a type of *factive* construction whose complement proposition is presupposed to be true regardless of whether the higher predicate is affirmative or negative:

(11) a. I regret that Art left (= Art left)
    b. I don't regret that Art left (= Art left)

These complements are typically set off by *that* complementizers and are usually prohibited from undergoing the kinds of deletions and word order dislocations seen with certain other types of higher predicates.

Karttunen (1971 a, c) had pointed out several infinitive constructions with implications about the truth of the complement proposition. *Implicatives* like *manage* imply the truth of the complement if the higher predicate is affirmative, but imply the falsity of the complement if the higher predicate is negative. *If-verbs* like *force* imply the truth of the complement if the higher predicate is affirmative but give no conclusion if the higher predicate is negative. And *only-if* verbs like *able* imply the truth of the complement only if the higher predicate is negative:

(12) IMPLICATIVES
    a. Art managed to leave (= he left)
    b. Art didn't manage to leave (= he didn't leave)

(13) IF-VERBS
    a. Meg forced Art to leave (= he left)
    b. Meg didn't force Art to leave (= no conclusion)

(14) ONLY IF-VERBS
    a. Art was able to leave (= no conclusion)
    b. Art wasn't able to leave (= he didn't leave)

Although these complement types were identified by Karttunen as having infinitive complementizers, there are also cases of *that* clauses that can have the same types of meaning:

(15) IMPLICATIVES
    a. It happens that Bob left (= he left)
    b. It doesn't happen that Bob left (= he didn't leave)

(16) IF-VERBS
    a. It is certain that Bob left (= he left)
    b. It isn't certain that Bob left (= no conclusion)

(17) ONLY IF-VERBS
    a. It is possible that Bob left (= no conclusion)
    b. It isn't possible that Bob left (= he didn't leave)

Karttunen had included *happen to*, the Subject Raising form of *happen that*, as an implicative, but because of his focus on the infinitive form, he did not include *happen that*, even though it can have the same meaning. Likewise, Karttunen did not notice that there are *that* clauses which correspond to if-verbs and only-if verbs and that these are related to the logicians' categories of *necessary* and *possible*.

Logicians, in their focus on truth values, had dealt with constructions like *be certain* and *be possible*, which take Truth Modality complements associated with *that* complementizers, but they had ignored constructions like *force* and *be able*, which take Action Modality complements associated with *for-to* complementizers. In looking at both types of complements forms and in looking at meanings beyond truth, one can see underlying similarities among these meaning types.

In the affirmative, "necessity" is defined as implying the truth of its argument, but in the negative, its argument has no conclusion, just as with if-verbs:

(18) a. 'It is necessary that S' implies 'S'
     b. It is certain that Helen won (= she won)
     c. Harry forced Helen to win (= she won)

(19) a. 'It is not necessary that S' implies 'possible not S'
     b. It is not certain that Helen won (= she may not have won)
     c. Harry didn't force Helen to win (= she may not have won)

Higher predicates like *certain* and *force* follow the "necessity" definition because when they are affirmative, their complements are interpreted as true, but when negative, their complements are interpreted as meaning "possible not".

"Possibility", in the affirmative, is defined as having no conclusion regarding the truth of its argument, but in the negative, its argument is interpreted as false, just as with only-if verbs:

(20) a. 'It is possible that S' implies not necessary 'S'
       b. It is not possible that Helen won (= she may have won)
       c. Helen is able to win (= she may win)

(21) a. 'It is not possible that S' implies 'necessary not S'
       b. It isn't possible that Helen won (= she didn't win)
       c. Helen isn't able to win (= she won't win)

Higher predicates like *possible* and *be able* follow the "possibility" definition because when affirmative, their complements are interpreted as meaning "not necessary", but when negative, their complements are interpreted as false, meaning "necessary not".

Horn (1972), dealt with both *that* clauses and infinitives, and with truth as well as action meanings. He pointed out a number of higher predicates like the if-verbs that seemed to share properties of logical necessity, and those like the only-if verbs that seemed to share the properties of logical possibilities, some one-sided like 'possible that S' and some two-sided like 'possible S or not S'. He also identified a set of higher predicates that seemed to fall between necessity and possibility, what he called the *mid-scalars*, a group of predicates including *believe, think*, and *suggest*, which do not presuppose or imply the truth of their complement and which take complements that can undergo neg-raising, a rule which is supposed to move a negative from the lower clause into the higher clause.

Hooper and Thompson (1973), and Hooper (1975), pointed out a class of higher predicates that they called *assertives*, which they subdivided into *strong (say)* and *weak (believe)* types. These predicates asserted the truth of the complement rather then presupposing it, and they tended to undergo syntactic variations called "root transformations" (cf. Edmonds 1970) that involved movement of complement elements to a more emphatic position, like VP preposing and participial preposing, or involved a foregrounding interpretation of the complement by parenthetical formation, tag-questions, and neg-raising.

Givón (1980) distinguished between *manipulation* verbs like *force* and *tell to*, *self-inducement* verbs like *manage* and *intend*, and *remote attitude* verbs like *hope*, *decide*, *know*, *think*, and *say*. These three types of verbs were compared on a semantic scale based on the semantic dependence of their complement event or proposition on the influence of an agent in the higher sentence. Highest on the scale were the implicative manipulation and self-inducement verbs (*force* and *manage*), because their agents have the greatest amount of influence over the complement. Lower on the scale were the nonimplicative manipulation and self-inducement verbs (*tell to* and *intend*), because their agents have less influence over the complement. Still lower were the verbs of remote attitutde, representing varying degrees of emotional commitment but little or no influence.

Givón also presented a syntactic scale based on the syntactic dependence of complement forms on the higher sentence. Those complements that lacked a complementizer (*make NP VP*), subject marking (*manage to*), and tense, aspect, or modality marking (*force NP to VP*) were treated as more syntactically dependent on the higher sentence and thus higher on the scale, while those with these markings (*know that*) were treated as more syntactically independent of the higher sentence and thus lower on the scale. Givón gave evidence for a parallel between the semantic scales, claiming that the more semantic dependence a complement had because of a higher agent's influence, the more syntactic dependence its complement form had, as with *make NP VP*.

Thus in the struggle to delineate types of meanings and their relationships to forms, there appeared to be a variety of unrelated meaning types: factives like *regret*, implicatives like *manage*, if-verbs like *force*, only-if verbs like *be able*, necessity like *be certain*, one-sided possibility like *be possible that*, two-sided possibility like *wonder if*, strong assertives like *say*, *claim*, and *predict*, weak assertives or midscalars like *believe*, *suggest*, and *intend*, as well as a cross-category of manipulation verbs, like *force* and *tell to*, self-inducement verbs like *manage* and *intend*, and remote attitude verbs like the assertives.

Because factives, implicatives, if-verbs, and necessity constructions were all defined according to their patterns of truth values when the higher predicate was affirmative and negative, no relationsip could be shown among them. If looked at when the higher predicate is affirmative, a similarity can be seen: the complements of each are interpreted by an audience as being the case, with no alternatives, regardless of whether they deal with truth or action:[6]

(22) a. FACTIVE
          I regret that Bart wrote the book
          (= The speaker presents it as certain that he did)
          *but it's not possible he did
          *but there's no expectation he did
          *but he may not have
          *or not

      b. EPISTEMIC NECESSITY:
          It is certain that Bart wrote the book
          (= The speaker presents it as certain that he did)
          *but it's not possible he did
          *but there's no expectation he did
          *but he may not have
          *or not

      c. IMPLICATIVE:
          Bart managed to write the book
          (= The speaker presents it as certain that he did)
          but there's no expectation he did
          *but it's not possible he did
          *but he may not have
          *or not

      d. IF-VERB:
          I forced Bart to write the book
          (= The speaker presents it as certain that he did)
          *but it's not possible he did
          *but there's no expectation he did
          *but he may not have
          *or not

The present analysis will focus on the similarities between these four constructions by treating the affirmative construction as the prime case and treating
the negative construction as governed by three separate types of narrow-
scope negation, as will be discussed in Chapter V.

  All the complements in (22) are interpreted by the audience as meaning
that the speaker believes that Bart wrote the book, with no alternatives
available. Consequently, conjoined expressions offering alternatives are
interpreted as contradictory. Because of the lack of alternatives, the modality

of these complements is called *Predetermined*. In the factive sentence (22a) and the necessity construction (22b), the complement has a Predetermined Truth Modality, and the propositional content is interpreted as true with no alternatives. In the implicative sentence (22c) and the if-verb sentence in (22d), the complement has a Predetermined Action Modality, and the propositional content is interpreted as a controllable act with no alternatives to its taking place. Thus factives, implicatives or self-inducement verbs, if-verbs or manipulation verbs, and necessity constructions are all shown to have Predetermined complements which are interpreted as being the case.

Another set of relationships can be shown to occur between strong assertives like *say* and *decide*, and weak assertives or midscalars like *believe*, *suggest*, *intend*, and *seem*. In these constructions, the audience interprets the complement as meaning that the speaker, unless otherwise indicated, is not committed to the complement proposition being the case, but presents it as likely or expected, with some alternatives available. Consequently, conjoined expressions offering some alternatives create no contradiction. However, those negating either the possibility or the expectation are interpreted as creating a contradiction, more so for the past oriented Truth constructions in (a) and (b) than in the future oriented Action constructions in (c) and (d):

(23) a. I've decided that Bart wrote the book
          (= The speaker presents it as likely that he did)
           *but it's not possible he did
           *but there's no expectation he did
            but he may not have
           *or not

      b. It seems to me that Bart wrote the book
          (= The speaker presents it as likely that he did)
           *but it's not possible he did
           *but there's no expectation he did
            but he may not have
           *or not

      c. I said for Bart to write the book
          (= The speaker presents it as likely that he will)
           ?but it's not possible he will
           ?but there's no expectation he will
            but he may not
           *or not

    d. Bart intends to write the book
        (= The speaker presents it as likely that he will)
        ?but it's not possible he will
        ?but there's no expectation he will
         but he may not
        *or not

Because these complements are interpreted as expressing a likehood but with alternatives available, they contrast with the Predetermined complements, and their modality is called *Determined*. In the assertive or remote attitude sentences (23a) and (23b), the complement consists of a Determined Truth Modality with the interpretation that the propositional content is likely to be true. In the non-implicative manipulative construction (23c) and the non-implicative self-inducement construction (23d), the complement consists of a Determined Action Modality with the interpretation that the controllable act described by the propositional content is likely to occur.

    A third set of relationships can be seen among remote attitude verbs like *hope*, only-if verbs like *be able* and possibility constructions like *be possible*. In these constructions, the audience interprets the complement proposition as meaning that the speaker, unless otherwise indicated, is not committed to its being the case and presents it as a possible consideration, but with many alternatives available. Consequently, conjoined expressions offering some alternatives, or even contrary expectations, do not create contradictions. However, expressions negating the possibility of alternatives are interpreted as contradictory, especially with the past - oriented Truth constructions in (a) and (b):

(24) a. I hope that Bart wrote the book
        (= The speaker presents it as possible that he did)
        *but it's not possible he did
         but there's no expectation he did
         but he may not have
        *or not

     b. It is possible that Bart wrote the book
        (= the speaker presents it as possible that he did)
        *but it's not possible he did
         but there's no expectation he did
         but he may not have
        *or not

c. I permitted Bart to write the book
    (= The speaker presents it as possible that he will)
     ?but it's not possible he will
       but there's no expectation he will
       but he may not
     ?or not[7]

d. I am able to write the book
    (= The speaker presents it as possible that he will)
     ?but it's not possible I will
       but there's no expectation I will
       but I may not
     ?or not

This type of construction corresponds to Horn's one-sided possibility, since one alternative is treated as possible but with many alternatives available. I call this type of complement an *Undetermined Evaluation*. In (24a), with the remote attitude or assertive predicate, and in (24b), with the possibility predicate, the complement consists of an Undetermined Truth Modality with the interpretation that the propositional content is possibly true. In (24c), with the non-implicative manipulative predicate, and in (24d) with the non-implicative only-if or self-inducement predicate, the complement consists of an Undetermined Action Modality with the interpretation that the propositional content is about the possibility of the controllable act occurring.

Finally, there are higher predicates like *wonder* that take indirect or embedded questions. In these constructions, the audience interprets the complement proposition as meaning that the speaker, unless otherwise indicated, is not committed to its being the case and presents it as possibe or not, with equal alternatives available. Consequently, conjoined expressions offering other than equal alternatives are interpreted as contradictory:[8]

(24.1)a. I wonder whether Bart wrote the book
          (= The speaker presents it as possible or not he did)
           *but it's not possible he did
           ?but there's no expectation he did
           ?but he may not have
           or not

     b. I wonder whether to write the book
         (= The speaker presents it as possible or not he will)
          *but it's not possible I will

> ?but there's no expectation I will
> ?but I may not
>   or not

This type of complement construction is comparable to Horn's two-sided possibility because consideration is given to both alternatives, and they are called *Indeterminate*. In the indirect or embedded question in (24.1a) the complement consists of an Indeterminate Truth Modality with the interpretation that the propositional content may or may not be true. In the indirect or embedded question in (24.1b) the complement consists of an Indeterminate Action Modality with the interpretation that the controllable act may or may not take place.

Looking then at the interpretation of complements embedded under affirmative higher predicates, four levels of meaning can be distinguished: *Predetermined*, *Determined*, *Undetermined*, and *Indeterminate*. These four meanings form a scale for the evaluation of alternatives and are called the *Evaluation Modalities*.[9]

Although English has complement forms that distinguish only two of these four levels (*whether* and *whether to* for Indeterminate and *that* and *for-to* for the other three), in other languages, we find more distinctions. Korean has forms that distinguish all four levels. The complementizer *kes* is used for complements with a Predetermined meaning, as in the complements of verbs like *forget that* and *forget to*. The complementizer *ko* is used for complements with a Determined meaning, as in the complements of verbs like *tell that* and *tell to*. The complementizer *ki* is used for complements with an Undetermined meaning, as in the the complements of verbs like *hope that* and *be easy*. And the complementizer *ci* is used for complements with an Indeterminate meaning, as in the complements of verbs like *wonder whether* or *wonder whether to*.

Further discussion of the meanings and forms associated with the Evaluation Modalities will be found in Chapter III, and an analysis of the effect of higher sentence negation and modality on the meaning of the complement will be found in Chapter V.

The Meanings of the Combined Modalities

From the preceding discussion, one can see the need to distinguish two sets of modality meanings: one set of four Information Modalities of Truth, Future Truth, Occurrence, and Action, which describe information about someone's knowledge or behavior in the world, and a second set of four Evaluation Modalities with a Predetermined, Determined, Undetermined, and Indeterminate meaning, which describe evaluations of alternatives. The next question that was raised was how these two sets of modality meanings were related. Previously, all analyses of modality had assumed a unitary set of modality meanings, but it looked as though these two sets functioned together to form sixteen different combinations of modality meanings:

Predetermined Truth	Predetermined Occurrence
Determined Truth	Determined Occurrence
Undetermined Truth	Undetermined Occurrence
Indeterminate Truth	Indeterminate Occurrence
Predetermined Future Truth	Predetermined Action
Determined Future Truth	Determined Action
Undetermined Future Truth	Undetermined Action
Indeterminate Future Truth	Indeterminate Action

In Table 1, examples of sixteen possible combinations of modalities are given using higher predicates whose complements typically have the specified combination of Information and Evaluation Modalities.

Table 1

Higher Predicates and their Combined Modalities

INFO: EVAL:	TRUTH	FUTURE TRUTH	OCCURRENCE	ACTION
PREDET	regret know(t) acknowledge	anticipate foresee forewarn	watch see(Ø) observe	force know(i) manage
DETER	state believe decide(t)	predict expect prophesy	tend wait about	command promise decide(i)
UNDET	hope(t) possible	want eager	like(i) fun	permit willing
INDET	wonder(w) know(w)	foresee(w)	watch(w)	wonder(wi) know(wi)

(t)=that, (i)=infinitive, (Ø)=null
(w)=whether, (wi)=whether to

The higher predicate *regret* in English, always takes a complement with a Predetermined Truth Modality. The higher predicate *know*, however, can take more than one type of complement: one with a *that* complementizer which has a Predetermined Truth Modality, one with a *whether* complementizer which has an Indeterminate Truth Modality, one with an infinitive complementizer which has a Predetermined Action Modality, and one with a *whether to* complementizer which has an Indeterminate Action Modality.

These sixteen combinations account for a variety of meaning contrasts, and they allow one to see regular patterns of cooccurrence with forms. In Chapter IV, we will discuss in more detail the ways the meanings combine. For now, one can see the patterns of similarities and differences more clearly by contrasting minimal pairs, that is, constructions with the same propositional content but different complement modalities.

First, there are constructions which differ only in their Information Modality:

(25) a. TRUTH: I know that I play chess tomorrow/
          that I am tall
      b. ACTION: I know to play chess tomorrow/
          *to be tall

(26) a. TRUTH: I told Sue that she plays chess tomorrow/
          that she is tall
      b. ACTION: I told Sue to play chess tomorrow
          *to be tall

(27) a. TRUTH: I suggest that Sue plays chess tomorrow/
          that she is tall
      b. ACTION: I suggest that Sue play chess tomorrow/
          *that she be tall

(28) a. TRUTH: I wonder whether Sue plays chess tomorrow/
          whether she is tall
      b. ACTION: I wonder whether to play chess tomorrow/
          *whether to be tall

In each pair of sentences, the only difference in meaning is that the first one is about the truth of the proposition and can take a stative or nonstative complement predicate while the second one is about the performance of an act and requires a nonstative controllable complement predicate. The only difference in form is that the first sentence of each pair has a finite complement while the second one has a nonfinite complement.

Next there are constructions that differ only in the Evaluation Modality of the complement. This meaning contrast can be shown more clearly with minimal pairs, though there are not as many variations of these in English as there are with the preceding type:

(29) a. PREDETERMINED TRUTH
          I know that I play chess tomorrow
      b. INDETERMINATE TRUTH
          I know whether I play chess tomorrow

(30) a. DETERMINED TRUTH
          I told Deb that she plays chess tomorrow
      b. INDETERMINATE TRUTH
          I told Deb whether she plays chess tomorrow

(31) a. PREDETERMINED ACTION
          I remembered to play chess tomorrow
      b. INDETERMINATE ACTION
          I remembered whether to play chess tomorrow

(32) a. DETERMINED ACTION
          I decided to play chess tomorrow
      b. INDETERMINATE ACTION
          I decided whether to play chess tomorrow

In each pair of the sentences, the only difference in meaning is that the first is about the necessity or expectation of the complement proposition being the case, with no or few alternatives available, while the other is about the possibility of the proposition being the case or not, with equal alternatives available. The only difference in form is that the first of each pair has either a *that* or a *for-to* complementizer, while the second one has either a *whether* or a *whether-to* complementizer.

Finally, there are constructions that differ in both the Information and the Evaluation Modalities of the complement, with all else remaining the same:

(33) a. PREDETERMINED TRUTH
          I like (it) that Alice plays chess
      b. UNDETERMINED OCCURRENCE
          I like for Alice to play chess

(34) a. INDETERMINATE TRUTH
         I asked whether Alice played chess
     b. DETERMINED ACTION
         I asked Alice to play chess

With the first pair of sentences, (a) is about the necessity of the complement proposition being true, with no alternatives, while (b) is about the possibility of the complement event occurring, but with alternatives available. In both cases, the higher sentence expresses a positive emotion about the complement, its being true or its occurring. With the second pair of sentences, (a) is about the possibility of the complement proposition being true or not, with equal alternatives available, while (b) is about the expectation of the complement act being performed, with some alternatives available. Both sentences have a higher predicate that describes a linguistic act of requesting, whether requesting behavior or knowledge. The only difference in form with each pair is the complementizers: in the first pair, one has a finite *that* and the other an infinitive; in the second pair, one has a finite *whether* and the other an infinitive.

In order to account for the similarities and differences in meaning among constructions like the ones we have discussed, modality has the be treated not as a unitary meaning, but as a combination of the Information and the Evaluation Modalities. Furthermore, one has to look at these meanings as residing in the complement rather than in the higher predicate, as some linguists have claimed. While certain higher predicates, like *true* and *possible*, contain the same meanings as certain combinations of the modalities, they do not represent them individually, and other higher predicates, like *tell* and *like* do not represent them even in combination. Consequently, complements must be treated as having their own modality meanings, separate from the meanings of their higher predicates, and higher predicates must be treated as having their own meanings and as selecting the kinds of complement modalities compatible with those meanings, just as they select the kinds of subjects and objects they take. Further discussion of the meanings and forms of the combined modalities will be given in Chapter IV.

Higher Sentences and the Complement Modalities

Although higher sentences have their own meanings and forms independent of their complements, they can affect the meanings and forms of their complements. The type of predicate in the higher sentence can have an important effect, as does its time reference and the type of nominal roles it takes. The polarity and modality of the higher sentence also can affect the complement.

First, let us look at some of the basic types of higher predicates. One distinction involves whether the higher predicate is subject or object embedding. Those that are object embedding make predications about animate, usually human, subjects, and will be called *reactions* because they describe a person's reaction to a proposition. Then there are subject embedding predicates which make predications about the subject proposition and will be called *appraisals* because they describe a person's appraisal of a proposition.

These reactions and appraisals can be broken into three semantic classes. One class consists of *emotive* predicates. There are emotive reactions, which involve someone's emotional response to a proposition (*regret, be afraid, hope, desire, like, be willing*), and emotive appraisals, which involve someone's emotional evaluation of a proposition (*be amazing, be hopeful, be desirable*). These higher predicates play an important part in influencing the meaning and forms of complements. It is this class, in combination with a Predetermined Truth complement, that makes up what Karttunen (1971) called *full factives*, which in some languages are treated differently from other Predetermined Truth complements by having a special marker. It is also this class, in combination with an Undetermined complement, that makes up the class of wishes and desires, which are often set off from other constructions by desiderative or optative markers.

A second class consists of *linguistic* predicates. There are linguistic reactions, which involve someone uttering a proposition (*say, predict, command, promise*), and linguistic appraisals, which involve someone's linguistic appraisal of a proposition (*be said, be rumored, be predictable*). Linguistic reactions differ from other types of higher predicates in their ability to imitate the speech situation. These are the predicates that take embedded statements, questions, and commands and can be used performatively as speech acts (cf. Austin 1968, Searle 1970, Ross 1970, and Sadock 1969) like an assertion with a Determined Truth complement, a prediction with a Determined Future Truth complement, a command, request, or suggestion with an unlike-subject Determined Action complement, a promise or agreement with a like-subject Determined Action complement, and permission with an unlike-subject Undetermined Action complement.

Finally, there are cognitive-physical reactions, which involve someone's cognitive or physical response to a proposition (*know, discover, believe, show, wonder, expect, watch, see, force, manage, try, be able, decide, intend*), and cognitive-physical appraisals, which involve someone's cognitive-physical appraisal of a proposition (*be known, be true, be likely, be possible, be necessary, be important, be acceptable, behoove, begin, take place*). These are the predicates which, in combination with a Truth complement, have been called verbs of propositional attitude, and in combination with a Predetermined Occurrence complement, have been called perception verbs (Rogers 1974). Some like *cause* and *make* have been called causatives, and another set like *begin* and *continue* have been called aspectuals (Newmeyer 1969). With a Predetermined Action and Occurrence complement, one frequently finds this type of predicate with the properties of implicatives and if-verbs, and with an Undetermined Action complement, with the properties of only-if verbs.

These syntactic and semantic classes of predicates contribute their own meaning to the meaning of the entire construction, but this meaning still remains separate from the meanings of the complement modalities. A further discussion of these meanings and their effects on complement meanings and forms will be found in Chapter V.

Complement meanings and forms are also affected by the polarity and the modality of the higher sentence. In some cases, negatives, questions, imperatives, modals, and other types of modality constructions, affect only the higher sentence and not the complement, as with *regret* and, by definition, all factives. The same type of effect occurs with predicates like *know whether* or *decide whether* when they occur with an Indeterminate Truth Modality:

(35) a.   He doesn't regret that she left
          (= He doesn't regret it; she left)
     b.   He doesn't know whether she left
          (= He doesn't know; she may or may not have left)
     c.   Does he regret that she left?
          (= Does he regret it; she left)
     d.   Does he know whether she left?
          (= Does he know; she may or may not have left)

In each case, the negation, or the question, affects only the higher sentence and not the complement modality.

Another type of effect of negatives and modalities is one which affects both the higher sentence and its complement. This type occurs with predicates like *manage*, which have been called implicative, and predicates like *be true*, which behave in the same way with respect to these. Furthermore, the same type of effect will be shown to occur with a type of higher predicate that is usually thought of as undergoing negative raising:

(35.1)a. He didn't manage to leave
　　　　　　(= He didn't manage; he didn't leave)
　　　b. He didn't happen to leave
　　　　　　(= It didn't happen; he didn't leave)
　　　c. Did he manage to leave?
　　　　　　(= Did he manage? Did he leave?)
　　　d. Did he happen to leave?
　　　　　　(= Did it happen? Did he leave?)

A third type of effect of negation, but not modality, on the higher sentence is one that affects not only the polarity of the higher predicate and complement, but it also causes the complement modality to shift. Higher predicates like *be certain* or *be necessary* have been noted by logicians as implying the truth of their complement when affirmative, but when negative, as with 'not necessary', they are interpreted as meaning 'possible not'. Thus they shift from an affirmative Predetermined meaning to a negative Undetermined meaning. Parallel with this are cases like *be possible* which shift from an affirmative Undetermined meaning to a negative Predetermined meaning: 'not possible' is said to be equivalent to 'necessary not'. These two types of predicates are comparable to Karttunen's if-verb *force*, which takes an affirmative Predetermined complement when affirmative and a negative Undetermined one when negative, and his only-if verb *be able*, which takes an affirmative Undetermined complement when affirmative but a negative Predetermined one when negative:

(36)　a. AFFIRMATIVE PREDETERMINED ACTION
　　　　　　Frank forced Bell to leave
　　　　　　(= He forced Bell; Bell left)
　　　b. NEGATIVE UNDETERMINED ACTION
　　　　　　(= 'He didn't force Bell; Bell may not have left)

(37)　a. AFFIRMATIVE UNDETERMINED ACTION
　　　　　　Frank was able to leave
　　　　　　(= He may have left)
　　　b. NEGATIVE PREDETERMINED ACTION
　　　　　　Frank wasn't able to leave

(= He wasn't able; he didn't leave)

This treatment of the polarity and modality of the higher sentence and their effect on the complement brings together phenomenon that have not previously been related and provides a systematic analysis for them. A further discussion of this treatment will be given in Chapter V.

Summary: How does Modality Fit into a Grammar?

We have seen a brief summary of evidence that complement constructions consist of a combination of two types of modality meanings, the Information and the Evaluation Modalities, both of which have consequences for the propositional content of the complement and its cooccurrence with different meanings and forms. The next question is how these modality meanings and their semantic and syntactic cooccurrence restrictions fit into a grammar. Let us look at some of the previous attempts to account for certain of these modality meanings.

Within generative-transformational grammar, most attempts to account for meaning have made use of morphemes and their lexical content. Consequently, some linguists have tried to associate modality meanings with the meanings of higher predicates; some have tried to associate modality meanings with forms within the complement itself; and a few have tried to associate modality meanings with the sentence, whether simple or embedded.

First let's look at the attempts to use higher predicates as the carriers of modality meaning. This approach was proposed in the late sixties by a group of linguists working within a generative semantics framework, including Ross (1970), McCawley (1968), Postal, (1970), R. Lakoff (1968), G. Lakoff (1971), and Sadock (1969), among others. They tried to account for the performative or speech act meanings, pointed out by Austin (1968) and Searle (1970), by analyzing the modality meanings of the predicate, as shown in the following sentences:[10]

(38.1)a. Harry said that Shawn had left
     b. Harry told Mary that Shawn had left
     c. Harry state that Shawn had left

(38.2)a. Harry said for Shawn to leave
     b. Harry told Shawn to leave
     c. Harry ordered Shawn to leave

(38.3)a. Harry promised to leave

    b.   Harry agreed to leave
    c.   Harry swore to leave

(38.4)a.   Harry permitted Shawn to leave
    b.   Harry authorized Shawn to leave
    c.   Harry granted Shawn the right to leave

The sentences in (38.1) were said to have declarative complements because they were embedded under 'verbs of saying'. The sentences in (38.2) were said to have an imperative complement because they were embedded under 'verbs of ordering'. Similarly, since the complements in (38.3) were embedded under verbs of promising, they were promises, and since those in (38.4) were embedded under verbs of permitting, they represented permission. Verbs like *tell*, which could take complements with more than one type of Information Modality, were called different verbs. R. Lakoff (1968) called *tell that* a verb of saying and *tell to* verb of ordering.

This higher predicate approach fails to account for evidence of identity based on conjunction reduction and gapping, which can apply to the conjunction of *that* and infinitive clauses as long as the higher predicate is the same (I told him that it was raining and to take his umbrella), but not if the higher predicates are different in any way (*I hear it raining and that he was taking his umbrella). Such an approach would have to treat verbs like *tell* as four different verbs, in order to account for their cooccurrence with *that*, *to*, *whether*, and *whether to* complements.

This approach also has difficulty with nonlinguistic higher predicates like *explain*, which resemble verbs of saying, and those like *pressure*, which resemble verbs of ordering, except that they cannot be used performatively. There were some attempts to deal with nonlinguistic higher predicates, like those of George Lakoff's (1970) in his analysis of *persuade that* as "cause to believe" and *persuade to* as "cause to intend", and Robin Lakoff's (1968) in her analysis of Latin optatives as containing the abstract predicate VEL and potential constructions as containing the abstract predicate POSS.

These attempts to use abstract higher predicates resulted in a proliferation of abstract predicates that could not be applied generally for all verbs. They could not account for the systematic similarities and differences in complement meaning and form, and they could not account for complement constructions, as well as other types of simple and embedded sentences, with the same modality meanings but no higher predicate to attribute the meaning to (The opportunity for him to leave (*be tall) arrived; Leave (*Be tall!);

He excused himself in order to leave (*be tall)). Further arguments will be presented in Chapter VI.

A slightly different type of higher predicate analysis was made by Givón (1980), in which he classified verbs not according to speech act or mood meanings but according to the degree of influence that their agents had over the complement proposition. Highest on the influence scale were verbs like *make* and *force*, which Givón called "manipulative" verbs, and *manage* and *promise*, which he called "self-inducement" verbs. These verbs are just those that take Action complements with controllable predicates and consequently involve influence that is either self-directed (= self-inducement verbs) or other-directed (= manipulative verbs).

Lower on Givón influence scale were emotive verbs like *want* and *hope*, which he felt expressed a lesser degree of influence through an emotional commitment. Lowest on the scale were verbs like *know* and *say*, which he called "epistemic" or "remote attitude" verbs, and which he felt expressed no influence. The emotive and epistemic or remote attitude verbs are just those that typically take Truth, Future Truth, and Occurrence complements. The only time that influence or emotional commitment can be expressed is when the complement proposition can be interpreted as controllable by a self-directed or other-directed agent at a future time. If the complement proposition cannot be interpreted as controllable, then no influence or emotional commitment is possible. Furthermore, when an epistemic or remote attitude predicate takes a complement that can be interpreted as controllable, it can express as much influence or emotional commitment as an emotive higher predicate:

(39) EMOTIVE
    a. I want to quit smoking (= commitment)
    b. I want to be tall (= no commitment)

(40) EPISTEMIC/REMOTE ATTITUDE
    a. I know I will quit smoking (= commitment)
    b. I know I will be tall (= no commitment)

Both (39a) and (40a) express the same degree of emotional commitment, but neither (39b) nor (40b) express any commitment at all.

Although Givón's analysis can deal with non-speech act constructions like *force* and *manage*, it cannot deal with higher predicates that have no agents, like the subject-embedding appraisals *be obligatory* and *behoove*, though these also express influence because they take Action complements requiring a controllability interpretation. His analysis can show the relationship between higher predicates high on the influence scale, like *force* and *make*, which are highest on the scale (Predetermined Action), and *tell to* and *pressure to*, which are a little lower (Determined Action), all of which take an Action Modality complement. However, it cannot show the relationship between, on the one hand, those predicates lower on the scale, like the *emotive regret* and the epistemic *realize*, which both take a Predetermined Truth complement, and on the other hand, the emotive *be afraid that* and the epistemic *believe*, which both take a Determined Truth complement, all of which take a Truth Modality complement. Also, his analysis cannot deal with cases like *tell* and *remember* that can take four types of complement modalities, as signalled by the complementizer *that*, *for-to*, *whether* and *whether to*.

Because Givón's analysis treats the higher predicate as containing the meaning of the complement modalities, his analysis cannot account for the systematic patterns of restrictions on meaning and form. His observation that predicates higher on the influence scale, like *make*, *force*, and *manage*, had more reduced clauses than those lower on the scale, like *know that* or *believe that*, is predictable from the complement modalities and their restrictions: Truth Modality complements take finite complement forms, and Action Modality complements take nonfinite complement forms with subject identity constraints that require deletion through Equi. Furthermore, Givón's analysis cannot account for cases like *watch* (Predetermined Occurrence), which express no influence at all but tend to have reduced complements across languages, which is probably related to the fact that these complements have to have a time reference that is the same as that of their higher predicate.

All of these higher predicate analyses fail to account for the full range of meaning relationsips and their cooccurrences with form. Now let us turn to the complement form analyses. Bresnan (1972: 60) made a strong case for having complementizers represent certain meanings, claiming that they had distinct semantic functions which affect their compatibility with various predicates. She associated certain meanings with the complementizers: definiteness with *that*, subjectivity, intention, and motivation with *for*, and an undetermined meaning with *wh-* complementizers. Although these meanings may be compatible with the modalites that each form occurs with, nevertheless, it will be shown that these complementizers cannot represent any of the modality meanings that we have discussed, either individually or in combination

Langendoen (1968 and 1970) and Postal (1970) both suggested the possibility of using modals in the complement to represent certain modality meanings. However, because the modals represent a limited number of particular combinations of modality meanings, they cannot either fully or unambiguously represent the sixteen modality meanings or their combinations. For example, *may* represents both an Undetermined and an Indeterminate Modality and can stand for a Truth, Future Truth, or Action complement. It overlaps with *can* to represent Undetermined Action meanings.

The same problem holds for mood. Jacobs (1981) tried to use mood to account for certain relationships between modality meanings and complement forms. He proposed that two moods, the indicative and the hypothetical, were basic to English. The indicative mood was associated with tensed (finite) constructions typically having the meaning of a declarative, interrogative, or exclamative sentence type. In the present analysis, these sentence types would be associated with Truth, Future Truth, and Occurrence complements.

The hypothetical mood was associated with tenseless (nonfinite) constructions, but not those derived from subject raising (which were mistakely derived only from indicative structures, though *require to* and others do undergo raising). The meaning of the hypothetical mood was basically irrealis, as found in what Jacobs called "imperative complements", like *tell to*, and future oriented complements, like *hope to*. However, this analysis could not deal with the nonfinite complements of verbs like *be pleased to*, which take a Predetermined Truth complement, those like *watch* or *begin*, which take a Predetermined Occurrence complement, and those like *force* and *manage*, which take a Predetermined Action complement, none of which could be interpreted as irrealis or hypothetical. This analysis cannot characterize the meanings of the sixteen modalities, either alone or in combination, and it cannot account for the systematic relationships between the modalities and their complement forms.

Thus if the modality meanings cannot be represented either by higher predicates or by complement forms such as a complementizers, modals, or moods, where can the meanings be located? No one has proposed the use of the nonsegmental signals associated with the modalities, like word order, grammatical relations, and the suprasegmentals of stress, pause, and juncture. Although these nonsegmentals can be used to signal certain modality meanings, they too would be unable to represent each modality meaning individually or in combination. However, the fact that modality meanings can be signalled by a variety of segmental and nonsegmental contrasts suggests that none of these constrasts should be singled out to represent modality. Rather, modality should be represented independently of the segmental and nonsegmental contrasts.

One analysis that avoids the use of segmental and nonsegmental contrasts to represent modality is that by Katz and Postal (1964). They proposed the use of abstract markers to accompany complements as well as simple sentences: a "Q" marker for questions, an "I" marker for imperatives, but no marker for declaratives:

(41)   a.   I say [he left] --› I say that he left
       b.   I ask [Q he left] --› I ask whether he left
       c.   I command you [I you leave] --› I command you to leave

This approach could allow for the treatment of modalities not only in complements of all types, but also in simple sentences, as well as in adjective an adverb clauses. It would avoid treating verbs like *tell* as more than one verb, since *tell that* would have no marker but *tell to* would have an *I*, and *tell whether* would a *Q*, though it's not clear what *tell whether to* would have. Still this approach cannot account for the individual and combined meanings of the modalities and forms associated with them.

What is needed instead is an abstract representation of each of the Information and Evaluation Modalities individually, yet allowing for their combination. In order for these modalities to be able to influence the choice of propositional content, they must be available before lexical insertion. Consequently, I propose a rule similar to one proposed by Fillmore (1968), where a sentence is said to consist of Propositional Modality (PM) and Propositional Content (PC), and then the Proposition Modality would be written as consisting of the Evaluation Modalities (EM) and the Information Modalities (IM), which would each be broken down into types:

(42)   S --› PM PC
       PM --› EM IM
       EM --› <Predetermined, Determined, Undetermined, Indeter-
                mined>
       IM --› <Truth, Future Truth, Occurrence, Action>
       PC --› NP VP

A further discussion of how these abstract meanings can be represented in the deep structure and how they can be made available to account for the restrictions on propositional content and cooccurrence with different meanings and forms, will be found in the last chapter.

In summary, I have shown how my analysis of modality meanings and their forms developed out of previous linguistic theories and what new ways of dealing with modality meanings are necessary. In spite of the multiplicity of meanings and forms that one sees on the surface tapestry, if one looks at the underlying complement modality meanings, one can find logical patterns, as Jespersen suggested. In Chapter II, we will look at one type of complement meaning: the Information Modalities.

NOTES

1) The use of the word *noun* in *noun clause* and *noun complement* has been avoided by some linguists because of doubts as to whether the complements of verbs like *be glad that, condescend to*, and *tempt someone to* are noun phrase complements, since they cannot be questioned by *what* (cf. Rosenbaum 1967). Nevertheless, in the present analysis, they will be treated as though they were noun phrases, in the same way as the complements of verbs like *regret that, decide to*, and *tell someone to*, which can all be questioned by *what*. Even if it turns out that they have a different syntactic relationship, what is said about their complement modality will still hold true.

In the present analysis the term *complement* is used to include not only finite sentences but also infinitives and gerunds, which the term *clause* traditionally excludes since it refers to finite sentences with subjects (implied or explicit) in the subjective case. Infinitives and gerunds, with or without explicit subjects, will be treated as sentential (contra Montague analyses of them as verb phrases). The absence of an explicit subject will be attributed to deletion of a specified subject on the basis of identity or indefiniteness (contra the Chomsky and Lasnik 1977 analysis of them as unspecified). The present analysis is motivated by the need for a semantic interpretation of the understood subject for reflexive objects and, in some languages, subject agreement on infinitives.

The term *complement* has, unfortunately, been used for various types of postverbal constructions: direct objects, predicate nouns, and predicate adjectives. What's more, the term *subject complement* has been used to refer not only to noun clauses used as subjects, but also to predicate nouns and adjectives used in simple sentences, and the term *object complement* has been used not only for noun clauses used as objects but also for predicate nouns and adjectives embedded under verbs like *make* and *call*.

2) Sentential noun phrases can occur not only as subjects and objects of predicates, but also as predicate nouns, appositives to nouns, and objects of prepositions:

   a. The conclusion is that Darla did it
   b. The idea that Darla did it startles me
   c. The opportunity for Darla to do it has arrived
   d. It is a question of whether Darla did it

These sentence types appear to have many of the same meanings and forms as found with subject and object types. However, their cooccurrence restrictions are based on another noun in the higher sentence rather the higher predicate. Consequently, they would pose a problem for any analyses that tried to treat their meanings as derived from a higher predicate.

3) Although one somtimes finds the terms *tense* and *time reference* treated as the same thing, *time reference* refers to meaning while *tense* refers to form. Sometimes one finds a one-to-one correspondence between the two, as when the past tense form in *He left* represents past time,

but there is not always such a correspondence, as is espAcially clear when present tense forms are used for future time and when sequence of tense causes a change in tense but not in time reference, as in *I thought the party was tomorrow*.

Philosophers sometimes treat tense as a type of time reference associated with modality rather than propositional content. However, in the present analysis, time reference will be associated with propositional content, although the modalities can influence the time reference. Tense forms will be associated with the representation of time reference and sequence of tense.

4) The names that I have used for the Action Modality include *Power* (1974) and *Control* (1977).

5) Other names that I used for the Information Modalities are *Propositional Modalities* (1974) and *Qualifying Modalities* (1981).

6) In trying to determine whose attitude is involved in the modality of the complement, one must consider the attitude of the speaker, the attitude or the desired attitude of the audience, and the attitude of the major participant, called here the "director", whether it be the subject of the higher predicate or, in subject embedding appraisals, a type of object. Some of the problems with determining who believes what will be discussed in Chapter V.

7) The higher predicates *permit* and *be able* appear to take complements which can be interpreted as having a Predetermined, an Undetermined, and an Indeterminate Modality, the latter allowing "or not" to cooccur with their complements.

8) Another kind of higher predicate that takes this type of complement is one like *know whether* or *predict whether*, which in themselves express a commitment to one alternative, but take complements that do not reveal which alternative. These constructions are dealt with more fully in Chapter III.

9) Previously, I have called the Evaluation Modalities by two other names: the Logical Modalities (1974) and the Quantifying Modalities (1980). The Logical Modalities were divided into only two types: the Necessity Modality, which corresponds to the Predetermined and Determined Modalities, and the Possibility Modality, which corresponds to the Undetermined Modality.

10) Austin's performative verbs are usually what we have called linguistic reactions, like *say*, *order*, or *promise*. With a first person subject (the speaker) and a present time reference (speech time), a sentence containing these verbs is interpreted as both an utterance and an act. Hence they are called illocutionary acts, and they are said to have an illocutionary force, like making a statement or giving an order. Their complements appear to be in direct discourse. With any other type of subject or time reference, these constructions are interpreted as reports of performatives, and their complements are in indirect discourse. Both Austin and Searle classified verbs according to the kind of illocutionary force they could indicate.

CHAPTER II

The Information Modalities

The Information Modalities reflect the way the speaker intends the propositional content to be taken: whether as information concerned with knowledge about the world or as information concerned with behavior in the world. This distinction underlies some current plays on language: 'No Shirt, No Shoes, No Service' or 'We aim to please; you aim too please.' It underlies the jestful reply of 'Yes' to the question 'Can you pass the salt?' And it underlies the indirect manipulation of those who make complaints while intending requests (mother to son: 'Your room's a mess!'), or who give compliments while expecting favors (wife to husband: 'Your clothes look so good on you!'), or who ask for information while expecting commitment (English chairman to untenured linguistics instructor: 'Would you be willing to teach composition?'), or the humor in a child's saying 'If you don't like this book, I'm gonna punch you in the nose.'

While giving or asking for information about the world is usually a pretty safe venture, trying to direct someone's behavior leads to an interaction of wills, a comparison of power status, and possible emotional clashes. Consequently, people often disguise their manipulative intentions by acting as though they were simply giving out or asking for information about the world.

The kind of information that is concerned with knowledge about the world corresponds to what philosophers have referred to as the *epistemic* value of a proposition, as exemplified by modal statements like 'That must/may be right' or 'That will/can happen.' In contrast, the kind of information that is concerned with behavior in the world corresponds to what philosophers have referred to as the *deontic* value of a proposition, as exemplified by modal statements like 'You must/will/may do it'. Linguists have preferred to use the broader term *root* value because the term *deontic* excludes the ability meaning exemplified in the modal *can* in 'You can do it if you try.' These epistemic and deontic, or root values, are closely related to the meanings referred to here as the *Information Modality* meanings.

The Information Modality includes both epistemic and root meanings. There are three types of epistemic meanings: one concerned with the truth of a proposition (the *Truth Modality*), a second one concerned with the future truth of a proposition (the *Future Truth Modality*), and a third one concerned with the occurrence of an event (the *Occurrence Modality*). Another type of Information Modality has a type of deontic or root meaning which is concerned with the performance of an act (the *Action Modality*). Each of these four modalities will be shown to have a characteristic set of meanings and forms, in English and other languages.

The Meanings of the Information Modalities

The Truth Modality

The *Truth Modality* is about the truth of the proposition, regardless of whether that truth value is certain or uncertain:

(1)   a.   I know that Dawn is a female
        b.   I believe that Dawn is a female.
        c.   I hope that Dawn is a female
        d.   I wonder whether Dawn is a female.

In (1a), the proposition is treated as definitely true; in (1b), as probably true; in (1c), as possibly true; and in (1d), as possibly true or false. Although they vary in the degree of certainty, nevertheless one can say that they are all *about* the truth of the complement proposition.[1] Thus if one inserts the expression 'be true,' it is redundant, but it does not change the meaning:

(1)   a'.   I know that *it is true* that Dawn is a female.
        b'.   I believe that *it is true* that Dawn is a female.
        c'.   I hope that *it is true* that Dawn is a female.
        d'.   I wonder whether *it is true* that Dawn is a female

Because the Truth Modality deals with the truth of a proposition, there are no restrictions on the type of subject, predicate, or time reference that the proposition can contain, as long as it can be evaluated as true or not. The complement subject has no restrictions on animacy or identity:[2]

(2)   a.   I know that *I/you/she/it* fell
        b.   I believe that *I/you/she/it* fell
        c.   I hope that *I/you/she/it* fell
        d.   I wonder whether *I/you/she/it* fell

The predicate can describe a state (be a female), an event (receive award), an act (left), or an appraisal (be true):

(3)   a. I know that Jo is a female/received an award/left
       b. I believe that Jo is a female/received an award/left
       c. I hope that Jo is a female/received an award/left
       d. I wonder whether Jo is a female/received an award/left

The complement can have any time reference, whether present, past, or future to the time of the higher predicate, as shown in the sentences in (4) and any aspect, whether simple, progressive, or perfect, as shown in the sentences in (5):

(4)   a. I know that Raul is/was/will be careful
       b. I believe that Raul is/was/will be careful
       c. I hope that Raul is/was/will be careful
       d. I wonder whether Raul is/was/will be careful

(5)   a. I know that Raul is being/has been careful
       b. I believe that Raul is being/has been careful
       c. I hope that Raul is being/has been careful
       d. I wonder whether Raul is being/has been careful

The examples in (4) and (5) all contain finite complements, but the same range of time reference and aspect can occur with nonfinite complements in the Truth Modality, as shown in the sentences (6):

(6)   a. Ella claims to play/be playing/have played chess
       b. It's good for Ella to play/be playing/have played chess
       c. We believe Ella to play/be playing/have played chess

With the simple infinitive, one can have a present habitual or, with a future time adverb, a future time reference. With the progressive infinitive, one can have a present or future time reference, and with the perfect infinitive, a past time reference.[3]

Truth Modality complements have a syntactic restriction called 'sequence of tense'. Although this restriction is not well understood, it seems to affect the tense form of the complement but not its time reference meaning. Traditionally, it is described as tense agreement between the complement and the higher sentence, but only when the higher sentence is in the past tense. Sequence of tense can apply to all finite, and nonfinite complements having a Truth Modality, and appears to be optional under certain conditions (cf. Kiparsky and Kiparsky 1971, Costa 1972, R. Lakoff 1970, and E. Riddle 1978):

(7) a. Jo was glad that Tim is/was leaving
          (that the earth is/was round)
     b. Jo was glad for Tim to leave/have left
          (for the earth to be/*have been round)
     c. Jo believed that Tim *is/was leaving
          (that the earth ?is/was round)
     d. Jo believed Tim to *leave/have left
          (the earth to be/*have been round)
     e. Jo wondered whether Tim *is/was leaving
          (whether the earth *is/was round)

Sequence of tense is possible with each finite complement. It is obligatory in certain ones, especially those involving doubt, as with the complement of *wonder*, but optional in certain cases, especially those involving accepted truths.

Thus, the Truth Modality is about the truth of the proposition, and that proposition can contain any type of subject, predicate, or time reference. There are a large number of higher predicates that take the Truth Modality in English and other languages. Some are emotive predicates like *regret that*, *be amusing that*, *be afraid that*, *hope that*, and *be concerned whether*; some of them are linguistic predicates like *inform that*, *say that*, *be rumored that*, and *ask whether*; some are cognitive-physical predicates like *know that*, *believe that*, *discover that*, *indicate that*, *be likely that*, *be possible that*, and *wonder whether*. When these predicates take complements with a Truth Modality meaning, they describe someone's response to the truth of the proposition, regardless of whether it is actually true or not.

The Future Truth Modality

While the Truth Modality is about a proposition's being true either in the present, past, or future, the Future Truth Modality is *about* a proposition coming true only in the future, regardless of whether it really will come true or not:

(8) a. Sam anticipates that Joan will be tall soon
     b. Sam expects that Joan will be tall soon
     c. Sam is eager for Joan to be tall soon
     d. Sam can predict whether Joan will be tall soon

These sentences are all about her becoming tall in the future. Each expresses varying degrees of certainty about whether it will actually come true: with *anticipate* there is a strong expectation that it will come true; with *expect* there is a weak expectation; with *eager* there is not so much an expectation as a consideration of its coming true; and with *predict whether* there is a consideration of its coming true or not

Because these sentences are all about the proposition coming true in the future, they can have 'come true' inserted at the expense of redundancy but without changing meaning:

(8) a'. Sam anticipates that *it will come true* that
         Joan will be tall soon
     b'. Sam expects that *it will come true* that
         Joan will be tall soon
     c'. Sam is eager for *it to come true* that
         Joan will be tall soon
     d'. Sam can predict whether *it will come true* that
         Joan will be tall soon

Because this modality is about the future truth of the complement proposition, it requires the propositional content to have a future time reference:

(9) a. *Doug anticipates that Lyn was tall before now
     b. *Doug expects that Lyn was tall before now
     c. *Doug is eager for Lyn to have been tall before now
     d. *Doug can predict whether Lyn was tall before now

Finite complements in the Future Truth Modality can occur with a *that* or *whether* complementizer accompanied by the modal *will*, by *be going to*, or by the simple or progressive present with nonstative predicates, as shown in the sentences in (10) below:

(10) a. Don anticipates that Kay will be tall soon
     b. Don anticipates that Kay is going to be tall soon
     c. Don anticipates that Kay plays chess soon
     d. Don anticipates that Kay is playing chess soon
     e. Don will predict whether Kay will play chess soon

Nonfinite complements in the Future Truth Modality can occur with an infinitive accompanied by either the simple aspect, or with nonstative predicates, the progressive aspect, as shown in (11) below:

(11) a. Hal is eager for Millie to be tall soon
     b. Hal is eager for Millie to play chess soon

c.   Hal is eager for Millie to be playing chess soon

The perfect aspect is possible with both finite and nonfinite forms, but only with a future perfect meaning, where the complement predicate must have a future time reference which precedes another future time reference, as shown in the examples below:

(12) a.   George anticipates that Terri will have played chess before noon
     b.   George aniticipates that Terri's going to have played chess before noon
     c.   George's eager for Terri to have played chess before noon
     d.   George anticipates her having played chess before noon

Finite complements with a Future Truth Modality, like those with a Truth Modality, usually undergo sequence of tense, so that when the higher predicate is past in form, the complement predicate must also be past in form, even though in meaning, the time reference is still future to the time of the higher predicate, as shown in (12) below:

(13) a.   Joe expected that Merle ?will/would be tall soon
     b.   Joe expected that Merle ?is/was going to be tall soon
     c.   Joe expected that Merle ?plays/played chess soon
     d.   Joe expected that Merle ?is/was playing chess soon

Nonfinite complements with a Future Truth Modality, unlike those with a Truth Modality, do not undergo sequence of tense.

(14) a.   Morgan expected Pat to be tall soon
     b.   Morgan expected Pat to play chess soon
     c.   Morgan expected Pat to be playing chess soon
     d.   *Morgan expected Pat to have played chess soon

In order for something to come true in the future, it must be capable of undergoing change from one time to another, and thus it can be a changeable state like becoming tall or being happy, an event like raining or being taken by surprise, or an act like singing or leaving. Permanent states, like being a female, an Aries, or a human being, are unacceptable unless one can force a changeable interpretation on them, like having a sex change, changing your birthdate, or taking on new properties that are more humane:

(15) a.   Bill anticipates that Diane will receive the award/chose one
     b.   Bill expects that Diane will receive the award/choose one
     c.   Bill is eager for Diane to receive the award/choose one

      d. Bill can predict whether Diane will receive the award/choose
          one

(16) a. *Jerry anticipates that Judy will be a female soon
      b. *Jerry expects that Judy will be a female soon
      c. *Jerry is eager for Judy to be a female soon
      d. *Jerry can predict whether Judy will be a female soon

There are no restrictions on the identity of the participants in the proposition; they can be like or unlike any other participant in the sentence:

(17) a. He anticipates that *you/he* will go
      b. He expects that *you/he* will go
      c. He is eager *for you/Ø(= for him)* to go
      d. He can predict whether *you/he* will go

Thus the Future Truth Modality is about a proposition coming true in the future, so that the predicate must be capable of change and the time reference must be future to the time of the higher predicate.

Only a small number of predicates take this modality in English and other languages. There are emotive predicates like *want* and *anxious for*, linguistic predicates like *predict* and *prophesy*, cognitive-physical predicates like *anticipate, expect, forewarn*, and *wait*, and appraisals like *be predictable* and *be desirable for*. When they take complements with a Future Truth meaning, they describe a response to the future truth of a proposition, regardless of whether it actually comes true or not.

There are predicates like *hope*, which can take both a Truth and a Future Truth Modality:

(18) a. Mike hopes that Linda left/is leaving/will leave
      b. Mike hopes for Linda to leave/be leaving/have left

In (a), *hope* takes a *that* complementizer and can occur with a present, past, or future time reference. In (b), *hope* takes an infinitive complementizer and can occur only with a future time reference. Consequently , the complement in (b) is defined as taking a Future Truth Modality while that in (a) is defined as taking a Truth Modality, even when it takes a future time reference.[4]

The Occurrence Modality

While the Truth and Future Truth Modalities are about the truth of a proposition, the Occurence Modality is about the occurrence of an event, regardless of whether it actually occurs or not:

(19) a. It took place that Bo received the awards.
       b. They watched Bo receive/receiving the awards.
       c. Bo tends to receive the awards.
       d. They like for Bo to receive the awards.
       e. They watched whether Bo received the awards.

In each of these sentences, the complement proposition is treated as an occurrence: the event of Bo's receiving the awards. With *take place* and *watch*, the event is expected to have occurred, with no alternatives available. With *tend*, there are weak expectations that the event occurred, but with alternatives available. With *like*, there is no expectation but rather a preference or positive consideration of the event when it takes place. With *watched whether*, there is no preference, but only a consideration of the possibility that it did or did not occur.

Because the complements of these sentences are all about the occurrence of an event, they have restrictions on cooccurrence with other expressions and on the content of the proposition. Thus they can cooccur with predicates like *occur* and *take place* with redundancy, but with no change in meaning; *be true* or *come true* would not be acceptable:

(19) a'. It took place that *it occurred (*was true/*came true)* that Bo received the awards
       b'. They watched *it occur (*be true/*come true)* that Bo received the awards
       c'. It tends to *occur (*be true/*come true)* that Bo receives the awards
       d'. They like for *it to occur (*be true/*come true)* that Bo receives the awards
       e'. They watched whether *it occurred (*was true/came true)* that Bo received the awards

The occurrence meaning requires the complement proposition to have a predicate that can be interpreted as an event. Nonstative predicates, like *receive*, *arrive*, and *choose*, are acceptable because they can be more easily interpreted as events than stative predicates like *be tall* or *have cold*:

(20) a. *Jane watched them *be/being tall*[5]
       b. *It took place that they *were tall*
       c. *Jane tends to *be tall*
       d. *Jane likes for them to *be tall*[6]
       e. *Jane watched whether they *were tall*

(21) a. Jane watched them *choose* a winner
  b. It took place that they *chose* a winner
  c. Jane tends to *choose* a winner
  d. Jane likes for them to *choose* a winner
  e. Jane watched whether they *chose* a winner

Because the Occurrence Modality is about the occurrence of an event, it is strange if it is negative, since that would negate the occurrence of the event:

(22) a. ?It took place that Ralph *didn't* receive the awards
  b. ?They watched Ralph *not* receive/receiving the awards
  c. ?They tend *not* to receive the awards
  d. ?They like for Ralph *not* to receive the awards
  e. ?They watched whether Ralph *didn't* receive the awards

However, if the negated complement can be interpreted as a positive event, like interpreting 'not receiving the awards' as a positive occurrence, like receiving a rejection notice about the awards, then the preceding sentences would be more acceptable.

The occurrence meaning is also associated with a restriction on time reference. The complement proposition cannot be interpreted as having a time reference earlier than the higher sentence, but it usually has to have the same time reference as the higher sentence, regardless of whether the complement is finite or nonfinite:

(23) a. At 3, it took place that Pam received the awards (= at 3/*2/*4)
  b. At 3, they watched Pam receive the awards (= at 3/*2/*4)
  c. ?At 3, Pam tends to receive the awards (= at 3/*2/*4)
  d. ?At 3, they like for Pam to receive the awards (= at 3/*2/*4)
  e. At 3, they watched whether Pam received the awards (= at 3/*2/*4)

In these examples, the time of the higher sentence is taken to be 'at 3', and in each complement, the earlier time, at 2, is unacceptable, but the same time, at 3, or in some cases, the future time, at 4, is acceptable.

There are no restrictions on the participants in the proposition; they can be agents or not, and they can usually be like or unlike any participant in the higher sentence, though perception verbs, like the one in (24b), usually imply that what one perceives is outside oneself, so that a complement with a like-subject would have to be interpreted as an objectification of oneself, a kind of self-perception:

(24) a. It took place that *he/I/they* received awards
      b. Fred watched *him/me/?himself* receive awards
      c. Fred likes for *him/me/Ø (= himself)* to receive awards
      d. Fred watched whether *he/I/she* received awards

Thus in the Occurrence Modality, the meaning is about the occurrence of an event, and consequently, the predicate must be interpreted as an actual event and the time reference must be interpreted as the same as the time of the higher predicate.

In English and other languages, only a small number of predicates take the Occurence Modality. There are emotive predicates like *hate for* and *like for*; cognitive predicates like *watch* and *see*, which involve perception[7]; physical predicates involving causatives like *cause* and *allow* (in the sense of allow to happen); and appraisals like *take place* and *happen*[8] and the aspectuals of occurrence: *begin, continue,* and *tend*.[9] There do not seem to be any linguistic predicates that take this modality.[10]

The Action Modality

The Action Modality differs from the other modalities in that it is not about propositional truth or the occurrence of events but about the performance of a voluntary or controllable act, regardless of whether the act is actually performed or not:

(25) a. Mary forced John the leave
      b. It was necessary for John to leave
      c. Mary demanded that John leave
      d. Mary urged John to leave
      e. Mary told John whether to leave

(26) a. John managed to leave
      b. John decided to leave
      c. John promised to leave
      d. It was easy for John to leave
      e. John wondered whether to leave

In the sentences in (25), John's leaving is directed by others, while in (26) it is self-directed. Nevertheless, in each of these sentences, the complement proposition is about John's performing the act of leaving, regardless of whether the act has strong or weak expectations of being performed or no expectations at all.

Because these Action complements are about someone performing an act, the expression 'perform the act' can be inserted with redundancy but with no change in meaning, while neither *be true*, *come true*, nor *occur* can be used:

(27) a. Ed forced them to *perform the act* of leaving
      b. Ed urged them to *perform the act* of leaving
      c. Ed decided to *perform the act* of leaving
      d. Ed was able to *perform the act* of leaving
      e. Ed wondered whether *to perform the act* of leaving

(28) a. *Ed forced it to *be true/come true/occur* that they left
      b. *Ed urged it to *be true/come true/occur* that they left
      c. *Ed decided for it to *be true/come true/occur* that they left
      d. *It was easy for it to *be true/come true/ occur* that they left
      e. *Ed wondered whether for it to *be true/come true/occur* that
          they left

The interpretation of these complements as voluntary, controllable acts means that there are restrictions on the types of predicates that can occur in the complement. While acts like leaving are easily interpreted as controllable, permanent states like *be a female*, changeable states like *be tall*, nonstative events like *be taken by surprise* or involuntary acts like *sneeze* are not:

(29) a. Rose decided to *leave/*be tall*
      b. Rose persuaded Will to *leave/*be taken by surprise*
      c. Rose screamed for Will to *leave/*sneeze*

If one can imagine some way in which these normally uncontrollable states, events, or acts can be interpreted as controllable, then the sentence is acceptable, like Alice in Wonderland deciding to eat one side of the mushroom to be tall, or persuading someone to pretend that they are surprised, or pretending to sneeze. Thus, with the Action Modality, the complement predicate must be interpreted as a controllable act and must usually have a nonstative predicate.

Another requirement for the Action Modality is that the complement subject must be interpreted as an agent capable of performing the complement act, and so must usually be animate:

(30) a. Ilsa screamed for *Rick/*it* to move.
      b. It was obligatory for *Rick/*it* to move

Also, the complement subject has its identity constrained. With certain higher predicates, the complement action must be interpreted as self-directed, and consequently the complement subject must be interpreted as identical to a participant in the higher sentence who is responsible for the directing, whether implied or explicit:

(31) a. *José* managed *(= for José/*Pearl)* to leave
      b. *José* promised Pearl *(= for José/*Pearl)* to leave
      c. *José* was able *(= for José/*Pearl)* to leave
      d. *José* wondered whether *(= for José/*Pearl)* to leave

(32) a. *(= For José/*Pearl)* To leave was easy for *Jose*
      b. *(= For José/*Pearl)* To leave was wise of *Jose*

In each of the sentences above, the participant in the higher sentence responsible for the directing is José and the complement subject must be interpreted as identical to him; it would not be possible to interpret the subject to be Pearl.

Because the participant doing the directing is usually the subject of the higher sentence, as in the sentences in (31), the complement subject must be identical to that higher subject and consequently, this constraint has been described as a like-subject constraint (Perlmutter 1971). However, there are sentences like those in (32), where the participant who is doing the directing is not the subject of the higher sentence but rather some type of verbal object or prepositional object, and the complement subject must be identical to that object. In these cases, the term 'like-subject' is not appropriate. Since this constraint is not syntactic but semantic, and since the constraint functions between the complement subject and the participant in the higher sentence doing the directing, it would be more appropriate to call it a Self-Directed Constraint (cf. Givón's use of the term 'self-inducemenent verbs' (1980)). In the lexicon, those higher predicates requiring this constraint would have to be specially marked to specify which participant in the higher sentence the complement subject should be interpreted as identical to.

Another type of higher predicate taking Action Modality complements requires the complement action to be interpreted as directed by others. Consequently, the identity of the complement subject must be interpreted as different from the director of the higher sentence but identical to the receiver of the direction:

(33) a. Abby forced Roger (= for Roger/*Abby) to leave
      b. Abby beckoned for Roger/*herself to leave
      c. Abby allowed Roger (= for Roger/*Abby) to leave
      d. Abby told Roger whether (= for Roger/*Abby) to leave

(34) a. It behooved Roger (= for Roger/*Abby) to leave

     b. It was incumbent on Roger (= for Roger/*Abby) to leave

In the sentences in (33), Abby is the director and Roger is the receiver, whether explicit as in (33a, c, d) or implied, as in (33b). The complement subject must be interpreted as different from the director and as identical to the receiver.[11] Again, since the director is usually the subject of the higher sentence, Perlmutter called this constraint the Unlike-Subject Constraint. However, there are also sentences like those in (34), with no subject, only an implied director (someone) and an explicit receiver (Roger). In these cases, the complement subject must be interpreted as different from the implied director and identical to the receiver. To call this an 'unlike-subject' constraint would be as inappropriate as in the 'like-subject' constraint examples above. Consequently, it seems more appropriate to turn from these syntactic terms to semantic ones and to call this constraint an Other-Directed Constraint (cf. Givón's use of the term 'manipulation verbs' (1980)). In the lexicon, those higher predicates requiring this contraint would have to be specially marked to specify which participant in the higher sentence the complement subject should be interpreted as identical to or different from.

Still another type of higher predicate allows its Action Modality complement to be interpreted as either self- or other-directed action:

(35) a. *Jan is determined (= for Jan) to go*

     b. *Jan is determined for Max to go*

(36) a. It is important to *Jan (= for Jan)* to go

     b. It is important to *Jan for Max* to go

In each of these sentences, Jan is the director. In the (a) sentences, the complement subject is interpreted as identical to the director, so that the action is self-directed. In the (b) sentences, the complement subject is interpreted as different from the director and identical with the explicit or implied receiver, where there is one; in cases like *determined*, there is no explicit or implied receiver, but the identity of the complement subject still must be interpreted as unlike the director. In the lexicon, these higher predicates would have to be specially marked to specify that they can take a self-directed or an other-directed construction and, in each case, which participant in the higher sentence the complement subject should be interpreted as identical to or different from.[12]

Thus the subjects of Action Modality complements must be agents and must be interpreted as like or unlike a participant in the higher sentence, so that the action can be interpreted as either self-directed or other-directed.

The Action Modality also has a restriction on the time reference and the aspect of the complement act. Because the act is directed either by oneself or by another, the time of the act cannot precede the time of the direction, and in most cases, it must be future to it:

(37)　a.　Andy told Dan to *leave tomorrow/*yesterday*.
　　　b.　Andy permitted Dan to *leave tomorrow/*yesterday*.
　　　c.　Andy decided to *leave tomorrow/*yesterday*.

In these sentences, the leaving has to take place after the telling, permitting, or deciding; it can not take place before that, or even at the same time.

There are some predicates that require their complement to have the same time reference as they have, as with most Occurrence Modality complements, but reference to a prior time is still not possible:

(38)　a.　*Right now* Jack is forcing Lisa to leave.
　　　　　(= *right now/?tomorrow/*yesterday*)
　　　b.　*Right now* Jack is letting Lisa leave.
　　　　　(= *right now/?tomorrow/*yesterday*)
　　　c.　*Right now* Jack is trying to leave.
　　　　　(= *right now/?tomorrow/*yesterday*)

The normal interpretation of these sentences is that the leaving is taking place at the same time as the forcing, letting, and trying. It could not be taking place before that. However, some constructions can be interpreted as involving indirect causation, and then the complement event can be interpreted as occurring at a time future to the cause, as with causing someone to die by gradually poisoning them.

The Action Modality, then, cannot refer to a time prior to the time of the higher predicate; it must usually refer to a future time, or in some cases to the same time.

Aspects are also restricted with Action meanings. The perfect aspect form with its completion or precedence meaning can occur with Action complements only with a future perfect meaning: the complement act must precede some future point in time:

(39)　a.　Arthur told Jo to *leave/have left* by nine.
　　　b.　Arthur decided to *leave/?have left* by nine.
　　　c.　Arthur managed to *leave/*have left* by nine.

Although the perfect form is possible with a future perfect meaning, the same meaning can occur without the perfect form, which is the preferred way.

The progressive with its durative and accompaniment meaning is a little strange with Action complements unless there is a future point in time for the duration to accompany:

(40) a. Arthur told Jo/decided/managed to *leave/?be leaving*
      b. Arthur told Jo/decided/managed to *leave/be leaving* by nine.

Unlike the perfect aspect, the progressive does contribute a durative meaning not present otherwise, but the circumstances have to especially require it. Thus with the Action meaning, aspects are restricted even when they have the appropriate time reference.

There are a fairly large number of predicates taking this modality in English and other languages. A few are emotives like *desire*[13] and *be willing*; many are linguistic predicates like *command*, *suggest*, and *permit*, *promise*, *agree*, and *ask*; some cognitive predicates like *intend* and *decide*; some physical predicates like *force*, *enable*, *manage*, *attempt*, and *have time*; and some appraisals like *be essential*, *be acceptable*, and *be easy*.

Thus the Action Modality differs from the other Information Modalities in its performance meaning and in requirements that the proposition contain a predicate that is a controllable act, a subject that is in some cases identical to, and in other cases different from the director of the higher sentence, and finally, a time reference that is in most cases future to, and in a few cases the same as, the time of the higher predicate.

Now that we have seen how the four Information Modalities have different restrictions on complement meaning, let us turn to the restrictions that they have on complement forms.

The Forms of the Information Modalities

The Information Modalities can have a variety of forms. Typically lexical or morphological segments are used to represent the differences in information meanings, but word order, grammatical relations, and even suprasegmental contrasts could be used.

Lexical Segments

The most explicit way of representing the meanings of the Information Modalities is by the use of lexical segments, like certain higher predicates and sentence adverbs which have meanings closely related to the modalities:

(41) a. It *is true* that Jill left (Truth)
      b. It *took place* that Jill left (Occurrence)
      c. I *predict* that Jill will leave (Future Truth)
      d. It *is obligatory* that Jill leave (Action)
      e. I *permit* Jill to leave (Action)

(42) a. Bill said that Jill *obviously* had left (Truth)
      b. Bill said that Jill *hopefully* will leave (Future Truth)
      c. Bill said that Jill *intentionally* left (Action)

In their lexical content, these higher predicates and sentence adverbs contain meanings which make them compatible with only certain types of complement modalities. The higher predicates in (41) and the sentence adverbs in (42) carry the meaning that their complement takes a particular type of Information Modality. For example, the higher predicate *be true*, and the sentence adverb *obviously* both represent the meaning that the complement is about the truth of the proposition, and thus both are compatible only with a Truth Modality meaning. Similarly, *permit* and *intentionally* both carry the meaning that the complement is about the performance of an act so that they are compatible only with an Action Modality meaning. Because the meanings of these higher predicates and sentence adverbs literally convey the meanings of the Information Modalities, no special signals would have to be used to represent the type of complement modality used.

Semi-lexical Segments

With other types of predicates like *tell* and *insist*, the lexical content is general enough to allow many types of complement modalities, and thus other signals are necessary to specify which modalities are being used:

(43) a. I told them that she left (Truth)
      b. I told them to leave (Action)
      c. I told them that they should leave (Action)

(44) a. I insist that they left (Truth)
      b. I insist that they leave (Action)
      c. I insist that they should leave (Action)

In these sentences, it is not the lexical meaning of the higher predicate or of a sentence adverb that signals the type of modality meaning in the complement but rather forms which carry little or no lexical content of their own but which are used in contrasting patterns to signal the meanings of the

Information Modalities.

When these segmental forms, or morphemes, are used to set off complement clauses from the main clause, they are called complementizers; when they are used as auxiliary units within the verb phrase, they are called modals, and when they participate in the inflectional patterns of the verb, they are called mood.

Like higher predicates and sentence adverbs, these morphemes may represent the Information Modality meaning, but they do not usually contain particular lexical meanings, and thus they are said to be more 'grammaticized'. Many of these morphemes are clearly related to full lexical items, like the English complementizer *that* and the demonstrative pronoun, or the Thai quotative *wâa* and the verb 'to say', or the English modal *will* and the verb meaning 'to choose or desire'. Even though these morphemes no longer carry any lexical content, they still contain some properties of their earlier meaning which can be seen as compatible with the modality meanings they signal, like the definiteness of *that*, the assertiveness of Thai *wâa*, or the intentionality or futurity of *will*.

One can see a scalar progression from independent lexical forms with independent lexical content to varying stages of less independent forms with more bleached-out meanings.[14] Thus one finds that the Information Modality meanings can be represented by segments which contain complex lexical specifications or by segments which function as more specialized grammatical signals.

In English complements, the Information Modalities can be represented by complementizers, mood, modals, or by combinations of these. For complements taking the Truth Modality, one can predict the occurrence of the complementizers *that* or *whether* combined with the indicative mood, depending on the accompanying Evaluation Modality.

(45) a. We remembered/believed *that* Dawn was a female (Truth)
     b. We remembered/wondered *whether* Dawn was a female (Truth)

For complements taking the Future Truth Modality, one can predict the occurrence of the complementizers *that*, *for-to*, or *whether*, depending on the accompanying Evaluation Modality:

(46) a. We predict/expect *that* Russ will leave
     b. We will predict *whether* Russ will leave
     c. We hope/are eager *for* Russ *to* leave

For complements taking the Occurrence Modality, one cannot clearly predict any complement forms without reference to the higher predicate. They can be represented by a variety of complement forms: by the null complementizer with a nonfinite complement, as with *watch*, by the complementizers *that* and *whether* with a finite complement in the indicative mood, or by a *for-to* infinitive:

(47) a. We watched Russ leave early
       b. It took place *that* Russ left early
       c. We watched *whether* Russ left early
       d. We like *for* Russ *to* leave early

Complements taking the Action Modality are typically represented by the *for-to* infinitive complement, or a truncated form of it, and by *whether-to*, depending on the accompanying Evaluation Modality:

(48) a. We beckoned/signalled *for* Bart *to* leave
       b. We told/persuaded Bart *to* leave
       c. We remembered/tried *to* leave
       d. We remembered/wondered *whether to* leave

The occurrence of the preceding semi-lexical segments is predictable on the basis of the type of Information Modality in the complement, or its combination with certain Evaluation Modalities, as will be discussed in Chapter III.

There are also other occurrences of complementizers that are not predictable on the basis of the Information or the Evaluation Modalities, but must be associated with particular predicates, representing, perhaps, fossilized versions of earlier patterns or attempts to signal different meanings. These will be discussed in Chapter IV.

Like English, other languages also make use of complementizers to represent distinctions between the Information Modality meanings, especially between the Truth and Action Modalities, as shown in the following examples from Basque, Thai, and Kanuri:

(49) Basque (Bakaikoa - native consultant)
       a. *Nik esan dut Jon joan* **dela**
            I   said AUX   left AUX-COMP
            I said that John left

       b. *Nik esan dut   Jon jo*a**teko**
            I   said AUX   leave COMP
            I said for John to leave

(50) Thai (Surrintramont - native consultant)

    a. *Kháw bòok chán* **wâa** *pay talaat*
       She   told   me   COMP go market
       She told me that she went to the market

    b. *Kháw bòok chán* **hây** *pay talaat*
       She   told   me   COMP go market
       She told me to go to the market

(51) Kanuri (Hutchinson 1976)

    a. Kamu-nze su-luwuna-***dero*** *njeskono*
       wife-his   go out COMP forgot
       He forgot that his wife had gone

    b. *Luwo -* **ro** *njeskono*
       He forgot to go out

Basque makes a contrast between Truth and Action by the two complementizers *-ela* for Truth and *-teko* for Action. Thai uses the complementizer *wâa* for Truth and *hây* for Action. Kanuri uses *dero* for Truth and *ro* for Action.

Modals are used in English, and other languages, primarily to represent the Evaluation Modalities. However, one finds some interaction with the Information Modalities. In English, each modal is ambiguous as to the Information Modality it represents, having both an epistemic (Truth, Future Truth, or Occurrence) meaning and a deontic or root (Action) meaning. Thus *must* can represent either a Truth or an Action Modality:

(52) a. We decided that the author of that book *must* be a woman
     b. We decided that you *must* nominate a woman for president

Will usually represents a Future Truth or an Action Modality; and with an Action Modality, it can either have a self-directed intention meaning or an other-directed command meaning:

(53) a. We predict that the winner *will* be a woman
     b. I say that I *will* nominate a woman
     c. I say that you *will* nominate a woman

May represents either a Truth, Future Truth, or an Action Modality; and with an Action Modality, it can only have an other-directed permission meaning:

(54) a. We think that the author of that book *may* be a woman
     b. We think that tomorrow's winner *may* be a woman

    c. We decided that you *may* nominate a woman

Can represents either an Occurrence Modality with the meaning of capable of happening, or an Action Modality with the meaning of able (self-directed), or in many dialects, despite the efforts of purists, permission (other-directed):

(55) a. It is hopeful that a woman *can* be elected
       b. I am glad that I *can* swim
       c. I promise that you *can* go with us

The Information Modalities are represented implicitly by the modals in combination with the meanings of the Evaluation Modalities.

In other languages, one finds some cases where modals are ambiguous in much the same way as in English, having both an epistemic and a deontic or root meaning, but one also finds cases where some modals are not ambiguous but represent a particular Information Modality:

(56) Thai (Steele 1975)
      a. *fŏn **khong** kamlang tòk*
             must
             It must be raining (Truth)
      b. *chăn/Maalii **tông** pay*
                  must
             I/Mali must go (Action)
      c. *khăw **khuan** cà? tua yay maak*
             should
             He should be really big (Truth)
      d. *khăw **khuan** tii măa kong khăw*
             should
             He should hit his dog (Action)

(57) Kapampangan (Steele 1975)
      a. **balamu** *maseya = iya i wan*
          certain happy = SM   John
          It's almost certain that John is happy (Truth)
      b. **kaylangan** *= iya = ng magalutu*
          required = SM   cook
          He must cook (Action)
      c. **malyari** *= ng sali = iya = ng bestido*
          might   buy = SM   dress
          She might buy a dress (Truth)

d. **malyari** = *ng muko* = *iya potang mayari=iya*
 may   leave = SM when finish=SM
He may leave when he is finished (Action)

Thai and Kapampangan use separate words to represent the Truth and Action meanings of English *must*. Thai uses *khong* for the Truth interpretation of *must*, and *tông* for the Action meaning. Kapampangan uses *balamu* for the Truth form and *kaylangan* for the Action form. However, for other modal meanings, they use the same forms. Thai uses *khuan* for both the Truth and the Action meanings of *should*, and Kapampangan uses *malyari* for both the Truth and the Action meaning of *may*.

Another set of semi-lexical segments used to represent the Information Modalities is one that is disappearing rapidly in English, the mood system. English has an indicative mood, which is associated with the epistemic meanings (Truth, Future Truth, and Occurrence) and a few fossilized occurrences of what has been called the present subjunctive mood, which is associated with the root meanings (Action):

(58) a. INDICATIVE MOOD: TRUTH
 I insist that Wally plays well
 b. PRESENT SUBJUNCTIVE MOOD: ACTION
 I insist that Wally play well

English also has the remnants of a past subjunctive mood, but this occurs in the complement of only one higher predicate, *wish that*, and it is associated with a counterfactual meaning:

(59) PAST SUBJUNCTIVE MOOD: NEGATIVE TRUTH
 I wish that Beth were president

In many dialects of British and American English, these subjunctive forms are being replaced by forms which are indistinguishable from the indicative, so that mood no longer functions as an effective signal for differences in the meanings of the Information Modalities.[15]

In other languages, mood forms are found which distinguish more systematically between the Truth and Action Modalities. One usually finds the indicative mood form with the Truth Modality and the subjunctive mood form with the Action Modality, as shown in the following examples from Lori and Shona:

(60) Lori (Noonan to appear)

    a. *zine   eteqad dar ke   pia tile-ye*   **dozid**
       woman belief have COMP man chicken-Obj stole/Ind
       The woman believes the man stole the chicken

    b. *zine   pia-ye   vadast ke   tile-ye*   **bedoze**
       woman man-Obj forced COMP chicken-Obj steal/Subj
       The woman forced the man to steal the chicken

(61) Shona (Dembetembe 1976)

    a. *Podzorimwa abvuma   kuti   **akatadza***
                 admitted COMP erred/Ind
       Podzorimwa admitted that he made a mistake

    b. *vakomana ave   varangana kuti   **vatize***
       boys   those planned   COMP run away/Subj
       Those boys have planned to run away

In Korean, the indicative mood form is used with the Truth Modality, but a nonfinite form is used with the Action Modality:

(62) Korean (Kong - native consultant)

    a. *John-in   ssileyki-lil   **peli-ess-ta***
             top garbage-ACC dump-PST-DCL
       nin-kes-lil   ic-ess-ta
       COMP-ACC forgot
       John forgot that he had dumped the garbage

    b. *John-in ssileyki-lil   **peli***
             top garbage-ACC dump
       nin-kes-lil   ic-ess-ta
       COMP-ACC forgot
       John forgot to dump the garbage

Although one finds some examples of mood forms being used to contrast between the Information Modalities, they are more likely to be used to distinguish between the Evaluation Modalities or certain combinations of these and the Information Modalities, as will be discussed in the next two chapters.

Nonsegmental Signals

    Turning now from segmental signals to the use of nonsegmental signals like word order, grammatical relations, and suprasegmentals, I have not found systematic contrasts. In English, one does find certain tendencies to use word order patterns with one modality but not another. Certain higher predicates take a construction called Subject Raising when their complement is in the Truth Modality but not when it is in the Occurrence Modality, as with the verb *happen*:[16]

(63) a. It happened (= turned out/took place) that Wally was drafted (Truth and Occurrence)
b. It happened to Wally (= took place) that he was drafted/*was 21 (Occurrence)
c. Wally happened (= turned out) to have been drafted/to be 21 (Truth)

Nevertheless, Subject Raising occurs with all Information Modalities. One finds a few higher predicates like *be exciting* which take a construction called Object Raising when their complement is in the Occurrence Modality but not the Truth modality:[17]

(64) a. It was exciting for Dennis to receive the award (Truth and Occurrence)
b. It was exciting for Dennis to deserve the award (Truth)
c. The award was exciting for Dennis to receive/*deserve (Occurrence)

Nevertheless, there are no systematic distinctions between Information Modalities made by word order and grammatical relations. They are all dependent on the particular higher predicate, as will be discussed in Chapter V.

As for suprasegmental distinctions between the Information Modalities, I have found none with complement constructions in English or other languages. The following sentence seems ambiguous as to Truth and Action meaning regardless of the intonation or juncture patterns:

(65) I insist that Belinda hit the nail

Whether Belinda did hit the nail or should hit the nail, the intonation gives us no clue.

Thus English and other languages primarily make use of various segmental forms to represent the Information Modalities. These forms can sometimes be combined. There can be higher predicates and sentence adverbs which express modality meanings, and these can be accompanied by complementizers, mood, or modals, and all of these could be accompanied by word order or suprasegmental distinctions. The only forms that do not work in combination are moods and modals. The following sentences show examples from English of ways in which these forms can be combined, more or less redundantly:

(66) a. Jim *realizes that* he *absolutely must* leave
      b. I *say that* it *probably should* rain
      c. Jim *hopes that perhaps* it *may* rain
      d. They *wonder whether* it *could possibly* rain
      e. We *predict that* it *probably will* rain
      f. She *recommended that* Jim *truly should* leave

The constraints on such combinations need further research.

The Four Information Modalities

The four Information Modalities of the complement have been shown to differ in restrictions on meaning and form. The first three types of modality, the Truth, Future Truth, and Occurrence Modalities, resemble what is called the epistemic modality, because they are about the knowledge of states, events, or acts in the world, or appraisals of the world, and their past, present, or future truth or occurrence. The fourth type of modality, the Action Modality, resembles what logicians have called the deontic modality, because certain cases involve obligation, permission, or intention. Linguists have preferred the name "root" rather than "deontic", because they wanted to include with the deontic meanings the ability meaning found in the modal *can* and the complement of *be able*. For convenience, I will sometimes refer to the Truth, Future Truth, and Occurrence Modalities as the epistemic modalities when I want to contrast them with the Action Modality.

The question has been raised as to whether these four modalities are discrete or scalar. Michael Silverstein (personal communication) pointed out a kind of implicational scale for the predicate restrictions, whereby the acceptability of a predicate interpreted as a permanent state implies the acceptability of one describing a temporary state, which implies the acceptability of an event, and it implies the acceptability of a controllable act. Yet other than this, each of the four modalities has its own separate set of restrictions, and there are no degrees of Truth that fade into Future Truth which fade into Occurrence which fade into Action.[18]

Nevertheless, there are ways in which these four types appear to overlap. While Action complements can take only controllable acts like "leave" as predicates, Occurrence complements can take any events, including controllable acts:

(67)   a.   Action: Jo forced Dick to leave/*sneeze
      b.   Occurrence: Jo watched Dick leave/sneeze

A verb like *watch*, when it takes a controllable act like *leave*, is still considered to have an Occurrence complement, not only because it can take noncontrollable events like *sneeze*, but also because even the controllable act is treated as an event, something that happened rather than a self-directed or other-directed act that was performed.

A problem arises with verbs like *cause* which can take both noncontrollable events like *sneeze* and controllable acts like *leave*, because the controllable act can be interpreted as an other-directed act that was performed:

(68)   Jo caused Dick to leave/sneeze

With *sneeze*, the only interpretation is one of an event: Jo caused something to happen so that Dick sneezed. With *leave*, one can either have the event interpretation, Jo caused something to happen so that Dick left, or the controllable interpretation, Jo caused Dick to perform the act of leaving. The difference between them is usually called indirect vs. direct causation, though the same contrast happens with *allow* (cf. Schmerling 1978) and *begin* (cf. Perlmutter 1970). In the present analysis, cases like *cause* are treated as being able to take either an Occurrence or an Action complement.

Other cases of overlap occur between Truth complements and the other types, since Truth complements can take the full range of predicates and time references. The higher predicate *hope* can take a Truth or a Future Truth complement. When it has a *for-to* complementizer, it clearly requires a Future Truth complement, but when it has a *that* complementizer, it can take any type of predicate and any time reference, including the future:

(69)   a.   Jo hoped to be *an Aries/tall
      b.   Jo hoped that she was an Aries/tall

In (a), *hope* is considered to have a Future Truth complement, because it requires a predicate that can be interpreted as changeable and a time reference that can be interpreted as future. Consequently unchangeable states like being an Aries are incompatible but changeable states like becoming tall are compatible. In (b), *hope* is thought to have a Truth complement, since it allows an unchangeable state and a past time reference. A problem arises when *hope* takes a *that* complementizer with a future time reference:

(70)   Jo hoped that she would be *an Aries/tall

In this case, *hope* appears to take a Truth complement in form, but in meaning, it appears to take a Future Truth complement.

We run across the same type of overlap with a verb like *say* when it takes an Action complement and when it takes a Truth complement containing a modal with an Action meaning:

(71) a. The coach says for you to practice
      b. The coach says that you must practice

These sentences are parallel in meaning, but in (a), *say* takes an Action complement while in (b) it appears to take a Truth complement with an Action Modality meaning.

In the present analysis, *hope* and *say* will be treated as taking more than one type of complement. When they, or any other higher predicates, take a Truth complement with a modal, they will be treated as having both the Truth modality and, embedded under it, the modality signaled by the modal. The example in (70) will be treated as taking a Truth complement containing an embedded Future Truth complement, paraphrasable by "Jo hoped that it was true that it would come true that she would be tall". This paraphrase shows the parallel that this construction has with the simple Future Truth complement, "Jo hoped that it would come true that she would be tall". Similarly, (71 b) would have a paraphrase like "The coach says that it's true that you must practice", which parallels the paraphrase for the plain Action complement in (71 a) as "The coach says that you must perform the action of practicing"

The verb *promise*, as pointed out to me by Bernard Comrie (personal communication), is peculiar in its distribution in English and other languages. It typically takes a self-directed Action complement, with a controllable predicate and a future time reference. However, it can also take a complement that appears to be a Truth complement:

(72) a. ACTION
          Will promises to marry Sadie/*be tall
      b. TRUTH (with deontic modal *will*)
          Will promises that he will marry Sadie/
          *that he will be tall
      c. TRUTH
          Will promises that he married Sadie/that he is tall

While (72 a) clearly takes an Action complement in meaning and form, (72 b) appears to have the form of a Truth complement but the meaning of an Action complement, since its predicate must be interpreted as controllable and self-directed, perhaps because of the deontic interpretation of the modal *will*. In many dialects of English, and in many languages, the complement of verbs like *promise* has to have an Action interpretation, and sentences like (72 c) are not acceptable.

In the present analysis, *promise* would be treated as being lexically specified for both an Action and a Truth complement, and in most dialects, and languages, the Truth complement would also have to be lexically specified as taking the deontic modal *will*, which signals a self-directed Action complement with future time reference.

Summary

Thus one can see that in English and in other languages, the Information Modalities are distinct in meaning and frequently in form. These differences are summarized in Table 2 and the types of predicates that take each of these complement modalities are listed in Table 3. Now we will turn to another set of complement modalities, the Evaluation Modalities, which interact with the Information Modalities.

Table 2
Characteristics of the Information Modalities

Truth:
1)   about the truth or falsity of a proposition
2)   subject - no restrictions
3)   predicate - no restrictions: interpreted as a proposition about permanent or temporary state, event, or act
4)   time reference - no restrictions
5)   aspect - no restrictions
6)   tense - required if finite; sequence of tense constraint
7)   complementizers: *that*, *whether*, or *if*, some higher predicates take infinitives also
8)   mood - indicative
9)   modals - *must*, *may*

Future Truth:
1)   about the future truth of a proposition
2)   subject - no restrictions
3)   predicate - interpreted as temporary, changeable state, event, or

act and usually incompatible with permanent states
4)   time reference - future
5)   aspect - no restrictions
6)   tense - required if finite; sequence of tense constraints
7)   complementizers: *that* or infinitives, depending on the Evaluation Modality
8)   mood - future indicative
9)   modals - *will, may*

Occurrence
1)   about the occurrence of an event
2)   subject - no restrictions
3)   predicate - interpreted as an event; usually takes nonstative events or acts; states usually incompatible
4)   time reference - same time as higher verb
5)   aspect - in finite complements, same as higher verb; in nonfinite complements prohibited
6)   tense - required in finite complements; must be same as higher predicate
7)   complementizers: inifinitives and null complementizers, depending on Evaluation Modality, and *that* with certain higher predicates
8)   mood - indicative
9)   modal - *can*

Action:
1)   about the voluntary performance of an act
2)   subject agent of act; identity restricted (self- and other-directed)
3)   predicate - interpreted as controllable act; takes voluntary acts; usually prohibits states, events, or passives
4)   time reference - most constructions require future; some require same time as higher predicate
5)   aspect - usually prohibited or strange unless relative to a future time; even then unnecessary
6)   tense - prohibited, except in those dialects that have no subjunctive form
7)   complementizers: infinitives basic; *that* subjunctive with a few higher predicates
8)   mood - subjunctive
9)   modals - *must* and *may* (other-directed) *will* and *can* (self- and other-directed)

Table 3

Higher Predicates and their Information Modalities

Truth	Future Truth	Occurrence	Action	
			Self Dir.	Other Dir.

Linguistic Reactions

Truth	Future Truth	Occurrence	Self Dir.	Other Dir.
inform (t)	predict (t/wf)	-	promise (i)	command (i)
announce (t)	prophesy (t)	-	swear (i)	order (i)
say (t/wf)	pray (i)	-	demand (i)	demand (i/ts)
assert (t)		-	propose (i)	say (i/wi)
claim (t)		-	refuse (i)	insist (i/ts)
pray (t)		-	beg (i)	beg (i)
ask (wf)		-	ask (i/wi)	ask (i)

Cognitive-Physical Reactions

Truth	Future Truth	Occurrence	Self Dir.	Other Dir.
assume (t)	anticipate (t)	cause (i)	aim (i)	expect (i)
aware (t)	expect (t/or)	hear (Ø)	decide (i)	plan (i)
believe (t)	foresee (t)	observe (Ø)	intend (i)	intend (i)
know (t/wf)	foretell (t)	ready (i)	know (i/wi)	pressure (i)
remember (t/wf)	forewarn (t)	wait (i)	remember (i/wi)	let (Ø)
wonder (wf)		watch (Ø)	willing (i)	signal (i)
convince (t)			able (i)	beckon (i)
discover (t)			arrange (i)	compel (i)
see (t)			have time (i)	make (i)
hear (t)			hesitate (i)	force (i)
persuade (t)			manage (i)	allow (i)
show (t)			try (i)	persuade (i)

Emotive Predicates

Truth	Future Truth	Occurrence	Self Dir.	Other Dir.
amazed (t)	afraid (i)	hate (i)	willing (i)	want (i)
enjoy (t)	anxious (i)	like (i)		wish (i)
fear (t)	eager (i)	love (i)		desire (i/ts)
glad (t)	hope (i)	dislike (i)		
hope (t)	want (i)			
like (t)	wish (i)			

Appraisals

Truth	Future Truth	Occurrence	Self Dir.	Other Dir.
amaze (t)	predictable (t)	begin (sr)	clever (i)	behoove (i)
true (t)	preferable (i)	fun (or)	easy (i/or)	necessary (i)
seem (t)	desirable (i)	exciting (or)		essential (i)
happen (t/sr)		happen (t)		preferable (i)

possible (t/i)	take place (t)	acceptable (i)
unknown (wf)	tend (sr)	unknow (wi)
unclear (wf)	about (sr)	unclear (wi)

(t)	= *that*	(ts) = *that*-subjunctive
(i)	= infinitive	(Ø) = null complementizer
(wf)	= *whether*-finite	(sr) = subject raising
(wi)	= *whether*-nonfinite	(or) = object raising

NOTES

1) The use of the expression *about* in this case is an attempt to show the similarities between factives and nonfactives by saying that they are both *about* the truth of their complement propositions, regardless of whether that truth is based on preknowledge, expectation, consideration of possibility, or even an open question. The differences between them are treated as differences in the evaluation of that truth and will be accounted for by the Evaluation Modalities. The expression will also be used for other types of meaning, like the occurrence of events and the performance of actions.

This use of the expression *about* is an extension of Morgan's use of the term (1973). He tried to show the similarities between factives and nonfactives by saying that they both dealt with truth, but distinguished between them by saying that factives like *regret* presupposed the truth of their complements while nonfactives like *believe* were simply *about* the truth of their complements.

2) I know of two higher predicates that are important exceptions to this generalization, and a few other suspicious ones. The verbs *pretend* and *claim*, when they take an infinitive complement, require the complement subject to be identical to the higher subject, so that they have what Perlmutter called a like-subject constraint, or what I have called a *self-directed* constraint, since non-subjects can be involved, as will be shown in the section on the Action Modality:

    a.   Alicia pretended that she/he had seen the movie
    b.   Alicia pretended (Ø= for her/*him) to have seen the movie
    c.   Alicia claims that she/he had seen the movie
    d.   Alicia claims (Ø= for her/*him) to have seen the movie

These two verbs are peculiar in other ways too. The verb *pretend*, like the verb *wish that*, is counterfactual because its complement must be interpreted as false, while *claim*, though not counterfactual, can have two possible interpretations, one that it is a serious claim capable of being substantiated and one that it is a dubious claim unlikely to be substantiated, what one might call a dubitative:

    e.   Val pretended/wished that she had seen the movie (= she hadn't)
    f.   Val pretended to have seen the movie (= she hadn't)
    g.   Val claimed that she had seen the movie
           (= I think she probably had/hadn't)
    h.   Val claimed to have seen the movie
           (= I think she probably had/hadn't)
    i.   I claim that I have the right answer

(= I think I do, but I could be wrong)
j.   I claim to have the right answer
(= I think I do, but I could be wrong)

Within the present analysis, *pretend* and *wish that* are described as taking a Negative Predetermined Truth complement, and *claim* is described as taking both a Negative Determined Truth complement and an Affirmative Determined Truth complement. The complement forms of *pretend* and *claim* do not have to be specially marked for taking the predictable *that*-indicative, but they do have to be marked for taking the unpredictable *for-to* complementizer with a *self-directed* constraint. The verb *wish*, when it occurs with a Negative Predetermined Truth Modality, has to be marked for taking a *that* complementizer with a past subjunctive complement mood (I wish that I were you); when it takes a *for-to* complementizer, it has the meaning of either a Future Truth or an Action Modality (I wish (for you) to leave). Thus, these verbs are irregular both semantically and syntactically.

Another set of higher predicates that appears to have a constraint on the identity of their complement subject includes verbs like *admit*, which are perfectly regular in form:

j.   I admit that I/*you/*he did it
k.   I admit that I/you/he tried

In (j), the expected interpretation is one of a confession, an admission of one's own guilt, which requires an incriminating statement about oneself, while in (k), the expected interpretation is one of a concession, an admission of evidence for the benefit of someone else's side, which does not require a statement about oneself.

It is not clear what the relationship is between the complement subject constraints with predicates like *admit*, predicates like *claim* and *pretend*, and predicates taking an Action complement. Are they the same constraints? I think the constraint with *admit* differs from the others in that there are no syntactically definable constraints on subject identity. Rather subject identity depends on the interpretation of the complement. If it is interpreted as an admission, the complement has to contain a statement about the person making the admission, but that person does not have to be the subject of the complement (e.g. "I admit that he gave me the loot"). With the other types of predicates, identity constraints can be specified in the lexicon.

3) When the infinitive is used with a Truth Modality, it cannot have tense forms, but it has many of the same constraints on stativity, time reference, and aspect as finite verbs, and it can represent almost the full range of time reference and aspect meanings.

In Truth complements with finite stative predicates, present time is represented by the simple present tense and with finite nonstative predicate, by the progressive present tense:

a.   We are glad that Les is here now
b.   We are glad that Les is leaving now

In Truth complements with nonfinite stative predicates, present time is represented by the simple infinitive, while with nonfinite nonstative predicates, it is represented by the progressive infinitive:

c.   We are glad for Les to be here now
d.   We are glad for Les to be leaving now

In sentences (a-d), Les's being here and his leaving are all interpreted as present time. The stative predicates, in the complements in (a) and (c), take a simple aspect and the nonstative predicates, in the complements in (b) and (d), take a progressive aspect.

Future time in Truth complements with finite verbs is represented in a variety of ways. For both stative and nonstative predicates, it can be represented by modals or paraphrastic constructions, and for nonstative verbs, it can also be represented by a simple or progressive present tense:

e.   We are glad that Less will be here/leave tomorrow
f.   We are glad that Les is going to be here/leave tommorrow
g.   We are glad that Les *is here/leaves tomorrow
h.   We are glad that Les *is being here/is leaving tomorrow

Future time in Truth complements with nonfinite predicates is highly restricted. Not only are modals prohibited, as in all infinitives, but the paraphrastic future, which is acceptable in Future Truth complements, is prohibited in Truth complements, as shown in (i) and (j) below:

i.   *We are glad for Les to will be here/leave soon
j.   *We are glad for Les to be going to be here/leave soon
k.   *We are glad for Les to be here/leave soon
l.   We are glad for Les to *be being here/be leaving soon

In (k), one can see that the simple infinitive cannot be used for a future time reference with either stative or nonstative predicates. However, the progressive infinitive can represent a future time with nonstative predicates, as shown in (1) above. Consequently, when stative predicates have a nonfinite form, they cannot represent future time in Truth complements.

Past time is usually unaffected by stativity and can be represented by finite verbs with the simple past tense or with the present or past perfect tense. Although nonfinitie verbs cannot use tense, they can use the perfect infinitive:

m.   We are glad that Les was here/left (yesterday/?before now)
n.   We are glad that Les has been here/has left (*yesterday/before now)
o.   We are glad for Les to have been here/have left (*yesterday/before now)

In the finite Truth complements in (m) and (n), the simple past tense represents a punctual past time like *yesterday*, and the perfect aspect represents a precedence relationship like *before*.
In the nonfinite Truth complements in (o), the perfect can be used to represent a past time, but it carries its meaning of precedence, so that a past punctual meaning is not possible.

Thus nonfinite Truth complements have many of the same constraints as finite Truth complements and can represent almost the same range of time reference and aspectual relations. The exceptions to this are the impossibility of representing a future time reference in a nonfinite stative Truth complement, and the impossibility of representing a past punctual meaning in any type of nonfinite Truth complement. Since Truth complements always allow a finite complement, these restrictions can be easily overcome.

4) While Truth complements can have any time reference, including the future, Future Truth complements can have only a future time reference. When a Truth complement has a future time reference, it has the same semantic constraints as a Future Truth complement. They both refer to a future change and thus prohibit permanent states which cannot be interpreted as capable of undergoing change in the future:

a.   I *am glad/*foresee that Wanda will be an Aries
b.   I *believe/*expect that Wanda will be an Aries
c.   I hope *that Wanda will be an Aries/*for Wanda to be an Aries

In spite of their semantic congruence, these Truth and Future Truth complements with a future time reference differ in the nonfinite forms they can use. As shown in examples (k-l) in footnote 3 above, repeated below as (d-e), nonfinite Truth complements can represent future time only with a progressive form. In contrast, nonfinite Future Truth complements can have a progressive form or, for both stative and nonstative verbs alike, they can have a simple aspect form, as shown in examples (f-g) below:

d. I am glad to *be there/*leave soon
e. I am glad to *be being there/be leaving soon
f. I expect to be there/leave soon
g. I expect to *be being there/be leaving soon

In the nonfinite Truth complements in (d), the future cannot be represented by nonfinite forms with a simple aspect, whether stative or nonstative, and in (e), it can be represented by a progressive aspect if the verb is nonstative. In comparison, in the nonfinite Future Truth complements in (f) and (g), the future can be represented by a simple aspect, regardless of stativity, and by a progressive aspect if the verb is nonstative.

Consequently, one can see that nonfinite Future Truth complements differ from nonfinite Truth complements in the use of simple aspect to represent the future depending on whether the complement takes a Truth or a Future Truth Modality. This provides motivation for keeping the two modalities separate when they both refer to the future. See also sequence of tense.

5) The verb *watch*, when it takes a nonfinite complement, has no complementizer. It is peculiar in that it takes either an infinitive form of the verb (e.g., *receive*) or an *-ing* form (e.g., *receiving*). Although the verb *to be* cannot be used with the infinitive form, it can be used with the *-ing* form as long as it has a nonstative interpretation:

a. Dylan watched Muffy *be/being given the award

The *-ing* form can take a nonstative *be*, but it cannot take the progressive *be* form (*being giving*), possibly because of the double *-ing* constraint (cf. Ross 1972). Nevertheless, it appears to be a reduced progressive rather than a gerund since its subject cannot be in the possessive case.

6) Certain emotive predicates such as *like* can take complements with a *that* complementizer or a gerund and then have a Truth Modality interpretation with no restrictions on the complement predicate, but when these emotives are used with infinitives, they have an Occurrence Modality interpretation and require a nonstative complement predicate. Thus, although one can say 'I like being tall,' there is something peculiar with 'I like to be tall.' Though the counterfactual Truth complement in 'I would like to be tall' is all right.

They differ from other Occurrence constructions in two ways. First of all, they do not seem as severely unacceptable when they occur with states (?I like to be tall/*It took place that I was tall), still they are strange and one would prefer to use a Truth Modality gerund (I like being tall).

These emotive higher predicates, as well as a few aspectuals like *continue* and *tend*, differ from the others in that they require a reiterative or habitual intepretation, as can be seen from the peculiarity of '?I like/tend to leave' or 'I like/tend to die'. One can interpret these only if one imagines, in the first case, that the speaker is a traveling salesperson or, in the second case, that the speaker is a science fiction character who has repeatedly died and come back to life. The Occurrence complements of the emotive predicates seem to be paraphrasable with a *when* clause: 'I like it when it rains/?I leave/?I die/*I am tall'.

7) The predicates *see* and *hear* take both a Truth and an Occurrence complement. When they take an Occurrence complement, they are interpreted as referring to the direct physical perception of an event (I saw/heard him leave), but when they take a Truth complement, they can be interpreted as more abstract cognitive evaluations of the truth of a proposition (I saw/heard that he'd left).

8) The higher predicate *happen* can take both a Truth and an Occurrence complement. When

it takes an Occurrence complement, it can be accompanied by a *to* patient phrase, and it can be used with a Cleft construction (What happened (to me) was that I received the award/*was tall). When it takes a Truth complement, it can have a Subject-Raising word order pattern (It happened (*to Holly) that she was tall/Holly happened to be tall).

9) Higher predicates of the *begin*-type can take both an Occurrence and an Action complement (cf. Perlmutter 1970). With an Occurrence complement, they describe an aspect or stage of the event, its beginning, continuance, or conclusion (It began to rain). With an Action complement, they describe a stage in the performance of an act (He began to type). When these higher predicates take an Occurrence complement, they can describe not only stages of events, but even stages involving a change of state like being tall (At the age of 9, Jill began to be tall).

10) There do not seem to be any linguistic predicates that take this modality. If there were, they would have to involve an utterance or a description of an utterance that caused or accompanied an event, perhaps something like 'She sang him to sleep,' 'He sang the sun in flight', 'She talked his ears off', or 'I bid you goodbye/farewell'.

11) Some of these other-directed constructions allow an interpretation in which one steps outside oneself and treats oneself as another person:

a.   I forced myself to read the news
b.   I yelled at myself to shape up
c.   I demanded of myself that I exercise every day
d.   I allowed myself to eat another piece

In these cases, there is a director and a recipient of the direction, but even though they have the same identity, the action is treated as other-directed. Thus an explicit receiver needs to be present, as shown in (e-g):

e.   ?Bess screamed for herself to read the news
f.   ?Webster recommended for himself to shape up
g.   ?I demanded that I eat another piece

and what is called Equi or Identical NP Deletion cannot take place, as shown in (h-k):

h.   *I forced (= myself) to read the news
i   *I yelled (= for myself) to shape up
j.   *I demanded (= of myself) to exercise every day
k.   *I allowed (= myself) to eat another piece

12) The easiest way to specify complement subject identity constraints is to list them in the lexicon in association with each higher predicate, along with constraints on the types of complement modalities each can take (cf. Grimshaw 1979). Thus each predicate specified as taking an Action complement would be marked with its particular type of complement subject identity:

a.   *decide*:   [NPa ____ [Action: NPa VP]]
b.   *persuade*:   [NPa ____ NPb [Action: NPb VP]]
c.   *behooves*:   [[Action: NPa VP] ____ NPa]
d.   *easy*:   [[Action: NPa VP] ____ for NPa]
e.   *necessary*:   [[Action: NPa VP] ____ to NPa/b]

In the *whether to* constructions, which occur only with the Action Modality, the complement subject must always be deleted on identity with an explicit or implied participant in the higher sentence, whether of a self-directed type, as in (f) below, or an other-directed type, as in (g) below:

    f.   Bess decided whether (for her) to tell him

    g.   Bess told Em whether (for Em) to tell Webster

Sometimes the participant is an indefinite NP which can be deleted:

    h.   It was unclear (to someone) whether (for someone) to leave

When these constructions take Action complements, they would have the identity of their complement subject specified in the lexicon, but not when they take Truth complements:

    i   *decide*:
        NPa____[Determined Action: NPa VP]
        "____[Indetermined Action: NPa VP]
        "____[Determined Truth: S]
        "____[Indeterminate Truth: S]

    j.   *tell*:
        NPa____NPb [Determined Action: NPb VP]
        "   [Indeterminate Action: NPb VP]
        "   [Determined Truth: S]
        "   [Indeterminate Truth: S]

    k.   *unclear*:
        [Indeterminate Action: NPa VP]____to NPa
        [Indeterminate Truth: S]   "

13) Some emotive predicates which typically occur with a Future Truth Modality can also take complements with an Action Modality. In some cases, there is little difference between the Future Truth and the Action Modality meaning:

    a.   I *desire* for you to leave (Future Truth/Action)

In this case, the expression of a desire about a future act coming true is equivalent to expressing a request for someone to perform that act, an equivalence that is used in a number of the American Indian languages. The Action interpretation is possible only when the construction has a performative structure, that is, when it has a first person subject and a present tense, present time predicate:

    b.   I *desire/*desired* for you to leave (Action)

    c.   I *desire/*desired* that you leave (Action)

In (b) and (c), the performative present tense form is acceptable, but the nonperformance past tense form is not acceptable with an Action meaning. While a nonperformative version of (b) would be acceptable with a Future Truth meaning, it would not be acceptable with (c). The *that*-(present) subjunctive complement is one used with Action complements embedded as object of certain linguistic predicates like *demand that*, and those embedded as subjects of predicates like *be necessary*. It cannot take uncontrollable acts, events, or states (*I desire that you be tall).

14) I am indebted to Joan Bybee for this idea. Across languages one finds forms with varying lexical content and varying degrees of syntactic independence. There are complementizers of different types. Some are free morphemes, as in English *that*; some are bound morphemes, as in Basque *-teko*. In Papago, one even finds a free complementizer form accompanied by person markers.

    Modals can be either free morphemes, as in English, or bound, as in Mojave. They usually have more distinct meanings than the complementizers and are more clearly combined with the Evaluation Modality meanings, as will be discussed in the next chapter.

Mood forms seem by definition to be bound morphemes, and they appear to be completely grammaticized in meaning. I have found no examples where their meanings are distinguishable from the modalities they signal or where their derivation can be traced back to a lexical item, though one would expect to be able to.

15) In English, the subjunctive forms are distinguishable from the indicative in only a few instances. While the present indicative has an *-s* ending for third person singular, the present subjunctive does not, and while the present indicative has the three forms *am*, *are*, and *is* for the verb *to be*, the present subjunctive has only *be*. The past indicative verb forms are identical to the past subjunctive verb forms except for the verb *to be* where the past indicative has the two forms *was* and *were* and the past subjunctive has only *were*.

There are few constructions in which the subjunctive occurs in English: in the complement of a few relatively unpredictable higher predicates and in adverbial clauses expressing condition:

Present Subjunctive
a.   I demand/insist/suggest that he *be* here on time
b.   If you *be* good, I'll get you a present
Past Subjunctive:
c.   I wish he *were* here now
d.   If he *were* here now, I'd be relieved

In the complement clause in (a) and in the adverb clause in (b), the present subjunctive represents a Determined Action Modality, while in the complement clause in (c) and the adverbial clause in (d), the past subjunctive represents a counterfactual or negative Truth Modality.

These subjunctive constructions seldom occur in informal discourse. In many British and American English dialects, the subjunctive forms have already been replaced with either modals or forms that are not distinct from the indicative. The survival of subjunctive forms is made unlikely by the lack of clear distinctions from the indicative and the limited number of constructions in which they can occur, along with a taint from the nonstandard use of the verb *be* for the indicative.

16) A sentence with a Subject Raising construction is one that is assumed to have undergone a rule which extraposes its complement to the end of the higher sentence and raises the complement subject into the higher sentence to assume the previous grammatical relation of its complement. This rule can occur with a small, unpredictable set of higher predicates about which more will be said in the following chapters.

17) A sentence with an Object Raising construction is one that, like Subject Raising, is assumed to have undergone a rule which extraposes its complement to the end of the higher sentence and, unlike Subject Raising, raises the object of the complement into the higher sentence to assume the grammatical relation of its complement. This rule occurs with a small, unpredictable set of higher predicates different from those that undergo Subject Raising. More will be said about these two types of raising in the following chapters.

18) Givón (1980) presented a scalar analysis of complement constructions based on the amount of influence that the agent in the higher sentence had over the success of the complement proposition. At the top of the scale was the greatest amount of influence with manipulative verbs like *make* and self-inducement verbs like *manage*, in other words, verbs that take an Action complement containing a controllable act. Below these were emotive verbs like *hope* and *want* that showed a small amount of influence resulting from emotional commitment. These correspond to emotive higher predicates taking Truth, Future Truth, and Occurrence complements. At the bottom of the scale were what he called epistemic verbs like *know* and *say* that expressed no influence, corresponding to linguistic and cognitive-physical predicates with Truth complements.

This scale was thought to be parallel with the syntactic dependence of the complement on the higher sentence, so that the greater influence over the complement (semantic dependence) was matched by a more reduced complement form (syntactic dependence).

The notion of "influence" plays an important part with sentences containing Action complements, even when there is no agent in the higher sentence, as with subject embedded constructions like *be essential*. It is that influence that determines whether the complement subject must be interpreted as self- or other-directed, indicating the identity relations that result in Equi deletion. It is also because of the notion of influence that the time reference of the complement must be either future to, or in a few cases the same as, the higher sentence, resulting in a nonfinite complement.

With emotive verbs taking Truth (*hope that*), Future Truth (*hope to/want to*), and Occurrence (*like to*), there may or may not be influence, depending on the content of the complement, whether it is controllable at a future time. If someone wants to jog, they can do something to achieve that end, but if someone wants to be tall, there is not much they can do. The same applies to epistemic verbs like *believe, know,* and *say*. If these take a complement which can be interpreted as controllable at a future time, as with believing you can or saying you can, then the positive attitude expressed by these verbs might lead you to expect that the agent would do something to achieve that end. Without a controllable content and a future time, there is no influence, as with believing you are tall, or saying you will be tall.

In English, and probably in other languages too, the reduction of complement form often results from redundancy of information (cf. Noonan (to appear)), which as we've seen, is related to the notion of influence only with Action Modality complements. The reduction of complement subjects is usually due to identity or indefiniteness, whether with Action complements or with other types. The use of nonfinite vs. finite complements is usually due to the type of complement modality. Truth complements, with their possibility of the full range of time references, usually have finite complements. The other types of complement modalities, which have either the same time reference as the higher sentence or a future time reference, usually have nonfinite complements. The use of a "null" complementizer, as with *make* and *watch*, occurs only with complements whose time reference has to be the same as their higher sentence.

CHAPTER III

The Evaluation Modalities

In the preceding chapter, we looked at the complement meanings and forms associated with the Information Modalities. We will now distinguish another type of complement meaning that accompanies the Information Modalities, what we will call the *Evaluation Modalities*. While the Information Modalities describe information about someone's knowledge or behavior in the world, the Evaluation Modalities describe someone's evaluation of the information either as being the case or as having alternatives available to it. Four types of Evaluation Modalities will be distinguished: *Predetermined* with no alternatives, *Determined* with few alternatives, *Undetermined* with many alternatives, and *Indeterminate* with equal alternatives.

In combination with the Information Modalities, the Evaluation Modalities can evaluate someone's knowledge of the world, as seen in such everyday expressions as 'I don't just think so, I know so', or they can evaluate someone's behavior in the world, as seen in such advertisement slogans as 'We don't just promise; we deliver'. These differences in the Evaluation Modalities also function in cultural misunderstandings, as in the difference in politeness conventions evidenced in the following scene that took place in the United States between a southern woman and a northern realtor: the southern woman, after seeing the house number they were looking for, said politely, 'I think we just passed 205 Main', but the northern realtor accompanying her assumed that the woman was not certain and said, 'No, I think its further down.' The differences in the Evaluation Modalities are also evidenced in the misunderstandings that occur when the modality signals are omitted, as when a student tells the university switchboard operator that she wants to speak to someone about dropping a course and is connected with counseling (uncertainty) instead of admissions and records (determination).

The Evaluation Modalities will be shown to differ in meaning, in cooccurrence restrictions, and in the forms used to represent them.

The Meanings of the Evaluation Modalities

The four Evaluation Modalities are alike in that they all assess the complement proposition according to the alternatives available to it. They differ from each other in the values of their assessment. Complements with a Predetermined Evaluation Modality are interpreted as being the case with no alternatives available, as in the complements of higher predicates like *regret*, *foresee*, *watch*, and *force*. Complements with a Determined Evaluation Modality are interpreted as having expectations of being the case, but with alternatives available, as in the complement of higher predicates like *believe*, *expect*, *be about to*, and *decide*. Those complements with an Undetermined Evaluation Modality are interpreted as expressing a preference or a positive consideration for one alternative over another, as in the complements of higher predicates like *hope*, *be eager*, *like to*, and *be willing*. Finally, complements with an Indeterminate Modality are interpreted as expressing an equal consideration of alternatives, with no expections, preferences, or other biases, as in the complements of higher predicates like *wonder*, *ask*, *be curious*, and *be unknown*.

These four Evaluation Modalities are shown on a scale in Table 4 with examples of higher predicates that typically take each modality:[1]

Table 4

A Linear Scale of the Evaluation Modalities

Predetermined No Alternatives	Determined Few Alternatives	Undetermined Many Alternatives	Indeterminate Equal Alternatives
regret	believe	hope	wonder
be true	be likely	be possible	ask (if)
foresee	expect	be eager	be curious
watch	be about to	like (to)	be uncertain
force	decide	be willing	be unknown
manage	be important	allow	be unclear

This scale has been divided into four types on the basis of differences in meaning, namely the degrees of alternatives available, and differences in form for English and other languages. For example, Korean has four complementizers, each of which tends to be associated with a different Evaluation

Modality regardless of the Information Modality: *kes* tends to be associated with Predetermined complements, both Truth and Action types, as occur with predicates like *ic* meaning 'forget that' and 'forget to'; *ko* tends to be associated with Determined complements, as occur with predicates like *malha* meaning 'tell that' and 'tell to'; *ki* tends to be associated with Undetermined complements, as occur with predicates like *pala* meaning 'hope that' and *swip* meaning 'easy to'; and finally *ci* tends to be associated with Indeterminate complements, as occur with predicates like *molik* meaning 'wonder whether' and 'wonder whether to'.

Although this scale is divided into four discrete types, nevertheless, there are other influences that seem to create varying degrees of alternatives on this scale, as seen in the following sentences:

(1)   a. I believe/Ann believes that he left
      b. I say/Ann says that he left
      c. I think/Ann thinks that he left

While the complement of each of these sentences has a Determined Modality, there are varying expectations about the truth of the complement proposition. When the speaker expresses his or her own attitude about a proposition, we tend to feel more assured that it is the case than if the speaker is describing someone else's attitude, as for example, Ann's. Also, we tend to be more trusting of cognitive evidence like the speaker's beliefs than of the speaker's linguistic testimony. Furthermore, higher predicates like *believe* express a more confident attitude than those like *think*. Finally, intonation contours in English can express determination (rising-falling) or doubt (falling-rising).

From these examples, one can see that the meanings of the higher sentence influence the meanings of the entire construction and thus appear to influence the interpretation of the complement. Nevertheless, each complement will be treated as having the unvarying interpretation of its own modality, and the differences in interpretation will be attributed to the meanings in the higher sentence.

In summary, the meanings of the Evaluation Modalities consist of a scalar assessment of the proposition as to whether it is necessarily the case with no alternatives available, probably the case with few alternatives available, possibly the case with some alternatives available, or possibly the case or not with equal alternatives available.[2] In order to illuminate and verify the meanings of these four modalities, we will conjoin them with expressions offering different degrees of alternatives. It is expected that those expressions which offer a different set of alternatives from the modality they are conjoined with will be judged contradictory or semantically incompatible by native speakers.[3]

Predetermined Evaluations

Predetermined Evaluations will be defined as evaluations by the speaker, or someone else, that the proposition is the case, with no alternatives available. Predetermined complements semantically entail the truth of their propositions, and native speakers interpret the propositions as being the case. Consequently any expressions negating that truth or offering other alternatives are judged as contradictory or semantically incompatible:

(2)　a.　I regret that Rod left
　　　　　*but it's not possible that he did
　　　　　*but there's no expectation that he did
　　　　　*but he may not have/*or not
　　　b.　I foresaw that Rod'd leave
　　　　　*but it's not possible that he did
　　　　　*but there's no expectation that he did
　　　　　*but he may not have/*or not
　　　c.　I watched Rod leave
　　　　　*but it's not possible that he did
　　　　　*but there's no expectation that he did
　　　　　*but he may not have/*or not
　　　d.　forced Rod to leave
　　　　　*but it's not possible that he did
　　　　　*but there's no expectation that he did
　　　　　*but he may not have/*or not
　　　e.　I managed to leave
　　　　　*but it's not possible that I did
　　　　　*but there's no expectation that I did
　　　　　*but I may not have/*or not

Each of these sentences is typically used by English speakers to mean that the speaker holds that the leaving occurred, with no other alternatives available. Consequently, expressions negating the proposition, negating expectations of it being the case, are incompatible with that belief and are judged as semantically incompatible. Translations of these sentences into other languages are judged in similar ways by native speakers of those languages.[4]

When the speaker is the subject of the higher sentence, as in (2), he or she is responsible for the attitude expressed by the Predetermined Evaluation of the complement proposition. When someone else is the subject of the higher sentence, as in (2.1), both that person and the speaker are considered responsible for the Predetermined attitude. Consequently, contradictions arise when alternatives are offered, regardless of whether the alternatives are offered by the subject or the speaker:

(2.1) a. She regrets that Rod left
          *but it's not possible that he did
          *but there's no expectation that he did
          *but he may not have/*or not

    b. She foresaw that Rod'd leave
          *but it's not possible that he did
          *but there's no expectation that he did
          *but he may not have/*or not

    c. She watched Rod leave
          *but it's not possible that he did
          *but there's no expectation that he did
          *but he may not have/*or not

    d. She forced Rod to leave
          *but it's not possible that he did
          *but there's no expectation that he did
          *but he may not have/*or not

    e. She managed to leave
          *but it's not possible that he did
          *but there's no expectation that he did
          *but he may not have/*or not

In each of the sentences in (2) and (2.1), the Predetermined Evaluation meaning combines with the meanings of the Information Modalities to provide four different combinations of meanings. When a Predetermined Evaluation meaning combines with a Truth Modality meaning, as in the complement of (2a) and (2.1a), or with a Future Truth Modality meaning, as in the complement of (2b) and (2.1b), the proposition is treated as being true, or coming true in the future, respectively, with no other alternatives possible. When a Predetermined Evaluation meaning is coupled with an Occurrence Modality meaning, as in the complement of (2c) and (2.1c), the proposition is treated as occurring, with no alternatives available. When coupled with

Action Modality meaning, as in the complements of (2d), (2.1d), (2e) and (2.1e), the proposition is treated as being performed, with no alternatives available.[5]

Determined Evaluations

The Determined Evaluation Modality will be defined as evaluations that the proposition is expected to be the case, though alternatives are possible. The expectation of it being the case is semantically entailed, and if the proposition is coupled with an expression asserting that it is not expected, native speakers will judge that a contradiction or anomaly arises, but if the expression merely asserts a possible alternative, no contradition is felt to arise, as can be seen from the following sentences:[6]

(3) a. I believe that he locked it
         *but it's not possible that he did
         *but there's no expectation that he did
         but he may not have/*or not

     b. I expect that he'll lock it
         *but it's not possible that he will
         *but there's no expectation that he will
         but he may not/*or not

     c. I tend to lock it
         *but it's not possible that I do
         *but there's no expectation that I do
         but I may not/*or not

     d. I commanded him to lock it
         ?but it's not possible that he will
         ?but there's no expectation that he will
         but he may not/*or not

     e. I intend to lock it
         *but it's not possible that I will
         *but there's no expectation that I will
         but I may not/*or not

These sentences are interpreted to mean that the speaker believes that the door was or will be locked. Consequently, the expression negating the proposition, the one negating the expectation, and the one offering equal alternatives are semantically incompatible, but the expression allowing a possible alternative is compatible.

When the speaker is the subject of the higher sentence, as in (3), he or she is responsible for the attitude expressed by the Determined Evaluation of the complement proposition. However, when someone else is the subject of the higher sentence, the speaker is not responsible for the attitude, but rather it is attributed to another person. The speaker is responsible only for the assertion that the other person holds that particular evaluation of the proposition. Consequently, no contradictions arise with the conjoined expressions unless the attitudes expressed by them are attributed to that same person rather than to the speaker, as shown in (4) below:

(4)   a.   Vi believes that he locked it
               but it's not possible that he did
               *but to her it's not possible he did
               but there's no expectation that he did
               *but to her there's no expectation he did
               but he may not have/*or not

      b.   Vi expects that he'll lock it
               but it's not possible that he will
               *but to her it's not possible he will
               but there's no expectation that he will
               *but to her there's no expectation he will
               but he may not/*or not

      c.   Vi tends to lock it (Vi is not the real subject of the higher
               predicate, but a subject-raised subject, so that the speaker
               is still responsible)
               *but it's not possible that she will
               but to her it's not possible she will
               *but there's no expectation that she will
               but to here there's no expectation she will
               but she may not/*or not

      d.   Vi commanded him to lock it
               but it's not possible that he will
               ?but to her it's not possible he will
               but there's no expectation that he will
               ?but to her there's no expectation he will
               but he may not/*or not

      e.   Vi intends to lock it
               but it's not possible that she will
               *but to her it's not possible she will

        but there's no expectation she that will
      *but to her there's no expectation she will
        but she may not/*or not

From these examples, one can see that Determined complements express an expectation that the proposition is or will be the case. The speaker can be responsible for the evaluation or can attribute it to someone else, taking no responsibility for it at all, unlike the Predetermined Evaluations which commit the speaker to a belief in the truth of the complement even when there is another person as subject of the higher predicate.

When the Determined Modality is coupled with a Truth or Future Truth Modality, as in (3a and b) and (4a and b), the proposition is interpreted with an expectation that it is or will be true, but with alternatives possible. When coupled with an Occurrence Modality, as in (3c and 4c), the proposition is interpeted with an expectation that it did or will occur, but with alternatives possible. When coupled with an Action Modality, as in (3d and e) and (4d and e), the proposition is interpreted with an expectation that someone did or will perform the action, though it is possible they may not.[7]

Undetermined Evaluations

Undetermined Evaluations express an evaluation that the proposition is possibly the case, but with alternatives available. This modality involves a preference or a positive consideration of one alternative, but with no expectation about that alternative. Because the possibility of the complement proposition is semantically entailed, expressions negating the proposition are usually judged by native speakers as incompatible, but those negating expectations or allowing other possibilities are judged as compatible:[8]

(5)   a. I hope that he locked up
         *but it's not possible that he did
         but there's no expectation that he did
         but he may not have/*or not
     b. I want him to lock up
         ?but it's not possible that he will
         but there's no expectation that he will
         but he may not/*or not
     c. I like for him to lock up
         *but it's not possible that he will
         but there's no expectation that he will

        but he may not/*or not
  d. I'm willing to lock up
        ?but it's not possible that I will
        but there's no expectation that I will
        but I may not/*or not
  e. I allowed him to lock up
        ?but it's not possible that he will
        but there's no expectation that he will
        but he may not/*or not

In these Undetermined Evaluation complements, there is no expectation that anyone did or will lock up, so that expressions cancelling that expectation are not contradictory. There is only a consideration of the possibility that they did or an inclination toward it, so that expressions allowing the possibility of alternatives are compatible. It is only the lack of alternatives that is incompatible, so that expressions completely negating the proposition are usually interpeted as incompatible, though because we can entertain emotions about things that are not possible, like wanting to see a unicorn, complements with emotive higher predicates are interpeted as only a bit whimsical but not unacceptable.

Like the Determined Evaluation complements, when the speaker is the subject of the higher predicate, he or she is responsible for the evaluation of the complement as possible, but when someone else is the subject of the higher predicate, the responsibility is attributed by the speaker to that person, and the speaker takes no responsibility for it. Consequently, an expression rejecting alternatives is not contradictory or anomalous unless attributed to the other person:

(6) a. Alison hopes that he locked up
        but it's not possible that he did
        *but to her it's not possible he did
        but there's no expectation that he did
        but he may not have/*or not
    b. Alison wants him to lock up
        but it's not possible that he will
        ?but to her it's not possible he will
        but there's no expectation that he will
        but he may not/*or not
    c. Alison likes for him to lock up
        but it's not possible that he will

      ?but to her it's not possible he will

        but there's no expectation that he will

        but he may not/*or not

  b. Alison's willing to lock up

      but it's not possible that she will

      ?but to her it's not possible she will

      but there's no expectation that she will

      but he may not/*or not

  e. Alison allowed him to lock up

      but it's not possible that he will

      ?but to her it's not possible he will

      but there's no expectation that he will

      but he may not/*or not

These sentences express Alison's attitude about the possibility of his or her locking up, so that the conjoined expressions create contradiction or questionableness only if they are expressly attributed to Alison.

    The Undetermined Evaluation differs from the Determined and Predetermined Evaluations in expressing no expectation, assertion, commitment, or presupposition, only a consideration or an inclination about the possibility. When the Undetermined Evaluation is coupled with a Truth and Future Truth Modality, as in (5a and b) and (6a and b), the proposition is interpreted to be about the possible truth of the proposition. When it is coupled with an Occurrence Modality, as in (5c and 6c), the proposition is interpreted to be about the possible occurrence of the event. And when it is coupled with an Action Modality, as in (5d and e) and (6d and e), the proposition is interpreted to be about someone possibly performing the action.[9]

Indeterminate Evaluations.

    The Indeterminate Modality will be defined as expressing an evaluation that the proposition may or may not be the case, with equal alternatives available. Thus, the availability of equal alternatives is semantically entailed, and expressions which specify or give a preference for one alternative over another are judged by native speakers as semantically incompatible; only those that allow for equal alternatives are judged as compatible:[10]

  (7) a. I wonder whether Kyle locked it

          *but/*and it's not possible that he did

        *but/*and there's no expectation he did
        *but/?and he may have
        or not

  b. I wonder whether to lock it
        *but/*and it's not possible that I will
        *but/*and there's no expectation I will
        *but/?and I may
        or not

Because the Indeterminate Modality offers equal alternatives, only the expression *or not*, which also offers equal alternatives, is fully acceptable. The other expressions are incompatible because they give a preference for one alternative over another.

There is another type of construction that occurs with Indeterminate complements, one involving higher predicates like *know whether* and *predict whether*, which we will call the *Committed* type, to distinguish them from those like *wonder*, which we will call the *Uncommitted* type. Committed predicates imply knowledge or expectation about one of the alternatives in the complement proposition, but without conveying which one, while the Uncommitted predicates show no preference. In spite of this difference, the Committed predicates take complements that allow equal alternatives, just as the Uncommitted ones do, as can be seen by the possibility of their complements cooccurring with *or not*:

(8) a. I know whether Barry left
        *but/ and it's not possible he did
        *but/*and there's no expectation he did
        *but/*and he may have
        or not

     b. I know whether to leave
        *but/ and it's not possible I will
        *but/*and there's no expectation I will
        *but/*and I may
        or not

     c. I predicted whether he would leave
        *but/*and it's not possible that he will
        *but/ and there's no expectation he will
        *but/ and he may
        or not

    d. I told Barry whether to leave
          *but/*and it's not possible that he will
          *but/ and there's no expectation he will
          *but/ and he may
          or not

In each of these sentences, although the predicate itself implies a preference, the complement is interpreted as expressing equal alternatives with no preference for one alternative over another, and consequently it can occur with *or not*, just as in the sentences in (7).

However, the Indeterminated complements of Committed predicates do have different cooccurrence restrictions with the other expressions. While the complements of the Uncommitted predicates cannot cooccur with expressions which affirm or negate the complement, or which show a preference for one alternative, complements of Committed predicates can. When the speaker has a preference because of knowledge, as with *know*, expressions corroborating that knowledge as affirmative or negative are compatible, but those offering alternatives, as with "there's no expectation" or "he may" are incompatible. But if the speaker has a preference based on expectation, as with *predict* and *tell*, the total affirmation and negation are not compatible while the expressions offering alternatives are compatible.[11]

When the Indeterminate Evaluation Modality occurs with a Truth or Future Truth Modality, the complement is about the truth or future truth of the proposition, with equal alternatives available. When it occurs with the Occurrence Modality, the complement is about the occurrence of the event described by the proposition, with equal alternatives available. And when it occurs with the Action Modality, the complement is about he performance of the act described by the proposition, with equal alternatives available.[12]

The Indeterminate Evaluation differs from the other Evaluations in offering equally available alternatives to the proposition. The Predetermined Evaluation offered only one alternative and no other, and the Determined and Undetermined Evaluations offered varying degrees of alternatives from expectation to weak possibility. Thus the four Evaluation Modalities have been shown to differ in meaning according to the alternatives available to each.

Now let us turn to the ways that these modalities differ with respect to cooccurrence with certain types of polarity items and other expressions.

The Cooccurrence Restrictions

Because the Evaluation meanings reflect different degrees of alternatives, they interact differently with expressions that may reflect one or the other of these degrees, expressions like *any*, *absolutely*, *for sure*, or *not only X but Y* (cf. Horn 1972).

Holistic and Partive 'Any'

There are two interpretations of *any*: one is a holistic, universal, all inclusive, distributed meaning, referring to *all*, *every*, and *each* member of a set, and the other is a partitive, particular, 'free choice' meaning, offering a choice between *one*, *some*, or *none* of a set. When *any* occurs with Indeterminate Evaluations, it is interpreted with the partitive or 'free choice' meaning, because that meaning is compatible with open alternatives:

(9) Indeterminate Evaluations
   a. I wonder whether Elsie eats any meat
   b. I anticipated whether Elsie'd eat any meat
   c. I watch whether Elsie eats any meat
   d. I asked whether to eat any meat

In the sentences above, the complement proposition is concerned with the alternatives of whether some meat is eaten or whether none is eaten.

When *any* occurs with the other evaluations, where one alternative is expected or preferred over another, it is interpreted with the holistic meaning of *all* or *every*:

(10) PREDETERMINED EVALUATIONS
   a. I am glad that Ada eats any meat
   b. I anticipate that Ada will eat any meat
   c. I watch Ada eat any meat
   d. I force Ada to eat any meat

(11) DETERMINED EVALUATIONS
   a. I believe that Ada eats any meat
   b. I expect that Ada will eat any meat
   c. I am waiting for Ada eat any meat
   d. I pressure Ada to eat any meat

(12) UNDETERMINED EVALUATIONS
   a. I hope that Ada eats any meat
   b. I want Ada to eat any meat

    c.   I like for Ada to eat any meat

    d.   I allow Ada to eat any meat

In each case, the complement is concerned not with some or no meat being eaten but with every kind of meat being eaten, regardless of what kind.

'Absolutely' and 'For Sure'

Certain expressions like, *absolutely* (Horn 1975) and *for sure*, express a conviction that something is or will be the case with no exceptions. These expressions occur readily though redundantly with the Predetermined Evaluation and with the Committed predicates taking Indeterminate Evaluations, but with the other types, which offer varying degrees of alternatives, they seem semantically anomalous:

(13) PREDETERMINED EVALUATIONS

    a.   I'm glad that Belle won,

        and she *absolutely did/did for sure*

    b.   I anticipate that Belle'll win,

        and she *absolutely will/will for sure*

    c.   I watched Belle win,

        and she *absolutely did/did for sure*

    d.   I forced Belle to win,

        and she *absolutely did/did for sure*

(14) DETERMINED EVALUATIONS

    a.   *I believe that Belle won,

        and she *absolutely did/did for sure*

    b.   *I expect that Belle'll win,

        and she *absolutely will/will for sure*

    c.   *I am ready for Belle to win,

        and she *absolutely will/will for sure*

    d.   *I'm pressuring Belle to win,

        and she *absolutely will/will for sure*

(15) UNDETERMINED EVALUATIONS

    a.   *I hope that Belle won,

        and she *absolutely did/did for sure*

    b.   ?I want Belle to win,

        and she *absolutely will/will for sure*

    c.   ?I like for Belle to win,

        and she *absolutely does/does for sure*

d. ? I'm willing for Belle to win,
and she *absolutely will/will for sure*

(16) UNCOMMITTED INDETERMINATE EVALUATIONS
a. *I wonder whether Belle won,
and she *absolutely did/did for sure*
b. *I wonder whether to win,
and I *absolutely will/will for sure*

(17) COMMITTED INDETERMINATE EVALUATIONS
a. I know whether Belle'll win,
and she *absolutely will/will for sure*
b. I know whether Belle'll win,
and she *absolutely will/will for sure*

These expressions tend to tease out a conviction that usually seems more appropriate with Predetermined Evaluations than with those evaluations that express weaker opinions.

Not Only X but Y

Differences in the Evaluation Modalities can also be observed in their cooccurrence with the expressions *not only X but Y* where Y adds to X (Horn 1975). The items *true S* and *probable S* are both evaluations of truth, and since *true S* can add certainty to *probable S*, it can serve as a Y:

(18) It's not only probable but true

However, the reverse ordering is semantically anomalous because *probable S* does not add anything new to *true S*:

(19) *It's not only true but probable

It is assumed that higher predicates like *true* and *probable* have meanings which parallel the meanings of their complements. Thus the meaning of *true* parallels the Predetermined Truth meaning of its complement, and the meaning of *probable* parallels the Determined Truth of its complement. Consequently, it is supposed that what the 'not only x but y' expression points up between *true* and *probable* is the difference in their complement evaluation meanings, the former being Predetermined, and the latter being Determined, so that the Predetermined meaning adds something to the Determined meaning.

Thus if all else is similar, those predicates whose complements are high on the Evaluation scale can add something new to those predicates whose complements are lower on the scale, but not vice versa. Consequently, this expression allows one to position predicate-complement constructions on the Evaluation Scale in relation to each other. The only difficulty is that one has to keep the meanings of the higher predicates similar in all respects so that the meanings compared are just those of the complement evaluations and not some other meanings of the higher predicate.[13]

First let us compare a set of predicates like *know, decide,* and *wonder,* which all have a basic cognitive meaning like to hold, or come to hold something in one's mind, and which differ mainly in meanings which parallel the differences in their complement modality meanings. The meaning of *know,* which is to hold something in mind with knowledge, is compatible with both the Predetermined and the Committed Indeterminate meaning of its complement. The meaning of *decide,* which is to come to hold something in mind with expectation, parallels the Determined meaning of its complement. Similarly, the meaning of *wonder,* which is to hold something in mind without knowledge or expectation, parallels the Indeterminate meaning of its complement. When used with the X-Y expression, these differences in Evaluation Modality meanings should stand out, regardless of whether they take complements with a Truth or an Action Modality:

(20) a.   I didn't just *wonder* if Carl did,
             I *decided/knew* that he did
       b.   I didn't just *decide* that Carl did,
             I *knew that/*wondered if* he did
       c.   I didn't just *know* that Carl did,
             I *decided that/*wondered if* he did

(21) a.   I didn't just *wonder* whether to do it,
             I *decided/knew* to do it
       b.   I didn't just *decide* to do it,
             I *knew/*wondered whether* to do it
       c.   *I didn't just *know* to do it,
             I *decided/*wondered whether* to do it

Since *know S* can be used as a Y to add something *to decide S,* but not vice-versa, its complement must be higher on the Evaluation Scale than the complement of *decide,* and since *decide S* can be used as a Y to add something to *wonder S,* but not vice-versa, its complement must be higher than that of *wonder.*

With linguistic higher predicates, one can see the same scalar contrasts between *say S* and *ask S* when they take complements with a Truth Modality:

(22) a. I not only *asked* whether it was so,
    I *said* that it was
  b. *I not only *said* that it was so,
    I *asked* whether it was

When *ask* takes a Truth complement with an Indeterminate Evaluation, it is lower on the scale than *said* S with its Determined Evaluation and can add nothing new to it.

When these same predicates take an other-directed Action complement, *ask* takes a Determined complement modality, and thus has the same modality as the complement of *say*. Consequently, if *say* can add anything to *ask*, it can only be a politeness meaning associated with the higher predicate rather than a complement modality meaning:

(23) a. ?I not only *asked* for Toni to leave
    I *said* for her to
  b. *I not only *said* for Toni to leave
    I *asked* for her to

With the emotive predicates *be afraid* and *be fearful*, since both take Determined Truth complements, neither one can add anything new to the other:

(24) a. *I am not only afraid that Randy left,
    but fearful that he did
  b. *I am not only fearful that Randy left,
    but afraid that he did

Because these predicates express a negative emotion, they cannot be used in the same expression with predicates like *hope*, which express a positive emotion:

(25) a. *I not only hope that Lyle left,
    but I am afraid that he did
  b. *I am not only afraid that Lyle left,
    but I hope that he did

As long as one can keep the information differences at a minimum, so that only the evaluation meanings vary, then this construction can point up differences on the evaluation scale.

Now that we have examined the meanings and the cooccurrence restrictions on the Evaluation Modalities, let us turn to the different kinds of forms they take.

The Forms of the Evaluation Modalities

The Evaluation Modalities occur in every complement and are typically signalled across languages by a system of contrasts, some lexical segments with content meaning, like higher predicates and sentence adverbs, some semi-lexical segments but with more bleached out meanings, like complementizers, modals, and mood, and some nonsegmental, like word order, grammatical relations, and the suprasegmentals of pitch, stress, and juncture. Below, we will examine a few brief examples of these from English and other languages, leaving a fuller discussion for Chapter V.

Lexical Segments

In English, with its rich heritage of Germanic and Romance higher predicates encrusted with nuances of meaning, as well as in other languages, one finds higher predicates, like *true*, *possible*, *command*, and *permit*, whose meanings tend to specify the Evaluation Modality meanings of their complements and consequently restrict the type of Evaluation Modality their complement can have. Examples of the types of higher predicates that take the different Evaluation meanings are shown in Table 5.

Table 5

Higher Predicates and their Evaluation Modalities

	TRUTH	FUTURE TRUTH	OCCURRENCE	ACTION
PREDET	regret	anticipate	watch	force
	realize	foresee	cause	manage
	true	foretell	take place	essential
	certain	predictable	begin	crucial
DETER	announce	predict	tend	command
	believe	expect	wait	intend
	probable	predictable	about	behoove
UNDET	hope	want	let	permit
	pray	eager	fun	willing
	worry	anxious	ready	try
	hopeful	preferable	like	easy
INDET	wonder	wonder	wonder	wonder
	know	predict	watch	know

Because the meanings of many of these higher predicates are so similar to the meanings of their complement modalities, linguists have sometimes tried to place responsibility for the complement modality meanings on the higher predicates themselves, rather than on their complements. Given such explicit modality meanings as found in higher predicates like *command*, one would not need any further signals to express the fact that it takes a complement with a Determined Action Modality of an Other-Directed type. However, there are other higher predicates, like *know*, *tell*, *decide*, and *ask*, that can take complements with more than one type of Evaluation Modality, so that other signals are needed besides the meaning of the higher predicate.

Sentence adverbs are lexical segments that are often closely related in meaning to particular higher predicates and are frequently used to represent the Evaluation Modalities, as shown in Table 6.

Table 6
Sentence Adverbs and their Evaluation Modalities

	TRUTH	ACTION
Predetermined	honestly	successfully
	clearly	obligatorily
	regretfully	necessarily
Determined	probably	intentionally
	supposedly	decisively
Undetermined	possibly	possibly
	hopefully	easily

These sentence adverbs differ from higher predicates in their form and in their location in the independent or complement sentence they modify.

Complementizers

Complementizers are semi-lexical forms that occur within the complement, setting it off from the main clause and, at the same time, signalling its modality. Although they are frequently derived from lexical items with full lexical content, like the English complementizer *that* from the demonstrative pronoun *that*, their meanings have been bleached out and have become more 'grammaticized'. In English and other languages, the Evaluation Modality is typically associated with certain complementizers. Examples from English are shown in Table 7.

Table 7

Complementizers and their Evaluations Modalities

	TRUTH	FUTURE TRUTH	OCCURRENCE	ACTION
PREDET	that	that	null/that	for-to
DETER	that	that	for-to	for-to
UNDER	that	for-to	for-to	for-to
INDET	whether	whether	whether	whether-to

In English, *that* and *for-to* are used with the more determined modalities while *whether* is used with the Indeterminate Modality. In Korean, complementizers appear to distinguish only the Evaluation meanings, with the Information meanings represented by tense and mood forms:

(26) Korean Complementizers: (Kim 1974; Kong-native consultant)

	TRUTH	ACTION
PREDET	*kes*	*kes*
DETER	*ko*	*ko*
UNDET	*ki*	*ki*
INDET	*ci*	*ci*

(27) PREDETERMINED TRUTH and ACTION

    a. *John-in   [ssileyki-lil   peli- ess-ta*
          top garbage Acc dump Pst Dcl
        ***nin-kes**-lil]   ic-   ess-ta*
        COMP Acc   forgot Pst Dcl
        John forgot that he had dumped the garbage

    b. *John-in   [ssileyki-lil   peli **nin-kes**-lil]*
          top garbage Acc dump   Comp ACC
        ic - ess-ta
        forgot Pst Dcl
        John forgot to dump the garbage

(28) DETERMINED TRUTH AND ACTION

    a. *Han-ka [John-ka ttena-ess-ta **ko**]   malha-ess-ta*
        he Nom   Nom leave pst dcl COMP said
        He said that John had left

    b. *Na-nin ki-eke ka [ttena-ess-ta **ko**]   cean-ha-ess-ta*
        I   top him   leave pst dcl COMP suggested
        I suggested to him to leave

(29) UNDETERMINED TRUTH and ACTION
   a. *Han-ka [John-ka ttena-ess-**ki** - lil] pala-ess-ta*
       he   nom   nom leave pst COMP Acc hoped
       He hoped that John had left
   b. *[ki-ka ttena **ki** - ka] swip-ta*
       He Nom Leave COMP   Nom easy
       It is easy for him to leave

(30) INDETERMINATE TRUTH and ACTION
   a. *[John-i mikukin-in **ci**] molik-ess-ta*
             AmericanCOMP wondered
       I wondered whether John was an American
   b. *Mary-nin [ka-ya ha-nin- **ci** an-inci-lil]   molik-ess-ta*
             top go   COMP   COMP Acc wondered
       Mary wondered whether to go or not

In Korean, the complementizer *kes* tends to occur with both Predetermined
Truth and Action, *ko* with Determined Truth and Action, *ki* with Undetermined Truth and Action, and *ci* with Indeterminate Truth and Action. These
four complementizers are used to distinguish four different degrees on the
scale of alternatives, regardless of the Information meanings.

   In Basque, complementizers are used to distinguish the Evaluation Modalities in combination with the Truth Modality and, to a certain extent, the
Action Modality:

(31) Basque Complementizers: (Bakaikoa: native consultant)

	TRUTH	ACTION
PREDET	-elako	-teko
DETER	-ela	-teko
UNDET	-ela	-teko
INDET	-en	-en

(32) a. PREDETERMINED TRUTH
          *Ni pozik nago [Jon etorri **delako**]*
          I happy   came COMP
          I am happy that John came
      b. PREDETERMINED ACTION
          *Marik Jon bultzatu zuen informea idaz**teko***
          Mary John forced   report write COMP
          Mary forced John to write the report

(33) a. DETERMINED TRUTH
      *Nik esan dut Jon joan **dela***
      I   said   left   COMP
      I said that John left
    b. DETERMINED ACTION
      *Nik esan dut Jon joa**teko***
      I   said   leave
      I said for John to leave

(34) a. UNDETERMINED TRUTH:
      *Uste dut Jon Leo **dela***
      hope   COMP
      I hope that John is a Leo
    b. UNDETERMINED ACTION
      *Poemak errexak dira Marirentzat idaz**teko***
      Poems   are easy   Mar   write COMP
      Poems are easy for Mary to write

(35) a. INDETERMINATE TRUTH
      *Mari galdetzenzuen [Jonek atea itxi zu**en**   edo ez]*
             asked   door lock COMP or   not
      Mary asked whether John locked the door or not
    b. INDETERMINATE ACTION
      *Mari galdetzen zuen [atea itxi z**en**   edo ez]*
          asked   door lock   COMP or   not
      Mary asked whether to lock the door or not

In certain dialects of Basque, one finds the complementizer -*elako* used with Predetermined Truth, in particular with the complements of emotive factives and with adverbial *because* clauses. The complementizer -*ela* is used with Determined and Undetermined Truth, especially with nonfactives and semi-factives. The complementizer -*en* is used with Indeterminate Truth. One does not find such divisions among the Action Modality constructions, where -*teko* is the only complementizer that is unique for this modality.

In Jacaltec, there are two separate complementizers for Predetermined and Determined Truth (Noonan).

(36) a. *xal naj [**chubil** chuluj naj presidente]*
                COMP
      He said that the president will come

b. *xal naj [**tato** chuluj naj presidente]*
    COMP
He said that the president would come

The use of *chubil* signals the absence of alternatives, while the use of *tato* signals the presence of alternatives.

Modals

Another type of signal typically used for the Evaluation meanings is the modals, and in English as well as in other languages, these forms tend to be ambiguous as to their Information meaning. The English modals and their modality meanings are represented Table 8.

Table 8
Modals and their Evaluation Modalities

	TRUTH	FUTURE TRUTH	OCCURRENCE	ACTION
PREDET	have to must	will		have to must will
DETER	should ought to	should ought to		should ought to
UNDET	may could might	may could might	can could	may can could
INDET	may could	may could	could	may

In English, the modals are auxiliary verbs used within the complement to signal its modality. In other languages, one finds a similar use of modals to represent the Evaluation Modality meanings, though the modal form may function as an auxiliary verb as in English or as a modal particle, comparable to sentence adverbs and sometimes, when a bound form, it can be indistinguishable from mood.

In the following simple sentence examples from Thai and Kapampangan, the modals appear to be auxiliary verbs, and, like English, they represent the Evaluation Modalities, sometimes representing more than one Information Modality and sometimes not:

Thai (Steele 1975)

(37) fŏn **khong** kamlang tòk
  must(PT)
  It must be raining

 b. chăn/Maalii **tông** pay
      must (PA)
  I/Mali must go

(38) a. khăw **khuan** cà? tua yày maak
      should (DT)
  He should be really big

 b. khăw **khuan** tii măa kong khăw
      should (DA)
  He should hit his dog

(39) a. khăw **àat** róng phleeng
      might (UT)
  He might sing a song

 b. chăn wîng **dâay**
        can (UA)
  I am able/allowed to run

Kapampangan (Steele 1975)

(40) a. **balamu**   maseya = iya i wan
  certain (PT) happy = SM   John
  It's almost certain that John is happy

 b. **kaylangan** = iya = ng magalutu
  required (PA) = SM   cook
  He must cook

(41) a. **siguru**   mwa =iya
  probable (DT) angry   SM
  It's probable that he is angry

 b. **dapat**   = iya = ng magalutu
  should (DA) = SM   cook
  He should cook

(42) a. **malyari** = ng sali = iya = ng bestido
  might (UT)   sali = SM   dress
  She might buy a dress

    b. **malyari**   = ng mako = iya potang mayari = iya
       may (UA)   leave = SM when   finish = SM
       He may leave when he is finished

In Thai and in Kapampangan, one finds modals representing the Predetermined, Determined, and Undetermined Evaluation meanings, just as in English.

Mood

Mood is another type of signal which can be used for representing the Evaluation meanings. The indicative and subjunctive moods are typically used for the more determined modalities, and the optative is used for the less determined modalities, as shown in Table 9.

Table 9
Moods and their Evaluation Modalities

	TRUTH	FUTURE TRUTH	ACTION
PREDET	indicative	fut indicative	subjunctive
DETER	indicative	fut indicative	subjunctive
UNDET	optative	fut optative	fut optative
INDET	optative	fut optative	fut optative

The indicative mood is usually associated with assertion, which means it involves expectations of a proposition being true and consequently falls within the Determined Truth range. According to Lightfoot (1979), the indicative in Classical Greek is used to express "existential presupposition" or near certainty. In Classical Latin, the indicative occurred in *quod* clauses to represent factuality.

The present subjunctive mood is often associated with obligation, necessity, expectation that a thing will happen, or willing a thing to happen. Like the indicative, it seems to involve few if any alternatives. In numerous languages that use mood, one finds the present subjunctive occurring with verbs of ordering and requesting, what is called the "jussive subjunctive":

(43) a.   Latin (PL. Men. 840) (Wales 1981)
        Imperat ut   illi   oculos exuram
        order   COMP that one eyes   burn out SUBJ
        He orders that I should burn her eyes out

b. Lithuanian (Maxwell 1971)
    Mano draugas prase, kad   as tai padaryciau
    my   friends asked COMP I it do SUBJ
    My friend asked that I do it
c. Bemba (Givón 1971)
    n-a-koonkomeshya Robert uku-ti   a-boomb-e
    I-PST-order   COMP he-work-SUBJ
    I ordered Robert to work

This jussive use of the present subjunctive, which represents the Predetermined and Determined Evaluation range, has to be kept distinct from uses
involving negative evaluations, like counterfactuals, which in certain dialects
of English would be represented by the past subjunctive (cf. *wish* and adverbial *if* clauses), and dubitatives.

The optative mood is typically described as expressing wishes, likeli-
hood, potentially, or possibility, as shown in the following examples:

(44) a. Classical Greek: Odyssey 1.402
          *ktḗmata   d'   autòs **ékhois** kaì dṓmasin*
          possessions pte. self   have   and in-house
                                    2s OPt

          *hoîsin **anássois***
          in-own rule
                  2s Opt
          But you yourself may *keep* your possessions and you may *rule*
          over you own house.
      b. Sanskrit: RV8.48.10
          *rūdárena   sákhiā **saceya**   yó má **nárísyed***
          wholesome friend associate who me not injure
                                1s Opt   3s Opt
          I wish *to associate* with a wholesome friend who *would not
          injure* me.
      c. Navajo: Young and Morgan (1980)
          *yiską́ą́go **hahółtą́ą́'** lágo*
          I hope that it doesn't *rain* tomorrow

All of these sentences with optative moods have the meaning that there are
alternatives available, as in the example of the permission being granted to
keep your possessions and rule over your own house, or a wish for it to be
possible to associate with a wholesome friend, or a hope that it is possible

for it to rain. Whether the optative occurs with Truth or Action meaning, it tends to carry an Undetermined meaning, distinguishing it from the more determined indicative and subjunctive meanings.

Since mood forms are the least independent segments in form and have the most bleached out meanings, they tend to be more affected by language change than the other types of segments. Consequently, one finds forms like the subjunctive and the optative merging and the meanings that they represent shifting. Nevertheless, when viewed from a general pattern of Evaluation and Information Modalities like the one presented here, it may be possible to make more sense out of the fluctuations.

Word Order and Grammatical Relations

There are certain variations in word order and grammatical relations that tend to be intertwined with the Evaluation Modalities, but not systematically enough to be predictable. First of all, the position at the front of a sentence tends to be occupied by definite noun phrases (cf. Givón 1976 and Comrie 1981), and the complements that can occupy this position tend to be Predetermined.

One example of this definiteness constraint appears to function with extraposition, a rule which moves a complement to the end of the main clause leaving an *it* as a dummy subject. Although the extraposition of a subject complement is usually an optional rule if the predicate is an adjectival predicate like *be true* and *be likely*, or a transitive verb like *please NP*, it is usually an obligatory rule if the predicate is a single word intransitive verb like *happen* and *seem*. However, if the single verb is accompanied by a longer phrase, extraposition becomes optional for verbs taking a Predetermined subject complement, like *happen*, but not for verbs taking a Determined subject complement: like *seem*:

(45) a. That Glenn played well happened to him again
      b. *That Glenn played well seemed to him again

In the preceding sentences, when the single verb *happen* has a long phrase after it, extraposition is optional, possibly because its Predetermined complement is definite. In contrast, the same long phrase after *seem* does not make extraposition optional, possibly because of the less definite Determined complement.

Another example of the definiteness constraint involves the topicalization of an object complement. Again, it is the Predetermined complement that is most satisfactory with this construction:

(46) a. That Deanna played well, I regret
      b. *That Deanna played well, I think
      c. *That Deanna played well, I hope
      d. That Deanna play well, I insist
      e. *That Deanna play well, I suggest

Another set of variations in word order and grammatical relations involve complements that are predominately Determined, though some are Predetermined and some Undetermined. The higher predicate appears to govern which variations its complement can undergo, as will be discussed in Chapter V.

One type of variation involves word order inside the complement. As pointed out by Hooper and Thompson (1973), and Hooper (1975), the complements of assertives, or what we would call Determined complements, tend to undergo certain root transformations (Edmonds 1970), which typically occur in main clauses and create emphatic focus: topicalization, VP Preposing, and Participal Preposing. When applied to complements, these transformations involve the moving of complement elements to the front of the complement, but not outside of it:

(47) a. *Stacy regrets that Gina he likes
      b. *Stacy knows that marry her he will
      c. Stacy discovered that standing there was Joe.

(48) a. Stacy said that Gina he likes
      b. Stacy believes that marry her he will
      c. It seems that standing there was Joe

(49) a. *Stacy hopes that Gina he likes
      b. *It's hopeful that marry her he will
      c. *It's possible that standing there was Joe

(50) a. *Stacy wonders if Mary he likes
      b. *Stacy asked if marry her he will
      c. *It's unclear if standing there was Joe

Although these word order variations occur predominately with Determined complements, they sometimes occur with other types too, as for example semifactives like *discover* with a Predetermined complement, as in (47c) above.

Another type of variation in word order and grammatical relations occurring predominately with Determined complements involves the disruption of the complement integrity by complementizer deletion, subject extraction by wh-movement, or noun phrase raising, a rule which raises a noun phrase out of the complement to assume the grammatical relation of its complement:

(51) a. *Betty regrets Pete left
b. *Who does Betty know left?
c. Pete was discovered by Betty to have left

(52) a. Betty says Pete left
b. Who does Pete think left?
c. Pete seems to have left

(53) a. Betty hopes Pete left
b. ?Who does Betty hope left?
c. *Pete was possible to have left

(54) a. *Betty wonders Pete left
b. *Who does Betty wonder left?
c. *Pete was unclear to have left

These rules typically apply to Determined complements, but some can apply to the complements of semifactives like *discover* which are within the Predetermined range, and some can apply to Undetermined complements. Although the majority of complements that can undergo these disruptions fall within the Determined range, they cannot be predicted on the basis of complement modality, but are governed by the higher predicate, and these too will be discussed further in Chapter V.

Finally, there are variations applying typically to Determined complements which seem to involve foregrounding of the complement itself. Sometimes the foregrounding is accomplished through movement to the front, as with complement preposing, also known as parenthetical formation, and sometimes with tag-question formation on the complement:

(55) a. *Cory left, Peggy regrets
b. *I know that Cory left, didn't he?

(56) a. Cory left, Peggy said
b. I think that Cory left, didn't he?

(57) a. Cory left, I hope
b. *It's hopeful that Cory left, didn't he?

(58) a. *Cory left, Peggy wonders

b. *I wonder if Cory left, didn't he?

The successful examples of complement preposing and tag-question formation on the complement cause the complement to be foregrounded, as though it were the sentence being asserted or questioned rather than the main clause. These complements tend to be Determined, though one does find examples of certain Predetermined and Undetermined compatible with such rules. Again, it is the higher predicate that determines which variations its complement can undergo, as will be discussed in Chapter V.

Suprasegmentals

Now let us turn to one final nonsegmental contrast, one which involves the relation that suprasegmentals of pitch, stress, and juncture have with the Evaluation Modalities. First of all, these suprasegmentals are thought to be main clause phenomena so that they interact with the modality of the higher sentence rather than that of the complement. Nevertheless, because complement modalities do affect the meaning of the overall sentence, they do have some effect on the choice of suprasegmentals.

In English, pitch, stress, and juncture make up intonation contours which can signal differences in meaning. Halliday (1976) describes the typical intonation pattern for assertions and other expressions of certainty as mid (2)-hi(3)-low(1), with a rising-falling contour, and he describes the typical pattern for questions and other expressions of uncertainty as mid (2)-low(1)-hi(3), with a falling-rising contour. Bolinger (1982) distinguishes two basic contour contrasts: a falling contour for conclusiveness and a rising contour for inconclusiveness, surprise, or wonderment.

In complex sentences, if the higher sentence is declarative, the entire sentence will typically have a rising-falling contour, even with *whether* clauses. However, there is a modified rising-falling (2-3-2) contour, or what Bolinger calls an arrested fall, which is used when the discourse is expected to continue. This modified rising contour can also be used to signal uncertainty, surprise, or what Bolinger calls "wonderment," just as the regular rising contour does. When this contour is used with declarative sentences containing a Predetermined or Determined complement, as in (59b), a continuation is usually expected. If the discourse were terminated at the end of the sentence, it would be as though the sentence had simply ended with *but*:

(59) a. I regret(2) that Eric prac(3)ticed(1)
      b. ?I regret(2) that Eric prac(3)ticed(2)

(60)   a.   I said(2) that Eric prac(3)ticed(1)
      b.   ?I said(2) that Eric prac(3)ticed(2)

However, with a declarative sentence containing an Undetermined or Indeterminate complement, the discourse could be terminated without the sentence seeming unfinished:

(61)   a.   I hope(2) that Eric prac(3)ticed(1)
      b.   I hope(2) that Eric prac(3)ticed(2)

(62)   a.   I won(2)der whether Eric prac(3)ticed(1)
      b.   I won(2)der whether Eric prac(3)ticed(2)

In (61) and (62), the higher predicate *hope* and *wonder*, which are compatible
with the alternatives available in their Undetermined and Indeterminate
complements, are also compatible with the notions of uncertainty, inconclusiveness, surprise, or wonderment associated with the rising contour. In (59)
and (60), on the other hand, the higher predicates *regret* and *said* are compatible with a lack of alternatives, as found in their Predetermined and Determined complements, and are then less likely to be compatible with the meanings associated with the rising contour and more likely to be compatible with
certainty and conclusiveness which is associated with a falling contour.

Thus one can see that suprasegmentals play a minor role in distinguishing
the Evaluation Modalities of the complement, at least in English.

The Four Evaluation Modalities

Four Evaluation Modalities have been distinguished on the basis of
meaning, cooccurrence restrictions, and the kinds of forms that each type is
associated with. Although the evaluation meanings consist of a scale of alternatives, from no alternatives to equal alternatives, with varying degrees in
between, languages segment this scale with lexical, grammatical, and sometimes phonological markers.

Just as logicians have distinguished between a scale of necessary, probable, one-sided possibility, and two-sided possibility, one finds languages
signaling two, three, or four of these, but I know of none that signal more.
In English, the complementizers make two distinctions: *that/for-to* = necessary, probable, and one-sided possibility (Predetermined, Determined, and
Undetermined), and *whether/whether to* = two-sided possibility (Indeterminate). The modals in English make three distinctions: *must/will* = necessary
(Predetermined); *should* = probable (Determined); and *may/can* = one-

and two-sided possibility (Undetermined and Indeterminate). In Korean, complementizers seem to make four distinctions: *kes* = necessary (Predetermined); *ko* = probable (Determined); *ki* = one-sided possibility (Undetermined); and *ci* = two-sided possibility (Indeterminate).

As seen from these examples, languages may choose to represent all four of these evaluation modalities, as with Korean, or different combinations of them, as with English. I have found no clear cut examples of forms that signal more than four types or that signal different boundaries within the four types. Based on meaning, one might expect to find distinctions made between, on the one hand, strong assertions like *insist* or the strong sense of *believe* and *think*, and on the other hand, weaker assertions like *guess* or the weaker sense of *believe* and *think*, which are more truly midscalar. The closest one comes to formal distinctions between these in English is with certain variations in word order and grammatical relations pointed out by Hooper and Thompson (1973) and Hooper (1975).

Since one finds as many as four formal distinctions made and not more than four, and since the formal distinctions made do not apear to violate the boundaries of the four evaluation modalities described, these four modalities are treated as discrete. The gradations in meaning that occur with higher predicates like *insist* and *guess* are treated as resulting from the predicates themselves and not from the complement modalities. The same holds for gradations caused by sentence adverbs, word order, grammatical relations, and suprasegmentals: the differences are attributed to these sources rather than to the complement modalities.[14]

Summary

Having distinguished between the meanings, restrictions, and forms that characterize the four Evaluation Modalities, we can now summarize differences in Table 10. In the next chapter, we will examine the ways that the Evaluation Modalties interact with the Information Modalities.

Table 10
Characteristics of the Evaluation Modalities

I. THE PREDETERMINED MODALITIES
   a) no alternatives to a proposition
   b) cannot be conjoined with expressions offering alternatives like "but not S", "but it's not expected S", "but I doubt S", and "or not".

c) can occur with expressions like "absolutely" which offer no alternatives

d) with expressions like "any", only a holistic interpretation is possible

e) with expressions like "not only X but Y", can only appear as a Y

f) complementizers with Predetermined complements:

ENGLISH: *that* (predictable with Truth and Future Truth, unpredictable with a subset of Occurrence and Action); *for-to* (predictable with Action; unpredictable for a subset of Truth and Occurrence)

KOREAN: *kes* (predictable with Truth and Action); KANURI: *de-ro* (predictable with Truth); BASQUE: *elako* (predictable with Truth and Future Truth); THAI: *thîi* (predictable with Truth);

g) mood: indicative with Truth; present subjunctive with Action

h) modals: ENGLISH *have to* and *must*

II. THE DETERMINED MODALITIES

a) expected to be the case with few alternatives

b) cannot be conjoined with expressions rejecting the proposition like "but not S"; with those denying expectations of the proposition, like "but I doubt S", or with those offering equal alternatives, like "or not"

c) can be conjoined with expressions adding a slim possibility, like "but maybe not S"

d) cannot be conjoined with expressions like "absolutely"

e) with expressions like "any", only a holistic interpretation is possible

f) with "not only X but Y", can be an X only if Y is Predetermined, all else being equal

g) complementizers with Determined complements:

ENGLISH: *that* (predictable with Truth and Future Truth; unpredictable with subset of Action); *for-to* (predictable with Action)

KOREAN: *ko* (predictable with Truth and Action); KANURI; *ro* (predictable with Truth and Action); BASQUE: *ela* (predictable with Truth and Future Truth); THAI: *wâa* (predictable with Truth)

    h)   mood: indicative with Truth; present subjunctive with Action

    i)   modals: ENGLISH: *should* and *ought to*

III.   THE UNDETERMINED MODALITIES

    a)   preference or positive consideration for it to be the case with no expectations and many alternatives

    b)   cannot cooccur with expressions rejecting the proposition, like "but not S" or with those offering equal alternatives like "or not"

    c)   can cooccur with expressions denying expectation like "but I doubt it", or with expressions allowing a slim possibility of an alternative like "but maybe not S"

    d)   cannot cooccur with expressions like absolutely, which offer no alternatives

    e)   with "any", can only be interpreted as partitive (some or none) and not as holistic (all)

    f)   with "not only X but Y", can be X only if Y is Determined or Predetermined

    g)   complementizers with Undetermined complements:

        ENGLISH: *that* (predictable with Truth; never occurs with the other Information Modalities); *for-to* (predictable with all Future Truth, Occurrence, and Action)

        KOREAN: *ki* (predictable with Truth and Action); KANURI: *ro* (predictable with Truth and Action); BASQUE: *ela* (predictable with Truth and Future Truth); THAI: *wâa* (predictable with Truth)

    h)   mood: ENGLISH: indicative with Truth; NAVAJO: optative with Truth and Action

    i)   modals: ENGLISH: *may* with Truth, Future Truth and Action; *can* with Occurrence and Action

IV.   INDETERMINATE

    a)   equal alternatives to proposition

    b)   cooccurs with expressions like *or not* which express equal alternatives

    c)   cannot cooccur with expressions rejecting one of the alternatives like "but not S", with expressions denying expectations of one alternative, like "but I doubt S", with expressions allowing a slim possibility like "but maybe not S"

d) cannot cooccur with expressions like "absolutely" which allow no alternatives

e) with "any" can only have the partitive and not the holistic meaning

f) with "not only X but Y", can be X but not Y

g) complementizers with Indeterminate complements:

ENGLISH: *whether* and *if* (predictable with Truth, Future Truth, and Occurrence); *whether to* (predictable with Action)

KOREAN: *ci* (predictable with Truth and Action); BASQUE: *en* (predictable with Truth and Action)

NOTES

1) The Evaluation Scale presented here is a representation of affirmative evaluations, but it is assumed that there is a parallel scale of negative evaluations, as shown in Table 11A.

Table 11A

A Linear Scale with Affirmative and Negative Poles

AFFIRMATIVE S No Alternatives to S			Equal Alternatives		NEGATIVE S No Alternatives to not S	
Predet	Det	Undet	Indet	Undet	Det	Predet
true	probable	possible	unknown	unlikely	improbable	false
remember	decide	willing	wonder	unwilling	refuse	forget
force	pressure	allow	question	doubtful	forbid	prevent

In addition to a linear scale, one can also use a circular model like the one in Table 11B.

Table 11B

A Circular Scale of the Evaluation Modalities

	AFFIRMATIVE 5/-5%	NEGATIVE 5/-5%
PREDETRMINED:	99/1%	1/99%
no alternatives		
DETERMINED:	75/25%	25/75%
some alternatives		
UNDETERMINED:	60/40%	40/60%
many alternatives		
INDETERMINATE:	50/50%	50/50%
equal alternatives		

This model, borrowed from the one used in political science to represent the common extremism of radicals and reactionaries and suggested to me by Mickey Noonan (personal communication), allows one to represent the distinction between the complements of affirmative and negative predicate pairs like *think* and *doubt* or *agree* and *refuse*, which are sometimes dealt with differently in other languages. For example, in some languages, the complements with affirmative evaluations use the indicative mood or an assertive marker, while the complements with negative evaluations use the past subjunctive mood or have a dubitative marker.

2) The values attached to these four evaluation types correspond for the most part to the logical values of necessity, probability, one-sided possibility, and two-sided possibility. However, there are a few differences between them which we will go into as we discuss the meanings of the Evaluation Modalities.

3) In trying to deal with the problem of how to verify meanings, I have turned away from the logicians' use of "logical entailments" to what I will call a linguistic use of "semantic entailments". Since logical entailments are based on systems of logic with truth values which are limited to true, false, and, in some systems, neither, they cannot capture the meanings found in human language involving questions, imperatives, performatives, metaphor and the various degrees in between necessary and possible. Furthermore, logical entailments are based on a correspondence between meaning and the real world ("The snow is blue" is true just in case the snow is blue), while the kinds of entailments that linguists are interested in are those that make up the interpretations of native speakers of a language. Consequently, in the present analysis, the meanings of a proposition will be verified by native speaker judgments about what is semantically compatible or incompatible. Based on these judgments, one can begin to delineate the semantic, rather than logical, entailments of the proposition, that is, how the native speaker interprets the proposition, rather than how it relates to the real world.

4) Because the Predetermined Modality is about the absence of alternatives, it corresponds to the epistemic and deontic values of "necessity" in a traditional logical system. The epistemic value is called "necessary" and the deontic value "obligatory". In a "possible worlds" logic system, the epistemic value would be described as "true in *all* possible worlds", and the deontic value would be described as "true in all morally or legally ideal worlds" (cf. Allwood et al. 1979: 111).

The meaning of the Predetermined Modality differs from that of "necessity" in several ways. First of all, the epistemic value "necessary" covers the meaning resulting from a combination of the meaning of the Predetermined Evaluation Modality with the meanings of the Truth, Future Truth, and Occurrence Information Modalities. The deontic value "obligatory" covers the meaning resulting from a combination of the meaning of the Predetermined Evaluation Modality with the meaning of the Action Information Modality, but only the Other-Directed type. Thus the meaning of "necessity" in traditional logic corresponds to certain combinations of the Predetermined Modality meaning with certain Information Modality meanings.

Secondly, the Predetermined Modality differs form the necessity of logic in certain implications. Logicians point out that the epistemic value of necessity has different implications from the deontic value of necessity, as shown in the following sentences:

a. Epistemic Necessity:
It is necessary that p implies p:
"she must be 6' tall" implies she is

b. Deontic Necessity
It is obligatory that p does not imply p
"she must do it" does not imply she will

While epistemic necessity seems to imply the truth of the proposition, deontic necessity, or obligation, does not. Most logicians, with the exception of Aristotle, and more recently Hare (according to Lyons 1978), have insisted on keeping the epistemic and deontic values separate because of these apparent differences in implications. With the Predetermined Modality, no distinction is made between epistemic and deontic. Rather, both are treated as having the same basic meaning: the absence of alternatives. The differences in implications are attributed instead to differences in the Information Modalities and the pragmatic interpretations of time reference and speaker-audience expectations.

On examining the sentences in (a) and (b) more closely, it appears that in (a), the time reference is past and thus realized, while in (b), the time reference is future, and thus unrealized. What is realized is easier to interpret as a known fact than what is not realized. Consequently, when both types of constructions are put in the past, there are more likely to be implications that the proposition is the case, as shown by the following sentences:

    c.   "Kerry had to be 6' tall" implies she was
    d.   "Kerry had to do it" implies she did

In traditional logic, both of these sentences would be interpreted as implying the truth of the complement proposition in the real world. In natural language, the tendency is also to interpret them as implying that the complement proposition is the case in the real world. However, natural language also allows for more complicated judgments based on the interaction between speakers and the audience.

It is expected that when the speaker chooses a complement proposition in the Predetermined Modality, the speaker is trying to convey that the proposition has no alternatives, regardless of whether in the real world it does or not. Furthermore, the audience, if not gullible, is expected to be aware of the possible discrepancy between what a speaker wants to convey and what the case actually is. Thus speakers can use sentences like "She must be 6' tall" or "She must do it" to convey an absence of alternatives but pragmatically will interpret these sentences to have implied alternatives: "She must/had to be 6' tall or else I'm mistaken" and "She must/had to do it or I expect that there will be negative consequences". In logic, such pragmatic interactions between the speaker and the audience are purposely excluded in order to give an unbiased, predictable assessment of the real world.

Thus the Predetermined Modality will be treated as expressing all types of necessity meanings, regardless of the difference in epistemic and deontic implications. The epistemic and deontic differences in meaning will be accounted for by the combined meanings of the Predetermined Evaluation Modality with certain Information Modalities, and by the pragmatic implications involving speakers and their audience.

5) When the Predetermined Modality is combined with the Information Modalities, some of the resulting meanings are those that have been identified with the meanings of certain types of higher predicates: the Kiparskys' factives (1970), Karttunen's implicatives and if-verbs (1971 a and c), and Hooper and Thompson's strong assertives (1973, and Hooper 1975). These will be discussed in more detail in the following chapter.

6) The Determined Modality relates to a value that falls between necessity and possibility. Although it is not dealt with by any logic systems as far as I know, if it were, one would expect traditional logic to describe it as "probable", associating it with the epistemic and deontic values of the modal *should*. In possible-worlds logic, one would expect it to be described as "true in *most* possible worlds".

7) When the Determined Modality is combined with the Information Modalities, some of the resulting meanings are those that have been identified with certain types of higher predicates like

Hooper and Thompson's assertives (1973, and Hooper 1975) and Horn's midscalars (1975, 1978). These will be discussed in more detail in the following chapter.

8) Because the Undetermined Modality is about the availability of alternatives, with a positive consideration or preference for one alternative over another, but with no expectations, this modality relates to what has been called one-sided possibility (Horn 1972). In traditional logic, this modality corresponds to the epistemic value "possible" or the deontic value "permitted". In possible worlds logic, it relates to the epistemic value described as "true in some possible worlds" and the deontic value "true in some morally or legally ideal worlds" (Allwood et al. 1979: 111).

This modality differs from the possibility of traditional logic in several ways. First of all, the epistemic value "possible" covers the meanings resulting from a combination of the Undetermined Evaluation Modality with the Truth, Future Truth, and Occurrence Information Modalities. The epistemic value "permitted" covers the meanings resulting from a combination of the Undetermined Evaluation Modality with the Action Information Modality, but only the Other-Directed type. In other words, the traditional notions of possibility consist of a complex of meanings, while the Undetermined Modality consists of only the meanings that evaluate alternatives.

Another way that the Undetermined Modality differs from traditional possibility is in the treatment of the difference between epistemic and deontic implications:

a.   Epistemic Possibility
      "It is possible that p" implies "p is possible but not necessary"
      "She may be 6' tall" implies "it is possible but not necessary that she is"

b.   Deontic Possibility
      "It is permitted that p" does not imply "p is possible but not necessary"
      "She is permitted to go" does not imply "it is possible but not necessary that she will"

Logically, a person can permit someone to do something that is not possible, because no one has complete control over future acts. Nevertheless, native speakers interpret permission to *mean* that an act has been said to be possible, whether it really is or not, just as they accept claims that something is possible to *mean* it is, whether it is or not.

As was mentioned in the discussion of necessity (footnote[4]), most logicians keep the epistemic and deontic values of possibility separate because of their different implications. However, with the Undetermined Evaluation Modality, as with the other Evaluation Modalities, no distinction is made between epistemic and deontic. Rather, the meaning of the Undetermined Evaluation Modality is treated as consisting of just the basic meaning that there are alternatives available. The differences in implications are attributed to differences in the combined meanings of the Undetermined Evaluation Modality and the Information Modalities, in conjunction with the pragmatic interpretations of speaker-audience expectations.

9) When the Undetermined Modality is combined with the Information Modalities, some of the resulting meanings are those that have been identified with the meanings of certain types of higher predicates. The predicates taking complements in this modality are nonfactive and nonassertive. They are typically emotive predicates expressing wishes, hopes, and desires, a group usually associated with what linguists call desideratives or the optative mood. There are also higher predicates dealing with potentiality or ability, a group associated with what linguists call the potential or optative mood.

10) Because the Indeterminate Modality involves the equal availability of alternatives, it is related to what has been called "two-sided possibility" (Horn 1972). This modality is not usually dealt with in traditional or possible worlds logic systems because it does not involve truth implications. However, linguists have identified constructions of this type as embedded or indirect questions (cf. Baker 1968; Karttunen and Peters 1976 and 1977; Keenan and Hull 1973).

11) Those higher predicates that we have described as Committed typically take a Predetermined or a Determined complement modality, but not an Undetermined complement modality, which would probably be incompatible with the committed meaning. Those higher predicates taking a Predetermined complement are the nonemotive ones that Karttunen called semi-factives, as will be discussed further in Chapter V. In Table 12, examples are given of the Committed higher predicates that can take Indeterminate complements as well as other types.

Table 12
Committed Predicates and their Complement Modalities

	TRUTH	FUTURE TRUTH	OCCURRENCE	ACTION
PREDET	know	foresee	watch	know
	remember	anticipate	see	remember
DET	decide	predict	-	decide
	tell	prophesy	-	tell
INDET	know	foresee	watch	know
	remember	anticipate	see	remember
	decide	predict	-	decide
	tell	prophesy	-	tell

Which higher predicates are interpreted as Committed will have to be specified in the lexicon along with the types of complement modalities they can take.

12) When the Indeterminate Modality is combined with one of the Information Modalities, one gets combinations of meanings which have not been classified by linguists. We will discuss these combinations in the next chapter.

13) It is not obvious how to discern whether we are dealing with the meanings of higher predicates or with the meanings of their complements. In the present analysis, we have hypothesized that certain modality meaninga are the property of the complement, even when the higher predicate contains the same or similar meanings. There are other meanings which could be thought of as belonging to either of them. Is the difference in degrees of expectation between *believe* and *think* a result of meanings associated with the higher predicate or with the scalar modality meanings of the complement? When dealing with the "not only X but Y" expressions, this question is especially problematic. These two higher predicates are both cognitive verbs and they both take the Determined Truth Modality, but nevertheless one can contrast them in the expression:

a.   I not only think it is true, I believe it is
b.   *I not only believe it is true, I think it is

Perhaps when the meanings of higher predicates have been more thoroughly analyzed, it will be clear where the responsibility for these meaning differences lies.

14) Givón (1980) presents a nondiscrete scale based on degrees of influence by the higher agent over the complement proposition. The highest amount of influence is found in implicative and manipulative verbs like *manage* and *force*, namely those predicates taking a Predetermined Action complement. Lower on the influence scale are higher predicates like *intend* and *tell to*, which take Determined Action complements, and still lower are higher predicates like *want*, which can take either an Undetermined Action or Future Truth complement. Lowest in influence are higher predicates like *know that* and *say that*, which take Predetermined and Determined Truth complements.

The reason for the nondiscreteness of the influence scale is that it is based on the meanings of the higher predicates rather than the meanings of the complement modalities.

CHAPTER IV

The Combined Modalities

Now that we have examined both the Information and the Evaluation Modalities separately, we will turn to the ways that these two Modalities can be combined to create a variety of complement meanings and forms.

The Meanings of The Combined Modalities

Every complement sentence has a combination of both an Information and an Evaluation meaning which affects the meaning of its proposition. The four Information Modalities of Truth, Future Truth, Occurrence, and Action combine with the four Evaluation Modalities, from Predetermined to Indeterminate, to create sixteen different types of complex modality meanings. Table 13 gives examples of higher predicates that typically take each type.

Table 13
Higher Predicates and their Combined Modalities

	TRUTH (__be a Leo)	FUTURE TRUTH (__be tall)	OCCURRENCE (__rain)	ACTION (__leave)
PREDET	be glad	anticipate	watch	force
	know	foresee	see	remember
DETER	state	predict	wait	command
	believe	expect	tend	intend
UNDET	hope	want	like	allow
	pray	prefer	ready	willing
INDET	wonder			wonder
	know	predict	watch	remember

The meanings associated with each of these sixteen types will be given, and each will be related to comparable descriptions by logicians and linguists.

Truth and the Evaluation Modalities

When the Information Modality of the complement sentence is Truth, the meaning of the complement is said to be about the truth of the proposition. The Evaluation Modality then evaluates what alternatives are available to that truth, whether the proposition describes a fact with no alternatives (Predetermined Truth), an assertion with some alternatives (Determined Truth), a possible consideration with many alternatives (Undetermined Truth), or an open question with equal alternatives (Indeterminate Truth):

(1)   a.   *Predetermined Truth*
           I was glad that Cal left early
      b.   *Determined Truth*
           I believe that Cal left early
      c.   *Undetermined Truth*
           I hope that Cal left early
      d.   *Indeterminate Truth*
           I wonder whether Cal left early

A complement taking any of these combinations of meanings would fall into a type of modal logic that logicians call "epistemic" because it deals with knowledge or belief about any state, event, or act in the world at any time.

The Predetermined Truth Modality corresponds in some ways to the value "necessary" in traditional modal logic, and in possible-worlds logic, to "true in all possible worlds." The Undetermined and Indeterminate Truth Modalities correspond to the traditional notion "possible", the former to "one-sided possibility, the latter to "two-sided possibility" (cf. Horn 1972), and in possible-worlds logic, they correspond to "true in some possible world". The Determined Truth Modality is not dealt with in traditional modal logic; but in probability theory, it would have the value "probable". Hintikka tries to handle sentences with this modality by extending the possible-worlds analysis to propositional attitudes: thus "A believes that B" is interpreted as "in all possible worlds consistent with A's beliefs, B holds" (Allwood et al.: 113).

Logicians have tried to deal with differences in meaning involving time reference with a "tense logic" system which parallels the possible-worlds logic (cf. Allwood et al.: 121-122). Thus a proposition with a Predetermined Truth Modality (epistemic necessity) would be described as true relative to a point in time t iff it is true relative to *all* points in time which precede/follow t, depending on the time reference of the proposition. A proposition with an Undetermined Truth Modality (epistemic possibility) would be described as true relative to a point in time *t* iff it is true relative to *some* point in time which precedes/follows *t* (Allwood et al.: 122).

Linguists have identified certain of these complement constructions as particular sentence types, depending on the kind of higher predicate used. Although these types will be discussed in more detail in the next chapter, a sketch of each will be presented here. Predetermined Truth complements can be embedded under higher predicates called "factives", like *regret* (the Kiparskys 1970), "semi-factives" like *know that* (Karttunen 1971b), or "strong assertives" like *be true* and *be certain* (Hooper and Thompson 1973; Hooper 1975). Determined Truth complements can be embedded under higher predicates that have been called "strong assertives", like *say that* and "weak assertives" (Hooper and Thompson; Hooper) or "midscalars" (Horn 1972) like *think that*. Verbs taking the Determined Truth Modality are often called "verbs of propositional attitude". Undetermined Truth complements and their higher predicates have not usually been treated separately from those that take the Determined Truth Modality. Constructions with Indeterminate Truth complements have been treated as indirect questions (cf. Karttunen 1977).

Future Truth and the Evaluation Modalities

Turning now to cases where the Information Modality is Future Truth, the meaning of the complement is said to be about the future truth of the proposition. The Evaluation Modality then evaluates what alternatives are available to that future truth, whether the proposition describes foreknowledge with no alternatives (Predetermined Future Truth), a prediction with some alternatives (Determined Future Truth), a possible future consideration with many alternatives (Undetermined Future Truth), or an open question about the future with equal alternatives (Indeterminate Future Truth):

(2) a. *Predetermined Future Truth*
         I foresee that Phil'll leave early
     b. *Determined Future Truth*
         I expect that Phil'll leave early
     c. *Undetermined Future Truth*
         I want Phil to leave early
     d. *Indeterminate Future Truth*
         I foresee whether Phil will leave early

Complements taking any of these combinations of meanings would also be called epistemic in modal logic, but they deal only with knowledge or belief about a future time (after the time of the immediate context). Consequently, they cannot describe permanent states, but only those states, events, or acts which can undergo a change in the future.

In trying to deal with truth conditions relative to a future time, logicians use a tense logic analysis which would describe a proposition with a Predetermined Future Truth Modality (epistemic necessity) as true relative to a future time t iff it is true relative to *all* points in time which follow t; it would describe a proposition with an Undetermined Future Truth Modality (epistemic possibility) as true relative to a future time t iff it is true relative to *some* point in time which follows t (Allwood et all.: 121-122).

Because an unrealized future state, event, or act is not thoroughly predictable, linguists have hesitated to treat higher predicates like *foresee* as factive in the same way they would *know* or *see that* even though the latter two can also occur with a future complement. Thus the Predetermined and Determined Future Truth constructions have usually been treated as describing predictions or expectations. The Undetermined Future Truth Modality, which consists predominately of emotive higher predicates, has been treated simply as desires or desiderative types. The Indeterminate Future Truth Modality, like the Truth Modality, would be treated as a type of indirect question.

Occurrence and the Evaluation Modalities

When the Information Modality is Occurrence, the meaning of the complement is said to be about the occurrence of the event described by the proposition. In this case, the Evaluation Modality evaluates what alternatives are available to that occurrence, whether the proposition describes an actual occurrence with no alternatives (Predetermined Occurrence), an expected occurrence with some alternatives (Determined Occurrence), a possible occurrence with many alternatives (Undetermined Occurrence), or an open question of occurrence with equal alternatives (Indeterminate Occurrence):

(3)   a. *Predetermined Occurrence*
          I watched Mona leave early
      b. *Determined Occurrence*
          Mona tends to leave early
      c. *Undetermined Occurrence*
          I like for Mona to leave early

    d. *Indeterminate Occurrence*
       I watched whether Mona left early

Complements taking any of these combinations of meanings would also be called epistemic, but they deal only with knowledge or belief about events, usually those taking place at the same time as the immediate context, so that they can describe only events or acts but not permanent or temporary states. Neither logicians not linguists have distinguished this modality from the Truth Modality.[1]

Action and the Evaluation Modalities

If the Information Modality is Action, the meaning of the complement is said to be about the performance of the act described by the proposition. In this case, the Evaluation Modality evaluates what alternatives are available to the performance of that act, whether the proposition describes an actual act with no alternatives (Predetermined Action), an expected act with some alternatives (Determined Action), a possible act with many alternatives (Undetermined Action), or an open question of an act with equal alternatives (Indeterminate Action):

  (4)   a. *Predetermined Action*
            Barb managed to leave early
            Barb forced them to leave early
        b. *Determined Action*
            Barb intended to leave early
            Barb pressured them to leave early
        c. *Undetermined Action*
            Barb tried to leave early
            Barb allowed them to leave early
        d. *Indeterminate Action*
            Barb wondered whether to leave early
            Barb told them whether to leave early

Complements taking any of these combinations of meanings would not be called epistemic, because they do not deal with knowledge or belief. Instead, they deal with someone's behavior that takes place either at a future time (after the time of the immediate context) or in some cases, at the same time as the immediate context. For those cases where the behavior is treated as obligatory or permitted, traditional logicians would call them deontic. Possible-world logicians would try to define them according to truth conditions within legally and morally ideal worlds. Thus a proposition with a Predetermined Action Modality, like the complement of *be necessary*, would be described as true in *all* legally and morally ideal worlds; a proposition with an Undetermined Action Modality, like *be permitted*, would be described as true in *some* legally and morally ideal world (Allwood et al.: 111).[2]

Linguists have identified certain of these complement constructions as particular sentence types, depending on the kind of higher predicates used. Although these types will be discussed in more detail in Chapter V, a brief sketch will be presented here. Predetermined Action complements can be embedded under higher predicates like *manage*, which Karttunen (1971 a and c) called "implicatives", and *force*, which he called "if-verbs". When Determined Action complements are embedded under linguistic higher predicates, they can be used as commands, as with *command* and *tell to*, or as promises or commissives (Austing 1968), as with *promise to* and *vow to*. When Undetermined Action complements are embedded under linguistic higher predicates, they can be used as permission, as with *permit* and *authorize*, and when embedded under higher predicates like *be able*, they represent Kartunnen's "only-if verbs" (1971 a and c). Finally, Indeterminate Action complements have been called "deliberative questions".

The sixteen types of modality meanings described here distinguish between the kind of information being presented and the kind of alternatives available to that information. In some languages, certain of these types are set off by particular forms, as we will see in the next section.

The Forms of the Combined Modalities

In looking at complement modalities individually, we found that a few forms were predictable on the basis of one type of modality. For the Information Modalities, we found that in English, Basque, and Korean, finite forms are always possible with Truth complements and nonfinite forms with Action complements. For the Evaluation Modalities, we found that in Korean, complementizers tend to represent the four evaluation levels. When we look at the complement modalities in combination, we find a far greater correspondence with complement forms. Again, the forms can consist of lexical segments like higher predicates or sentence adverbs, semi-lexical segments like complementizers, modals, and mood, or nonsegmental contrasts involving word order, grammatical relations, and the suprasegmentals of stress, pitch, and juncture.

Higher Predicates

Higher predicates are segmental forms with lexical content which can contain, along with more concrete descriptions of human reactions and appraisals, the meanings of the combined modalities, either fully or partially. The meanings contained in higher predicates like *be true*, *believe*, and *command* specify the kind of modality meanings their complements can have, and they usually specify a combination of the Information and the Evaluation meanings. Thus *be true* specifies that its complement takes a Truth Modality in combination with a Predetermined Modality. Similarly, *believe* specifies that its complement takes both a Truth and a Determined Modality, and *command* takes a complement with an Action and a Determined Modality. Because of the specific meanings contained in these higher predicates, they would not need any special forms to signal which modalities their complements take.

Some higher predicates like *hope*, only partially specify their complement modalities, requiring an Undetermined Evaluation Modality. These predicates cannot sufficiently distinguish their complement modalities without the use of special forms, like the use of the complementizer *that* for the Truth complement, and *for-to* for the the Future Truth. There are a fairly large number of predicates that take even more varieties of complement modalities and also need special forms to distinguish between them, predicates like *know*, *understand*, and *remember*, which can take a Predetermined Truth and Action or an Indeterminate Truth and Action, or predicates like *say*, *decide*, and *tell*, which can take a Determined Truth and Action or an Indeterminate Truth and Action:

(5) a. Kelly *remembered/said* that Gil left
     b. Kelly *remembered/said* for Gil to leave
     c. Kelly *remembered/said* whether Gil left
     d. Kelly *remembered/said* whether to leave

Languages can differ in the kind of modality meanings their higher predicates specify. English has the predicate *force* which requires a Predetermined Action complement, and the predicate *pressure* which requires a Determined Action complement. Lango, on the other hand, uses one predicate, *odio*, which requires an Action complement but takes either a Predetermined Evaluation, in which case it has the meaning of "force", or a Determined Evaluation, giving it the meaning of "pressure":

(6)   Lango (Noonan to appear)
   a.   *dákó   òdìò   ìcó   òkwàlò   cwènò*
        woman press man stole-INDIC chicken
        The woman forced the man to steal the chicken
   b.   *dákó   òdìò   ìcó   ní   'kwálo   cwènò*
        woman press man COMP steal-SUBJ chicken
        The woman pressured the man to steal the chicken

In Bemba, a Bantu language, (Givón 1980) the verb *koonkomeshya* is translated as "force" with a Predetermined complement and as "order" with a Determined one. In certain dialects of Basque, one finds the verb *esan dut* used with a Determined complement to mean "say" but with an Indeterminate one to mean "ask".

Languages could not rely solely on higher predicates to represent modality meanings, since for every special higher predicate meaning, they would need a different higher predicate for each combination of modality. At the opposite extreme, it seems unlikely, though theoretically possible, that one could find a language with a few higher predicates like *say*, *hold*, and *feel*, which would be completely unspecified as to the complement modality they took and which could be combined with sixteen different markers for each modality. Instead, languages seem to fit somewhere in between these two extremes, for example, English tends to make greater use of the higher predicate meanings while Korean and Basque tend to make greater use of complement forms.

Sentence Adverbs

Sentence adverbs, many of which seem to be derived from higher predicates, can also be used to signal modality meanings. These adverbs usually represent combinations of the Information and Evaluation Meanings. Thus *regretfully* is combined with the same Predetermined Truth meanings as the higher predicate *regret*, and cannot occur with alternatives the way *possibly* could, which is associated with the same Undetermined Truth meanings as the higher predicate *possible*:

(7)   a.   *Regretfully* Doc failed the exam,
             *but he may not have
      b.   I *regret* that Doc failed the exam,
             *but he may not have

(8)   a. *Possibly* Doc failed the exam,
         but he may not have
     b. It is *possible* that Doc failed the exam,
         but he may not have

Likewise, the adverbs *cleverly, intentionally*, and *willingly* have meanings like the higher predicates from which they were derived: *it was clever/intentional of NP* with their Predetermined and Determined Action complements, respectively, and *NP was willing* with its Undetermined Action meaning. Consequently, these sentence adverbs require that the propositions they modify be interpreted as controllable acts:

(9)   a. Mac *cleverly* avoided the problem/*liked her
     b. Mac was *clever* to avoid the problem/*like her

(10) a. Mac *willingly* avoided the problem/*liked her
      b. Mac was *willing* to avoid the problem/*like her

English has sentence adverbs for a large variety of modality combinations, as shown in Table 14, but as far as I can tell, there are none that have an Indeterminate meaning.

Table 14
Sentence Adverbs and their Combined Modalities

	TRUTH	FUTURE TRUTH	ACTION
Predet	honestly	foreseeably	cleverly
	of course	unforeseeably	successfully
Deter	probably	predictably	intentionally
	supposedly	unexpectedly	determinedly
Undet	possibly	preferably	willingly
Indet	-	-	-

Although sentence adverbs are not as plentiful as higher predicates, they can still reflect the modalities of the proposition that they modify.

Complementizers

Complementizers can be used either to represent the Information or the Evaluation Modalities individually, or more frequently, to represent them in combination. In English, the choice of a complementizer is dependent on the combined modalities. One can predict the possibility of a *that* complementizer for all complements taking a Predetermined, Determined, or Undetermined Truth Modality and a Predetermined or Determined Future Truth Modality. One can predict the possibility of a *for-to* complementizer for all complements taking a Predetermined, Determined, or Undetermined Action Modality, an Undetermined Occurrence Modality, and an Undetermined Future Truth Modality. Finally, one can predict a *whether* complementizer for Indeterminate Truth, Future Truth, and Occurrence, and a *whether-to* complementizer for Indeterminate Action. These predictable complementizers are represented in table 15.

Table 15
Complementizers and their Combined Modalities

	TRUTH	FUTURE TRUTH	OCCURRENCE	ACTION
PREDET	that	that	-	for-to
DETER	that	that	-	for-to
UNDET	that	for-to	for-to	for-to
INDET	whether	whether	whether	whether-to

While these complementizers are predictable for their particular combinations of complement modalities, they are not obligatory in all cases. There are other complementizers which do not appear to be predictable by a general rule, even though one can see tendencies, as we will discuss in the next chapter. The predictable occurrences of complementizers can be accounted for by each complementizer being listed in the lexicon with selectional restrictions for the combinations of modalities that it can occur with. The unpredictable occurrences can be accounted for in the lexicon by selectional restrictions on the particular higher predicate that they can occur with.

In Basque, the combination of complement modalities also affects the choice of complementizers. Predetermined Truth is represented in some dialects by *-elako* and in other dialects by *-ela*. Determined and Undetermined Truth are represented by *-ela*; Predetermined, Determined, and Undetermined Action are sometimes represented by *-teko*; and Indeterminate Truth and Action are represented by *-en*, as shown below:

(11) Basque (Arratibel Iza: native consultant)

	Truth	Action
Predetermined	-ela (ko)	-teko
Determined	-ela	-teko
Undetermined	-ela	-teko
Indeterminate	-en	-en

(12) Truth

a. *Marik atea hertsi zuela gogoratu zuen*
Mary door closed COMP remembered
Mary remembered that she locked the door

b. *Marik atea hertsi zuela esan zion*
Mary door closed COMP said
Mary said that she locked the door

c. *Marik atea hertsi zuela uste zuen*
Mary door closed COMP hoped
Mary hoped that she locked the door

d. *Marik atea hertsi zuen edo ez gogoratu zuen*
Mary door closed COMP or not remembered
Mary remembered wether she locked the door

(13) Action

Marik Jon atea hertsteko bultzatu zuen
Mary John door close COMP forced
Mary forced John to lock the door

b. *Marik Jon atea hertsteko eskatu zion*
Mary John door close COMP asked
Mary asked John to lock the door

c. *Mari atea hersteko gogoz zegoen*
Mary door close COMP with will was
Mary is willing to lock the door

d. *Mari atea hertsi zuen edo ez gogoratzen zen*
Mary door close COMP or not remembered
Mary remembered whether whether to lock the door

In Kanuri, an African language, there is one complementizer for Pre-determined Truth, *dero* (the definite article *de* plus the locative *ro*), which occurs with both full factives and semi-factives, and for other modalities, *ro* (the locative marker alone) for Determined Truth or Action:

(14) Kanuri (Hutchinson 1976) (# - no examples)

	Truth	Action
Predetermined	dero	ro
Determined	ro	ro
Undetermined	#	ro
Indeterminate	ro	#

(15) Truth

    a. *[Fanta isena **dero**]   Ali ye njeskono*
            come COMP   forgot
       Ali forgot that Fanta had come

    b. *[ishin **ro**   temangena*
       come COMP   think
       I think that he will come

    c. *[ishin au ishin-ba-**ro**]   nongenyi*
       come or come-neg-COMP know/1s neg perf
       I don't know whether he will come or not

(15.1) Action

    a. *[Luwo - ro]   njeskono*
       go out COMP forgot
       He forgot to go out

    b. *[nyi - ga   mato - nem lado - **ro**]   galazena*
       you - DO car   - P2s sell -VN-COMP advise
       He advised you to sell your car

    c. *[Ali Makka - ro le.te   - **ro**]   majin*
       Ali Mecca - to go VN - COMP look for
       Ali is trying to go to Mecca

Thus one can see that languages use complementizers to distinguish between the different types of Information and Evaluation Modalities, as well as between various combinations of these modalities.

Modals

Although modals typically represent the Evaluation Modalities, they are frequently ambiguous as to the type of Information Modalities they can specify. In English, the modals distinguish three levels of Evaluation Modalities: Predetermined, Determined, and Undetermined or Indeterminate. They are all ambiguous, some multiply ambiguous, as to the Information Modalities they can represent, as shown in Table 16.

Table 16
Modals and the Combined Modalities

	TRUTH	FUTURE TRUTH	OCCURRENCE	ACTION
PREDET	must	will		must/will
	have to			have to
DETER	should	should		should
	ought to	ought to		ought to
UNDET	may	may	can	may/can
INDET	may	may		may/can

While *must* and *have to* represent a Predetermined Modality, they are ambiguous as to whether they represent a Truth or Action Modality. The modal *may* is multiply ambiguous, since it can represent either an Undetermined or an Indeterminate Modality, as well as a variety of Information Modalities: Truth, Future Truth, and Action. It is unclear whether the modals should be counted as ambiguously including Occurrence.

In other languages, one finds modals that are not ambiguous, but may represent a particular combination of Information and Evaluation meaning. Thus in Thai (Steele 1975), there are separate modals for Predetermined Truth (*khong*) and Predetermined Action (*tông*), and a separate one for Undetermined Truth (*àat*) and Undetermined Action (*dâay*). However, the modal for Determined Truth and Determined Action is the same (*khuan*):

(16)   Thai (Steele 1975)

	TRUTH	ACTION
PREDET	*khong*	*tông*
DETER	*khuan*	*khuan*
UNDET	*àat*	*dâay*

In Japanese (Takahara 1972), there are modal infixes: while the suffix -.*oo* is said to reflect future necessity or intention (Predetermined Future Truth or Action), when it is preceded by -*u dar*-, the meaning changes to future possibility (Undetermined Future Truth):

(17)   a.   *boku wa miti or aruk.**oo***
             I will walk on the street
       b.   *boku wa miti o aruk.**u-dar.oo***
             I may walk on the street

In Navajo, there are large number of modal particles, which are the main way that modality is represented. Some of these particles represent combinations of the modalities. According to Young and Morgan (1980), when accompanying a verb, *t'aa aanii* means "it is true", representing a Predetermined Truth meaning; *sha'shin* means "probably" with a Determined Truth meaning; *daats'i* and *shii* mean "perhaps" or "possibly", with an Undetermined meaning.

Mood

Now let us turn to the uses of mood to distinguish between combinations of modality meanings. Typically, within the Predetermined and Determined range, Truth is associated with the Indicative Mood, Future Truth with the Future Indicative Mood, and Action with the Present Subjunctive. Within the Undetermined and Indeterminate range, Truth is associated with the Potential or Optative Mood, and Future Truth and Action with the Future Potential or Future Optative Mood. There do not appear to be any moods associated with the Occurrence Modality. In Table 17, the moods are listed with the combined modalities they are associated with.

Table 17
Moods and their Combined Modalities

	TRUTH	FUTURE TRUTH	ACTION
PREDET	indicative	fut. indicative	subjunctive
DETER	indicative	fut. indicative	subjunctive
UNDET	optative	fut. optative	fut. optative
INDET	optative	fut. optative	fut. optative

The *indicative* mood is usually described as the mood of fact or assertion, and consequently, it is compatible with the meanings of the Predetermined and Determined Truth Modalities. The *future indicative mood* is usually described as the mood used to express knowledge of future events or predictions about them, and thus is compatible with the meanings of the Predetermined and Determined Future Truth Modalities. The *present subjunctive* mood is usually concerned with obligations or requirements and thus is compatible with the Predetermined or Determined Action Modality. The *optative* or *future optative* mood is usually concerned with possibility or emotional reactions to a possibility, like hope, desire, etc. Consequently, these meanings are compatible with the meanings of the Undetermined Modality.

When negatives interact with these modalities, one often finds subjunctive mood forms in the complement. In English, we have one fossilized example in the complement of *wish that*, which must have a past subjunctive form, though in some dialects it is being replaced with a past indicative. The subjunctive is commonly used for counterfactual or doubtful evaluations in a number of languages. In some languages, one finds a mood referred to as the *dubitative*, which is used for doubtful situations, as in Uto-Aztecan.

There are less commonly mentioned moods that reflect combinations of the meanings of the modalities. The *necessitative, assertive, presumptive,* and *dubitative* moods reflect combinations of the Truth Modality with the meanings of various ranges within the Evaluation Modalities. The *potential* mood represents a combination of the Undetermined Truth Modality (meaning capable) or the (self directed) Action Modality (meaning able).

In English, the of use of mood forms to signal differences in modality has practically disappeared. At this time in English, the only regularly used mood is the indicative, which occurs with all Truth complements. In those few dialects of American English where the subjunctive is still used with noun complements, it occurs only with particular higher predicates, as will be discussed in Chapter V. The present subjunctive occurs with a few higher predicates taking a Predetermined or Determined Action Modality, and the past subjunctive with only one higher predicate, *wish*, which takes a counterfactual or negative Predetermined Truth Modality. Since the occurrence of these mood forms is not predictable by a general rule on the basis of combined complement modalities, we will put off discussion of them until the next chapter.

In Classical Greek, the indicative mood was typically used for the Determined Truth Modality while the present subjunctive was used for the Determined Action Modality:

(18)   Greek (Lightfoot 1979)
    a. *eìpen hóti hoi árkhontes apékteinan tòn Sōkrátē*
                (INDIC) (DT)
        He said the comissioners had put Socrates to death
    b. *hoi árkhontes apoktéinōsi tòn Sokrátē*
                (SUBJ) (DA)
        Let the comminssioners put Socrates to death

In Russian, one finds a similar contrast between the indicative and the subjunctive moods to distinguish the Determined Truth and Action Modalities:

(19)   Russian (Noonan-forthcoming)
    a. *on govoril [čto Boris **pridët**]*
       He said   COMP   come-Indic
       He said [that Boris will come]
    b. *ja prikazal [čtoby Boris **prišël**]*
       I   ordered COMP   come-Subj
       I ordered [Boris to come]

Syntax

The combined modalities can be represented not only segmentally but also nonsegmentally by syntax and grammatical relations.

The only clear case in English where syntax signals a contrast in modality occurs in simple sentences where an auxiliary inversion is used to form questions:

(20)   Jane was laughing/Was Jane laughing?

In other cases in English, syntax does not so much signal differences in modality as show tendencies for certain variations to be associated with certain modalities. There is one type of syntactic variation that tends to occur with Predetermined Modality complements, or complements high in the Determined range, but not in the Undetermined or Indeterminate ranges. This pattern is called Topicalization, a variation in word order that involves the fronting of a nonsubject noun phrase, interpreted as the topic, to sentence initial position. This topic fronting usually applies to definite but not indefinite noun phrases, and thus is comptatible with the Predetermined Modality and its lack of alternatives, but not those modalities with more alternatives available:

(21)   a.   That he left, she regrets/knows/*believes/*hopes
      b.   That he leave, she demanded/insisted/*suggested/*recommended

The next set of syntactic variations tends to occur with complements in the Determined range. Although these variations were linked with *assertives* (cf. Hooper and Thompson 1973 and Hooper 1975), which have a Determined Truth Modality, they can also be found to occur with other modalities besides Truth, and sometimes with Undetermined Modalities, but not usually with the Predetermined or Indeterminate Modalities:

(22) Complement Deletion
    a. I believe/regret that she was sad
    b. I believe/*regret she was sad
    c. I suggest/demand that she leave
    d. I suggest/*demand she leave

(23) Parenthetical Formation
    a. I believe/regret that she was sad
    b. She was sad, I believe/*regret
    c. I suggest/demand that you leave
    d. Leave, I suggest/*demand

(24) Tag-Question Formation on the Complement
    a. I believe/regret that she is sad
    b. I believe/*regret that she is sad, isn't she?
    c. I suggest/demand that you should leave
    d. I suggest/*demand that you should leave, shouldn't you

(25) So Substitution
    a. Barb believes/regrets that he left
    b. ...and I believe/*regret so too
    c. Barb expects/anticipates that he'll leave
    d. ...and I expect/*anticipates so too

(26) Subject Extraction by Question
    a. They believe/regret that someone was sad
    b. Who did they believe/*regret was sad?
    c. You suggested/demanded that someone should leave
    d. Who did you suggest/*demand should leave?

(27) Subject to Subject Raising
    a. That John is happy is likely/strange
    b. John is likely/*strange to be happy
    c. Jane's smoking cigars began a year ago
    d. Jane began to smoke cigars a year ago

(28) Subject to Object raising
    a. I believed/regretted that I was happy
    b. I believed/*regretted myself to be happy
    c. I expected/anticipated that I would be happy
    d. I expected/*anticipated myself to be happy

In English, Korean, and other languages, complements in the Determined, and sometimes the Undetermined range tend to be more malleable and less insulated with respect to insertion into or extraction from the complement than the Predetermined and Indeterminate Modalities, which do not usually allow the integrity of the complement to be disturbed by deletion, insertion, or extraction.

Suprasegmentals

The suprasegmentals of stress, pitch, and juncture that accompany a sentence appear to be related to the modality of the main clause but only indirectly to the modality of the complement. In Chapter II, we saw that there was no evidence for suprasegmentals being used to distinguish between the complement's Information Modalities of Truth, Future Truth, Occurrence, or Action. In Chapter III, we saw that there was an indirect relationship between the suprasegmentals and the Evaluation Modalities of the complement. While Undetermined and Indeterminate complement modalities could occur with a modified rising intonation (2-3-2) without requiring continuation of the discourse, the Predetermined and Determined complement modalities could occur with this contour only if there was a continuation of the discourse. Now let us look at the relationship that suprasegmentals can have with combinations of modalities.

In English, there does not appear to be any relationship between suprasegmentals and special combinations of modalities. However, in Yoruba (Lord 1976) there is high tone juncture that is used to distinguish between the following two types of sentences:

(29) a. *a   mo   '   wi   kpe...*
          we know HTJ say (say)
          We know how to say that...
      b. *a   mo   wi-kpe*
          we know (say say)...
          We know that...

The former sentence type appears to take an Indeterminate Action complement, and the latter a Predetermined Truth complement. Although it is not clear how systematic this use of suprasegmentals is, such examples suggest that a further study of the relation between suprasegmentals and modality in such languages could be fruitful.

Summary

We have now covered the sixteen types of combined complement modalities, examining their meanings and forms. A summary of these types with their meanings and forms is given in Table 18. Next we will investigate the contributions that higher predicates make to the meanings and forms of the complement.

Table 18
Characteristics of the Combined Modalities

1a) *Predetermined Truth*
- i) about no alternatives to the truth of the proposition; a fact
- ii) higher predicates: *regret, know, be true*
- iii) sentence adverbs: *regretfully, of course*
- iv) modals: English *must, have to*; Thai *khong*
- v) complementizers: English *that*; Kanuri *dero*; Japanese *koto*; Korean *kes*
- vi) mood: indicative
- vii) syntax: insulated complements; English allows topicalization of noun complement
- viii) suprasegmentals: English (2-3-1) not (2-3-2)

b. *Determined Truth*
- i) about few alternatives to the truth of the proposition; an expectation
- ii) higher predicates: *believe, say, show*
- iii) sentence adverbs: *probably, evidently*
- iv) modals: English *should, ought*; Thai *khuan*
- v) complementizers: Kanuri *ro*; Japanese *to*; Korean *ko*
- vi) mood: indicative
- vii) suprasegmentals: English (2-3-1) not (2-3-2)

c) *Undetermined Truth*
- i) about many alternatives to the truth of the proposition; a possibility or preference, with no expectation
- ii) higher predicates: *hope, possible*
- iii) sentence adverbs: *hopefully, possibly*
- iv) modals: English *may*; Thai *àat*
- v) complementizers: Kanuri *ro*; Japanese *to*; Korean *ko*

      vi) mood: indicative, optative, potential, dubitative

     vii) suprasegmentals: English (2-3-1) or (2-3-2)

  d) *Indeterminate Truth*

       i) about equal alternatives to the truth of the proposition; equal posssibilities, with no preference or expectation

      ii) higher predicates: *wonder*, *know*, *say*

     iii) complementizers: English *whether*, *if*; Japanese *ka do ka*; Korean ci; Basque -*en*

     iv) mood: indicative

      v) syntax: insulated

     vi) suprasegmentals: English (2-3-1) or (2-3-2)

2a) *Predetermined Future Truth*

       i) about no alternatives to the future truth of the proposition

      ii) higher predicates: *foresee*, *anticipate*

     iii) sentence adverbs: *foreseeably*, *of course*

     iv) modals: English *will*

      v) complementizers: English *that*

     vi) mood: future indicative

     vii) syntax: insulated complements; English allows topicalization of noun complement

    viii) suprasegmentals: English (2-3-2)

  b) *Determined Future Truth*

       i) about few alternatives to the future truth of the proposition; an expectation

      ii) higher predicates: *predict*, *expect*

     iii) sentence adverbs: *predictably*

     iv) modals: English *should*

      v) complementizers: English *that*

     vi) mood: future indicative

     vii) suprasegmentals; English (2-3-1) not (2-3-2)

  c) *Undetermined Future Truth*

       i) about many alternatives to the future truth of the proposition; a possibility or preference with no expectation

      ii) higher predicates: *eager*, *hope for*, *want*

     iii) sentence adverbs: *preferably*, *eagerly*

     iv) modals: English *may*

      v) complementizers: English *for-to*

     vi) mood: future optative or potential

vii) suprasegmentals: English (2-3-1) or (2-3-2)
d) *Indeterminate Future Truth*
    i) about equal alternatives to the future truth of the proposition; equal possibilities with no preference or expectation
    ii) higher predicates: *foresee, predict*
    iv) modals: English *may*
    v) complementizers: English *whether, if*
    vii) suprasegmentals: English (2-3-1) or (2-3-2)
3a) *Predetermined Occurrence*
    i) about no alternatives to the occurrence of the proposition; an event
    ii) higher predicates: *watch, begin, occur*
    iii) sentence adverbs: *continually*
    vii) suprasegmentals: English (2-3-1) not (2-3-2)
b) *Determined Occurrence*
    i) about few alternatives to the occurrence of the proposition; an expected event
    ii) higher predicates: *tend*
    iii) suprasegmentals: English (2-3-1) not (2-3-2)
c) *Undetermined Occurrence*
    i) about many alternatives to the occurrence of the proposition; a possible or preferred event with no expectation
    ii) higher predicates: *like to, be fun to*
    iv) modals: English *can*
    v) complementizers: English *for-to*
    vii) suprasegmentals: English (2-3-1) or (2-3-2)
d) *Indeterminate Occurrence*
    i) about equal alternatives to the occurrence of the proposition; equal possibilities, with no preference or expectation
    ii) higher predicates: *watch*
    iii) sentence adverbs: *regretfully, of course*
    v) complementizers: English *whether, if*
    vi) suprasegmentals: English (2-3-1) or (2-3-2)
4a) *Predetermined Action*
    i) about no alternatives to the performance of the act in the proposition; a fait accompli
    ii) higher predicates: *force, manage, necessary*
    iii) sentence adverbs: *regretfully, of course*

      iv) modals: English *must*, *have to*; Thai *tông*
      v) complementizers: English *for-to*; Kanuri *ro*; Japanese *koto*; Korean *kes*
      vi) mood: present subjunctive
     vii) syntax: insulated complements; English allows topicalization of noun complement
    viii) suprasegmentals: English (2-3-1) not (2-3-2)

b)   *Determined Action*
      i) about few alternatives to the performance of the act in the proposition; an expectation
     ii) higher predicates: *pressure*, *intend*, *decide*
    iii) sentence adverbs: *intentionally*, *probably*
     iv) modals: English *should*, *ought*; Thai *khuan*
     v) complementizers: English *for-to*; Kanuri *ro*; Korean *ko*
     vi) mood: present subjunctive
    vii) syntax: malleable complements
   viii) suprasegmentals: English (2-3-1) not (2-3-2)

c)   *Undetermined Action*
      i) about many alternatives to the performance of the act in the proposition; a possible or preferred act, with no expectation
     ii) higher predicates: *willing*, *able*, *permit*
    iii) sentence adverbs: *willingly*
     iv) modals: English *may* and *can*; Thai *dâay*
     v) complementizers:English *for-to*
     vi) mood: optative or potential
    vii) suprasegmentals: English (2-3-1) or (2-3-2)

d)   *Indeterminate Action*
      i) about equal alternatives to the performance of the act in the proposition; equal possibility with no preference or expectation
     ii) higher predicates: *wonder*, *remember*, *tell*
    iii) complementizers: *whether-to*
     iv) suprasegmentals: English (2-3-1) or (2-3-2)

NOTES

1) For example, logicians cannot distinguish between *happen* with a Predetermined Truth complement, as in (a) below, and *happen* with a Predetermined Occurrence complement, as in (b) below, because they both have the same truth values:

(a) *Predetermined Truth*
    i.   It happened (*to Sue) that she was an Aries
    ii. *It is happening that she is an Aries
    iii. Sue happened to be an Aries
    iv. *Sue is happening to be an Aries
    v.   *What happened (to Sue) was that she was an Aries

(b) *Predetermined Occurrence*
    i.   It happened (to Sue) that she lost the game
    ii. It is happening (to Sue) that she's losing the game
    iii. Sue happened (*to her) to lose the game (Truth)
    iv. *Sue is happening to lose/be losing the game
    iii. What happened (to Sue) was that Sue lost the game

While the acceptable sentences in (a) are about the truth of the complement proposition and have no restrictions on their propositional content, those in (b) are about the occurrence of the complement event and require the complement to have a nonstative predicate. When *happen* takes a Truth complement, as in (a), it cannot have a patient phrase like "to Sue"; it cannot take a progressive because it is stative; and it cannot undergo what has been called psuedo-cleft formation, as in (v), but can undergo subject to subject raising. When *happen* takes an Occurrence complement, as in (b), it can have a patient phrase; it can take a progressive because it is nonstative; and it can undergo pseudo-clefting; but it cannot undergo subject-to-subject raising. To linguists, these are important differences in meaning, cooccurrence restrictions, and form that cannot be captured by a truth value analysis.

2) As we discussed in Chapter III, the apparent differences in implication between epistemic and deontic values of necessary and possible led traditional logicians to postulate separate logic systems for the two, and it led possible-world logicians to postulate morally and legally ideal worlds. Since linguists are concerned about the way that native speakers interpret what speakers mean by what they say, the present analysis treats both the epistemic and deontic values as having similarities that transcend the epistemic and deontic differences. Consequently, necessary truth and necesary action (obligation) are both treated as having no alternatives, because that is what the speaker is interpreted as meaning, whether the real world allows alternatives or not. Similarly, possible truth and possible action (permission) are both treated as being possible but with some alternatives, even though in the real world there may be no possibility or no alternatives, simply because that is what the speaker is interpreted as meaning:

(a). i. He had to be 6' tall (?but he wasn't)
            (= he was or else the speaker is wrong)
     ii. He had to leave (?but he didn't)
            (= he did or else the speaker is wrong)
(b). i. He may be 6' tall (?but he can't be)
            (= he may be or the speaker is wrong)
     ii. He may leave (?but he can't)
            (= he may or else the speaker is wrong)

Logicians seem to treat declarative sentences as though they were the absolute truth, forgetting that their source is a fallible speaker.

CHAPTER V

The Higher Sentence and Its Complement Modalities

Now that we have examined the complement meanings and forms associated with the Information and Evaluation Modalities, both separately and in combination, we will look at the ways that these Modalities interact with the higher sentence.

The higher sentence provides the immediate context for the complement sentence in the same way that the speech situation provides the immediate context for a simple sentence or an independent clause. This context sets up the deictic references to person and time that affect the meanings and forms of the complement. Other meanings in the higher sentence that make up the context are the meanings of its higher predicate, the nominal roles of its noun phrases, its polarity, and its own modalities, which are distinct from those of the complement. One also finds certain combinations of higher sentence and complement meanings being singled out for special uses.[1]

Deixis and the Immediate Context

The higher sentence provides two important pieces of deictic information that affect the complement. It contains information about the participants in the sentence and the time reference of the construction relative to the speech situation.

All higher sentences have a major participant to whom the predicate reaction or appraisal is attributed. With object embedding reactions, the major participant is always the subject, but with subject embedding appraisals, the major participant can be the direct object, the indirect object or benefactor, or an implied participant:

(1)   a.   *Harold* heard that he had won
       b.   It pleased *Harold* to win
       c.   It seemed *to Harold* that he'd won
       d.   To win was easy *for Harold*

    e. It seemed that Harold had won

    f. To win was easy

    g. It was true that Harold had won

In (a) through (d), the major participant is Harold, since he is the one to whom the reaction or appraisal is attributed. In (e) through (g), there is no explicit major participant, but the appraisals can be attributed either to the speaker or to a nonreferential "one". The constraints on the identity of the complement subject in Action Modality complements are dependent on the deixis of the higher sentence, as will be discussed in more detail under nominal roles.[2]

If the major participant is the speaker, a Determined complement modality will be evaluated as more determined than if it is another person:

(2)   a. I think that Karen is right

      b. Ned thinks that Karen is right

(3)   a. It seems to me that Karen is right

      b. It seems to Ned that Karen is right

(4)   a. I suggest that Karen leave

      b. Ned suggests that Karen leave

(5)   a. It is important to me that Karen leave

      b. It is important to Ned that Karen leave

Although each of these sentences has a Determined complement modality, each pair varies as to who has what expectations. In the (a) sentences, the speaker is the major participant and is responsible for the attitude expressed, so that the hearer is led to expect the complement proposition to be the case. In the (b) sentences, the speaker attributes the attitude to Ned, taking no responsibility for it, so that the hearer is not led to expect the complement proposition to be the case. However, Ned is expected to have expectations that the complement proposition is the case, though with alternatives available.

Another piece of deictic information contributed by the higher sentence is time reference. The time reference of the higher sentence is relative to the speech act, but the time reference of the complement is relative to the higher sentence, as shown in the following examples:

(6)   a. Rudy is suggesting that Nell left

      b. Rudy suggested that Nell leave

      c. Rudy will watch Nell leave

In (6a), the time reference of the higher sentence is the same as the time of the speech act, while the complement time reference is before the time of the higher sentence and consequently before the time of the speech act. In (6b), the time of the higher sentence is before the time of the speech act, and the time of the complement is after the time of the higher sentence, which could be before, during, or after the speech act. In (6c), the time reference of the higher sentence is after the time of the speech act, and the time reference of the complement is identical to that time.

The time reference constraints on certain complement modalities all refer to the time of the higher sentence. Future Truth complements require a time reference after the higher sentence. Occurrence complements require the same time reference as the higher sentence. Action complements usually require a time reference after the higher sentence, but, depending on the higher predicate, some require the same time as the higher sentence. Only a Truth complement can have a time reference that is before the time of the higher sentence, and only this type can have a free choice of time reference.

Time reference constraints also affect the forms a complement can take. Since Truth complements can take any time reference, they have to have time specified in the complement. In languages with tense forms, the time is typically specified by using finite complements ("I am glad that she is/was here"). However, it can also be done by using nonfinite complements with aspectual markers ("I am glad for her to be/have been here"), as discussed in Chapter II.

The time reference of the other Information complements is completely restricted by the complement modality. Occurrence Modality complements and a few higher predicates with Action Modality complements require the same time reference as the higher sentence, and Future Truth Modality complements and all other Action Modality complements take a future time reference. These complements tend to have a nonfinite form.[3]

One complement form that is not predictable from time reference constraints but is clearly associated with them is the null complementizer, which in English occurs only in those complements that have to have the same time reference as their higher sentence. One finds this null complementizer with several higher predicates like *watch* that take an Occurrence complement and a few like *make* and *let* which take both Occurrence and Action complements.

Now that we have looked at the ways that the personal and temporal deixis of the higher sentence contributes to the meaning and form of the complement, let us turn to the contributions made by the higher predicate.

The Higher Predicate

Subject and Object Embedding Predicates

The first distinction that needs to be observed among higher predicates is the difference between subject embedding and object embedding types. Subject embedding predicates like *amaze*, *be rumored*, *be easy*, and *be true*, take a complement as a subject:

(7)   a.   *That she won* amazes them
        b.   *For her to win* is easy (for her)
        c.   *Whether she won* is unknown (to anyone)

In these sentences, the higher predicate describes an appraisal of the complement proposition. The emphasis is on the appraisal rather than the person doing the appraising, though that person is either explicit or implied. If the person is explicit, it functions as either the object of the verb, as in (a) above, or the object of a preposition, as in the other examples above. These subject embedding higher predicates, I have called *appraisals* and their complements, I have called by the traditional name of *subject complements*.

Object embedding predicates like *regret*, *say*, and *believe* take a complement as an object:

(8)   a.   We regretted that she left
        b.   We said that she left
        c.   We believe that she left

In these sentences, the higher predicate describes someone's reaction to the complement proposition. The emphasis is on the person doing the reacting, usually the subject of the verb, and that person's reaction. These object embedding higher predicates, I have called *reactions* and their complements, I have called *object complements*.

The meaning differences between these two types of higher predicates are mainly a matter of emphasis, but they affect the overall meaning of the complex sentence and the form of the complement.

One variation in complement form typical of subject embedding constructions results from extraposition, a rule which moves the subject complement to the end position of the higher sentence:

(9)   a.   That she left bothered me
        b.   It bothered me that she left
(9.1) a.   Whether to leave is unclear

    b. It is unclear whether to leave
(9.2) a. For her to leave is a shame
    b. It is a shame for her to leave

Although extraposition is usually an optional ordering, it is obligatory with certain higher predicates, as shown in the starred examples below:

(10) a. That she left is apparent/*appears
    b. It is apparent/appears that she left
(10.1)a. That she left came to pass/*happened
    b. It came to pass/happened that she left
(10.2)a. That she left was believed by all/*believed
    b. It was believed/rumored that she left

Extraposition appears to be obligatory if the higher predicate is a single word verb or a passive verb with no agent phrase. It appears to be optional for most higher predicates which consist of a phrase, like a verb and its object or a linking verb and a predicate adjective or noun. However, there is a very strong preference for the use of the extraposed construction in order to avoid a lengthy subject, so that many people find unextraposed subject complements unacceptable.[4]

    A few object embedding predicates are thought to allow extraposition:

(11) a. I dislike that she left (very much)
    b. I dislike (it) very much that she left
(11.1)a. He believes that he is right (very deeply)
    b. He believes (?it) very deeply that he is right
(11.2)a. She wants him to leave (very much)
    b. She wants (*it) very much for him to leave

The dummy subject *it* that is supposed to result from extraposition sounds peculiar in some of these sentences, and in many dialects it is prohibited or just omitted.

    Although the majority of *that* and *for-to* complementizer forms in English are predictable on the basis of complement modality alone, nevertheless, there is a tendency for subject complements with a Predetermined or Determined Modality to take a *that* complementizer where it might not be predictable by modality. While Action complements with a Predetermined or Determined Modality take *for-to* complementizers, those that are subject embedded can also take a *that* subjunctive:

(12) a. For him to leave is necessary

b. That he leave is necessary

(13) a. For him to leave is important
      b. That he leave is important

Aside from these subject embedding cases, the only time a *that* subjunctive complementizer can occur with an Action Modality complement is with a small, unpredictable set of object embedding linguistic predicates (*demand*) and emotives (*desires*).

There are no instances of *that* complementizers among object complements with an Occurrence Modality, but one does find them with subject complements:

(14) a. It took place that they left
      b. It came to pass that they left
      c. It developed that they left

One might speculate that the reason for this tendency for subject complements to take *that* has something to do with the fact that subjects tend to be definite (cf. Givón 1976 and Comrie 1981), and, as Bresnan (1972) showed, *that* complementizers tend to have a definite meaning.

In Thai, subject complements also have a tendency to occur with a certain complementizer, the complementizer *thîi*. Usually this complementizer occurs with only certain types of Predetermined Truth complements, but it can occur with many subject embedding appraisals that would regularly take other types of complements (data from Yuphaphann Hoonchamlong, native consultant):

(15) a. *chǎn sǐacai/ruu thîi John pen Leo*
         I regret/*know that John is a Leo
      b. *nâa pralàatcai/cing thîi John pen Leo*
         It is amazing/true that John is a Leo
      c. *cam pen thîi khǎw tôong pai*
         It is necessary that he leave
      d. *pen pai dâi thîi John ca pen rǐi mâi pen Leo*
         It is possible for John to be a Leo or not

Looking at related uses of *thîi*, it occurs as a relative or nominalization marker, as a noun meaning "place", and as a preposition meaning "at" (Surrintramont, native consultant). Like English *that*, the complementizer *thîi* may have definite properties that make it compatible with the definiteness of a subject.

Another way in which the forms of subject complements differ from those of object complements is in their resistance to complementizer deletion. While *that* and *for* can be deleted from the object complements of certain higher predicates, they cannot be deleted from any subject complements in initial position:

(16) a. She said/regretted that he left
      b. She said/*regretted he left

(17) a. She disliked/waited for him to sing
      b. She disliked/*waited him to sing

(18) a. That he left bothered her
      b. *He left bothered her

(19) a. For him to snore was strange
      b. *Him to snore was strange

One can speculate that sentence initial complementizers cannot be deleted because they provide a necessary signal that the following noun and verb are subordinate. This reasoning is more persuasive with *that* complementizers than with *for*.

If the subject complement is not sentence initial but is extraposed, a *that* complementizer, but not a *for*, can be more readily deleted if it occurs with certain higher predicates:

(20) a. It was likely/true that he left
      b. It was likely/*true he left

(21) a. It was difficult/fun for him to leave
      b. *It was difficult/fun him to leave

The constraints on which higher predicates allow complementizer deletion will be discussed under the section on the semantic classes of higher predicates.

Another difference in form resulting from the differences in subject and object complements is the possibility of extraction of subject or object noun phrases from the complement by wh-movement. There can be no wh-movement from clause-initial subject complements, but if the complement is extraposed, there can be wh-movement of the object, and if the higher predicate is a type like *be likely* which can also undergo complementizer deletion, there can also be wh-movement of the subject:[5]

(22) a. [That he wrote *the book*] is likely/true

    b. *What [that he wrote] is likely/true?
    c. *I saw the book which [that he wrote] is likely/true
    d. I saw the book which it is likely/true [that he wrote]
    e. I saw the guy who it is likely/*true [wrote the book]

(23) a. [For him to write the book] was difficult
    b. *What [for him to write] was difficult?
    c. *I saw the book which [for him to write] was difficult
    d. I saw the book which it was difficult [for him to write]
    e. *I saw the guy who it was difficult [to write the book]

With object complements, there are no constraints on wh-movement of the object, but wh-movement of the subject is possible only with higher predicates that can undergo complementizer deletion:

(24) a. She thinks/hates [that he wrote it]
    b. What does she think/hate [that he wrote?]
    c. I saw the book which she thinks/hates [that he wrote]
    d. I saw the guy who she thinks/*hates [wrote the book]

Another type of noun phrase extraction is raising, which also shows a difference between subject and object complements. With subject complements, raising involves the extraposition of the complement to the end of the higher sentence and the raising of a noun phrase from the complement into the higher sentence to assume the grammatical relations of the extraposed complement. There are two types of raising for subject complements: one in which the subject of the complement is raised into the subject of the higher sentence, called subject to subject raising, and one in which the object of the complement is raised into the subject of the higher sentence, called object to subject raising:

(25) a. That Margo sold the car is likely
    b. Margo is likely to have sold the car

(26) a. For Margo to sell the car was easy
    b. The car was easy for Margo to sell

In example (25b), the subject complement is extraposed and the subject of the complement, Margo, becomes the new subject of the higher sentence. In example (26b), the subject complement is extraposed and the object of the complement the car becomes the new subject of the higher sentence.

    With object complements, only one kind of raising is possible in English. It involves the extraposition of the object complement and the raising of the subject of the complement into the object of the higher sentence, what is called subject to object raising:

(27) a. He believes that *Margo sold the car*
b. He believes *Margo* to have sold the car

For various analyses and names for the raising phenomena, see Ross (1969), Perlmutter and Postal (1974), and Postal (1974).

These are the main differences in meaning and form that occur with subject and object complements. Now let us look at other meanings associated with higher predicates.

Stative and Nonstative Higher Predicates

Another important meaning difference between higher predicates is the stative-nonstative distinction. Stative reactions or appraisals, like the typical uses of *regret, amaze, believe, be likely*, and *be able*, describe permanent or temporary states taking place at a point in time with no duration, so that they cannot occur with the progressive aspect. Nonstative reactions or appraisals, like certain uses of *worry, say, be rumored, realize, take place*, and *try*, can be used to describe events or acts with duration in time, so that they can occur with the progressive aspect:

(28) a. I *regret/*am regretting* that she left
b. It *amazes/*is amazing* me that she left
c. I *am able/*being able* to leave
d. It *is likely/*is being likely* that she left

(29) a. I *worry/am worrying* that she left
b. I *say/am saying* that she left
c. It *is rumored/being rumored* that she left
d. I *tried/was trying* to leave

It is not usual to hear people use typically stative predicates with the progressive to add a nonstative flavor of duration, as in answer to the question "What are you doing?", in which case some of the starred examples would be a little irregular but acceptable.

Some higher predicates are stative with one type of complement modality and nonstative with another:

(30) a. I *heard* that she was a Virgo (DT)
b. *I *was hearing* that she was a Virgo (DT)
c. I *heard* her leave (DO)

    d. I *was hearing* her leave (DO)

(31) a. It *happened* that she was a Virgo (PT)
       b. *It *was happening* that she was a Virgo (PT)
       c. What *happened* was that she left (PO)
       d. What *was happening* was that she was leaving (PO)

These stative and nonstative differences in the meanings of higher predicates combine with other meanings to affect the meaning of the entire complement construction, but they do not appear to affect the complement form.

Semantic Classes of Higher Predicates

Another important set of meaning differences has to do with the semantic class of a higher predicate. Four semantic classes of higher predicates can be distinguished. There are emotive reactions like *regret, be afraid, hope, want, be willing*; and emotive appraisals like *be amazing, be hopeful,* and *be desirable*. There are linguistic reactions like *say, tell, assert, command, demand, promise*; and linguistic appraisals like *be rumored* and *be said*. There are cognitive-physical reactions like *know, think, believe, decide, intend, persuade, show, prove, force, manage, be able, enable*; and cognitive-physical appraisals like *be unknown, strike NP as, be apparent, be true, be likely, be possible, be necessary, be acceptable,* and *be easy*. Although each higher predicate has its own unique meaning contribution, it also has the more general meaning of its class which will be shown to affect the meanings and forms of the complement.

Emotive Higher Predicates

Emotive higher predicates describe someone's feelings about a proposition, either their emotional reaction to it or their emotional appraisal of it; whether it involves the truth or future truth of the proposition, or the occurrence or performance of it, and whether it is absolute, expected, possible, or questionable. Higher predicates of this type include *regret, be afraid, hope, want, be willing, prefer, amazing, be hopeful, be desirable, be concerned,* etc:

(32) a. I regret that he ate the pizza
       b. I'm afraid that he ate the pizza
       c. It is hopeful that he ate the pizza
       d. I am concerned whether he ate the pizza
       e. I wanted him to eat the pizza

    f. I was willing to eat the pizza
    g. It is desirable that he eat the pizza
    h. I am concerned whether to eat the pizza

These predicates are mostly stative, as with *regret* and *be afraid*, but a few are nonstative, like *enjoy* ("I am enjoying this").

Emotive higher predicates can take a variety of complement modalities. The different combinations create important meaning types, many of which have been examined independently by linguists.

A large number of emotive predicates take a Predetermined Truth Modality, like *regret*, *be glad*, and *be amazing*. There do not appear to be any that take a Predetermined Future Truth Occurence, or Action Complement.

Emotives that take a Predetermined Truth complement have been described by Karttunen as full factives, because, in contrast to other types of higher predicates that he calls semi-factives, only the emotive factives carry their presuppositions in the context of conditionals (cf. the Kiparskys 1970 and Karttunen 1971):

(33) a. If I regret that he left, maybe I'll call him (= he left)
      b. If I find out that he left, maybe I'll call him ($\neq$ he left)

An important difference between emotive and nonemotive factives is that with emotive factives, the Predetermined Truth complement is interpreted as directly causing an emotional reaction or appraisal, while with nonemotive factives it is not interpreted in a causal way:

(34) a. I am glad that he lied
         (= I am glad because he lied
      b. That he lied disturbed me
         (= I am disturbed because he lied)
      c. I know that he lied
         ($\neq$ I know it because he lied)
      d. I found out that he lied
         ($\neq$ I found it out because he lied)

It is interesting that in certain dialects of Basque, emotive factives take the complementizer *-elako*, which is the same form used with adverb clauses to mean *because*, while nonemotive factives take *-ela*. In Thai, emotive factives take the complementizer *thîi*, while other types of factives take *wâa*. So the distinction between emotive and nonemotive factives seems to be important enough that languages use different forms for the two.

When most emotive higher predicates take a Predetermined Truth complement, they can optionally take a *for-to* complementizer, along with the predictable *that* complementizer:

(35) a. That he is sick/For him to be sick is sad
      b. I was sorry that he was sick/for him to be sick
      c. I regretted that he was sick/*for him to be sick

All emotive appraisals and most emotive reactions can take this *for-to* complementizer, but a few like *regret* cannot. There is no apparent characteristic of reaction predicates like *regret* that allows one to predict which can and which cannot take the *for-to* complementizer, so that these would have to be specially marked in the lexicon.

The emotive higher predicate *wish* is unique in that it takes a Negative Predetermined Truth complement modality with a counterfactual meaning and has a *that* complementizer with a past subjunctive mood:

(36) a. I wish that I were a musician
      b. I wish that I had eaten anything ($\neq$ none)

This is the only higher predicate in English that requires a past subjunctive mood form in its complement. Also, this predicate is peculiar in that the negative interpretation of the complement does not have the expected interaction with the negative polarity *any*, which one would expect to be interpreted as nothing but instead is interpreted as something. This needs more investigation.

There do not appear to be any emotive higher predicates that take a Predetermined Future Truth, though it is easy to imagine expressing an emotion about a future fact. The absence of emotive predicates taking Occurrence or Action complements is more understandable: one can not so easily imagine emotions that represent the cause of an event, or act, or an aspect of it (?"I wished him on his way").

Not very many emotives take a Determined complement. A few take a Determined Truth Modality, like *be afraid*, *fear*, and *be worried*, which express an expectation about the truth of a proposition. These typically express a negative emotion. Even fewer take a Determined Future Truth complement, like *be apprehensive*, where an emotion is expressed about the future truth of a proposition. There are none taking Determined Occurrence complements, where an emotion would be expressed about the expected occurrence of an event happening at the same time as the emotion or at a future time.

The few emotives that appear to take a Determined Action complement are predicates like *desire* and *prefer* that typically take an Undetermined Future Truth or Action complement with an infinitive form. These emotives can be interpreted as taking a Determined Action complement only if the higher sentence is used performatively as a request. In other words, the higher sentence must contain a first person speaker as subject and a present time reference (= speech time), and the complement must have an other-directed Action Modality.

(37) a. I desire for you to leave (UFT, UA, DA)
      b. I desired for her to leave (UFT, UA)
      c. She desires to leave (UFT, UA)

In (37a), the sentence can be interpreted as a wish for a future event (Undetermined Future Truth), a wish for you to perform the action of leaving (Undetermined Action), or a performative request (Determined Action). The other two examples can be interpreted as having an Undetermined Future Truth or Action complement modality, but since they cannot be used performatively, they cannot have the Determined Action complement meaning.

When emotives like *desire* and *prefer* are used performatively as a request and thus are interpreted as having a Determined Action complement modality, at least in certain dialects, they can optionally take a *that* complementizer with a present subjunctive mood:

(38) a. I desire for you to leave (UFT/UA/DA)
      b. I desire that you leave (DA)
      c. ?She desired that he leave (DA)
      d. *I want that you leave (DA)

This construction appears to be in imitation of certain linguistic predicates like *demand that* with Determined Action complements. One cannot predict which emotive higher predicates can take a *that* subjunctive construction so that they would have to be specified in the lexicon.

Emotives taking an Undetermined complement are more plentiful. A few like *hope that* and *hopeful that* take an Undetermined Truth complement, describing an emotion about the possible truth of a proposition, and a fairly large number like *hope to*, *want*, and *be desirable* take an Undetermined Future Truth complement, describing and emotion about the possible future truth of a proposition. These two types of complement constructions make up the set of constructions called *wishes*, *desideratives*, or *optatives*.

Several emotive predicates such as *like* and *be fun* take an Undetermined Occurrence complement, describing an emotion about the possible occurrence of an event.

There are not many emotives that clearly take an Undetermined Action complement, describing someone's emotion about their own or another's possible performance of an act. The emotive reaction *be willing* and the emotive appraisal *be easy* clearly take Undetermined Action complements, which usually have a Self-Directed use, but in some dialects *be willing* can also be Other-Directed:

(39) a. I am willing (?for him) to leave (UA)
      b. For him to leave is easy (UA)

Emotive predicates like *desire* and *want* are not such clear cases, since they can be interpreted as taking either an Undetermined Future Truth complement or an Undetermined Action complement of either the Self-Directed or Other-Directed type:

(40) a. I desire to leave/for him to leave (UFT/?UA)
      b. I want to leave/him to leave (UFT/?UA)

There is a thin line between expressing an emotion about the possible future truth of a proposition and expresing an emotion about the possible performance of a future act:[6]

Certain emotive appraisals taking an Undetermined Occurrence or an Undetermined Action complement allow a construction that is called object-to-subject raising, also known as Tough Movement, where the object of the complement becomes the subject of the higher predicate:

(41) a. It is fun for Jan to do math (UO)
      b. Math is fun for Jan to do (UO)

(42) a. It is easy for Jan to do math (UA)
      b. Math is easy for Jan to do (UA)

This type of raising construction seems to occur only with the Undetermined Occurrence and Action Modality complements in English, but it is not predictable which of the subject embedding appraisals can undergo it, so that such predicates have to be lexically specified.

Few emotives occur with Indeterminate complements. Those that do take either a Truth or an Action complement, expressing an emotion about the question of a proposition being true or an act being performed:

(43) a. I am concerned whether he left
     b. I am concerned whether to leave

Linguists frequently talk about desiderative predicates, which are the emotive predicates that take Undetermined complements. These are often set off by special mood forms, like the optative, which is called a mood of wishing for something to be possible.

Emotive predicates thus form a semantic class that combines with the complement modalities and contributes to important meaning types and to the forms they can take. Now let us turn to another important semantic class.

Linguistic Higher Predicates

Linguistic higher predicates are those that involve someone uttering something to someone. They are unusual in that they can imitate the speech act. Most linguistic predicates are nonstative object-embedding reactions: *inform, say, tell, state, suggest, pray, predict, command, promise, warn, permit, ask*. A few linguistic predicates are stative and nonstative subject-embedding appraisals, which seem related to linguistic reactions, as with *be said* and *be rumored*,[7] and *be predictable* and *be permissible*.

The object embedding reactions, but not the subject embedding appraisals, can be used with reports of direct as well as indirect speech:

(44) a. Direct: Bill said, "You left early"
     b. Indirect: Bill said that you left early

Also, they can be used as a speech act; that is, an expression whose utterence constitutes a social act (cf. Austin 1968; Searle 1970 and 1979):

(45) a. I state that you left early
     b. I predict that you will leave early
     c. I command you to leave early
     d. I promise to leave early

(46) a. I say that you left early
     b. I say that you will leave early
     c. I say for you to leave early
     d. I say that I will leave early

In order to be used as a speech act, a sentence must have, either explicit or implied, a first person speaker, a second person audience, and a present time reference (= speech time: the same time as the immediate context). When used as speech acts, these higher predicates and their complement modalities often take on a conventional meaning associated with certain social acts. In our society, the sentences in (45) would be called a statement, a prediction, a command, and a promise, respectively, just as expressed by the individual meanings of the higher predicates *state*, *predict*, *command*, and *promise* (cf. Austin 1968, Searle 1970 and 1979, and Sadock 1974). Those in (46) would be called the same; however, *say* is unspecified with respect to any individual meanings other than the class meaning "for someone to utter something to someone else".

Relying on higher predicates like those in (45) above, linguists have usually identified the meanings of the complement modalities with the meanings of the higher predicate. Thus verbs like *tell* and *say* have been called "verbs of saying" when they occurred with a *that* indicative complement, as in (46a), and "verbs of ordering" when they occurred with an infinitive, as in (46c), (R. Lakoff 1968).

In the present analysis, verbs like *tell* and *say* will be treated as linguistic predicates which can either take a Truth Modality complement, in which case the combined effect makes it appear to be "a verb of saying" used to make a statement, or it can take an Action Modality complement, in which case the combined effect makes it appear to be "a verb of ordering" used to make a command. Thus the meanings of speech acts, like those in both (45) and (46), will be analyzed as a combination of the individual and class meanings of a linguistic higher predicate, the literal meanings of the complement modalities, and whatever conventional implications are associated with the construction when it is used as a social act (cf. Grice 1975):

Higher sentence individual + class meanings of the predicate	*Complement Sentence* info & eval modalities of the complement
declare= NPa utter to NPb S	[S be True] + [S Determined]
command=NPa utter to NPb S	[NPb perform S] + [S Determined]
say= NPa utter to NPb S	[Be True]/[NPb Perform S] + [S Determined]

In the following example, one can see how the individual and class meanings of the combined modalities contribute to the meaning of the entire construction:

(47) a. I warn you that the brakes are bad
      b. I warn you to drive slowly

The verb *warn* is a linguistic predicate that has as its individual meaning the expectation of something undesirable happening. It can take a Determined Truth complement, in which case it constitutes a warning about something being the case, as in (47a), or it can take a Determined Action complement, in which case it constitutes a warning to someone to do something.

Table 19 shows examples of speech acts and their related modalities.

Table 19
Speech Acts and The Combined Modalities

	TRUTH	FUTURE TRUTH	ACTION
PREDET	informing acknowledgement admission	foretelling prophesy	sentence
DETER	statement suggestion	prediction expectation	command suggestion request action
	warning agreement	forewarning	warning promise
UNDET	prayer	prayer	permission request of permission
INDET	question	question	question

A small number of linguistic predicates take a Predetermined Truth Modality: *inform*, *acknowledge*, and *admit*. These describe the utterance of a statement of fact and fall into the sentence type called "semi-factives" (Karttunen 1971b). The linguistic predicates that seem to take a Predetermined Future Truth Modality are verbs like *foretell* and *prophesy* which are not used very often today as performatives, except perhaps by fortune tellers, since most people do not believe in foreknowledge. In English, there do not appear to be any linguistc higher predicates that take an Occurrence Modality, nor do there appear to be any that take a Predetermined Action Modality.[8]

The most plentiful group of linguistic predicates is one that takes a Determined Truth Modality: *say*, *tell*, *announce*, *assert*, *suggest*, *etc.* These described the utterance of a statement which is expected to be true, but may not be, and make up a large part of the sentence type called "assertives" because they assert the truth of the complement and can occur with a variety of syntactic patterns used for emphasis (Hooper and Thompson 1973; Hooper 1975).

Although Determined Truth complements take a *that* complementizer, the linguistic predicate *claim* stands out in that it not only takes the predictable *that* complementizer, but it also takes an infinitive, in which case its complement subject has to be identical with the higher subject:

(48) a. She claimed that she/he had won
      b. She claimed (for her/*for him) to have won

In most common usage, the complement of *claim* is interpreted as open to doubt by the speaker but not usually by the subject of *claim*. However, there is a growing tendency, especially in the U.S., for *claim* to be used as a positive assertion, where neither the higher subject nor the speaker express any doubt. With this latter interpretation, only a *that* complement is used, making the dubitative interpretation the only one possible with the infinitive form, as one can see from the contradiction that seems to arise with the speaker as the subject:

(49) c. ?I claim to have won

This sentence can only be interpreted to mean that the speaker is knowingly making a dubious claim, perhaps for the sake of argument. It sounds peculiar because as the subject of *claim*, the speaker is making an assertion that the complement is true at the same time that the speaker is casting doubt on its truth.

Like *wish*, *claim* has a negative interpretation of the complement, and yet it does not allow the negative polarity item *any* to be interpreted as "none".

A few linguistic predicates take a Determined Future Truth complement like *predict*, *prophesize*, and *forewarn*, which describe types of predictions, but there are none that take a Determined Occurrence complement.

A number of linguistic predicates take Determined Action complements. Those with a Self-Directed Determined Action complement like *promise*, *agree*, *vow*, and *swear* represent promises or agreements, what Austin called commissives (1968). Those with an Other-Directed Determined Action complement, like *command*, *demand*, *suggest*, and *warn*, represent what have been called "mands" with different degrees of pressure for someone to do something. Although Action complements typically take a *for-to* complementizer, there are a few linguistic predicates with an Other-Directed

Determined Action complement that can also have a *that* complementizer with a present subjunctive mood:

(50) a. She requested for him to leave
      b. She requested that he leave

One cannot predict the predicates that allow this construction.

The combination of linguistic predicates with a Determined complement is one that has important consequences for the meaning and form of the complement. In numerous languages, one finds modality markers that are called Quotative or Reportative which occur with this construction. Some markers have been derived from the verb "to say" and have expanded their association from being a linguistic marker to being a marker of Determined Modality, as with Korean *ko*, or to being a marker of Truth or Future Truth, as with Thai *wâa*.

There is only one linguistic predicate that I know of in English that takes an Undetermined Truth or Future Truth complement: *pray that* and *pray for*, respectively. There are a few linguistic predicates that take an Other-Directed Undetermined Action complement, and these represent permission for someone to do something: *permit, authorize, empower*. A few linguistic predicates take a Self-Directed Undetermined Action, which represent requests to be allowed to do something: *ask, request, beg*.

Finally, linguistic predicates that take an Indeterminate Truth, Future Truth, or Action complement represent types of questions: questions of fact: *ask whether, tell whether*; questions of the future: *predict whether*, and questions of behavior: *ask whether to, tell whether to*.

Thus one can classify speech acts or reports of speech acts according to the linguistic and individual meanings of the higher predicate and the type of complement modalities it occurs with.

Cognitive-Physical Predicates

Another type of higher predicate is the cognitive-physical predicate, which describes someone's cognitive or physical reaction to or appraisal of the complement proposition. These predicates can be stative reactions like *know, think, wonder, intend, be able, have time*, stative appraisals like *be true* and *be necessary*, nonstative reactions like *decide, deduce, discover, find out, show, force, persuade*, and *try*, or nonstative appraisals like *begin* and *take place*. Unlike linguistic predicates, cognitive-physical predicates cannot be used to report direct discourse; nor can they be used as speech acts. Instead, they have been called "verbs of propositional attitude".

Cognitive-physical predicates taking a Predetermined complement are numerous. Many like *know*, *discover*, *be true*, and *be certain* take a Predetermined Truth complement, expressing a cognitive or physical reaction to or appraisal of the absolute truth of the complement:

(51) a. Ali knows that Ed lied
     b. Ali discovered that Ed lied
     c. It is true that Ed lied
     d. It is certain that Ed lied

Only a few predicates like *foresee*, *anticipate*, *foreseeable* take a Predetermined Future Truth complement, expressing a cognitive or physical reaction to or an appraisal of the absolute future truth of the complement:

(52) a. Ali foresaw that Ed would lie
     b. Ali anticipated that Ed would lie
     c. It was foreseeable that Ed would lie

Predicates like *know*, *discover*, and *foresee* are called factive because, regardless of whether they are affirmative or negative, their complements are interpreted as true, and thus the truth is considered to be presupposed (cf. Kiparskys 1970). The other predicates taking a Predetermined Truth or Future Truth complement are not said to presuppose the truth of their complements because their complements are interpreted as true only when the higher predicate is affirmative:

FACTIVE
(53) a. She knows/doesn't know that he lied (= he lied)
     b. She discovered/didn't discover that he lied (= he lied)
     c. She foresaw/didn't foresee that he would lie (= he lied)

NONFACTIVE
(53.1)a. It is true that he lied (= he lied)
      b. It isn't true that he lied ($\neq$ he lied)

(53.2)a. It is certain that he lied (= he lied)
      b. It isn't certain that he lied ($\neq$ he lied)

While emotive factives fit Karttunen's (1971b) category of *full factives*, cognitive-physical factives fit his category of *semi-factives*, because, unlike emotive factives, they lose their presupposition of truth in conditional clauses:

(54) a. If I regret that I have lied, I will confess (= I lied)
      b. If I discover that I have lied, I will confess (≠ I lied)

As mentioned in the discussion of emotive factives, in languages like Thai and Basque, one finds different forms used for full and semi-factives. This is a good example of the semantic class of the higher predicate influencing the meaning and the form of the complement.

There is a single higher predicate *pretend* which is usually interpreted as taking a negative Predetermined Truth complement. This predicate, like the counterfactual *wish* and the dubitative interpretation of *claim*, has a negative interpretation of the complement, but also like these other predicates, it does not take the negative interpretation of *any* that one would expect with a negative. While *wish* takes a *that* complementizer with a past subjunctive mood form, *pretend* takes a *that* complementizer with an indicative mood form, as found with other Predetermined Truth complements. However, *pretend*, like *claim*, can also take an infinitive form, in which case its complement subject must be identical with the higher subject:

(55) a. Ellen pretended that she/he was a wolf
      b. Ellen pretended (for her/*for him) to be a wolf
      c. Ellen pretended to have eaten any (≠ none)

Rosenberg (1975) and Riddle (1975) tried to show that *pretend to* had some action involved with it, as shown in a subtle contrast between pretending that you are a doctor and pretending to be a doctor. However, the complement has no firm constraints against having predicates that are states, so that one can pretend to be a Leo or to be tall without involving any action at all. It seems that one can interpret both *pretend that* and *pretend to* as either a mental act of pretending to oneself or a physical act of pretending to others.

What *pretend* shares with *wish that* and *claim*, as distinct from other predicates, is that its complement is open to doubt by the speaker: severe doubt in the case of *pretend* and *wish that*, but only moderate doubt in the case of *claim*. Perhaps the history of these forms and their meanings can reveal more about how they are different from the other types of predicates taking Truth complements.

With Predetermined Occurrence complements, one finds several types of cognitive-physical predicates that differ in meaning and in form. Some, like the subject embedding appraisals *take place* and *begin*, fall into the category of Karttunen's *implicatives*, because they imply the occurrence of their complement event when the higher predicate is affirmative, and they imply its nonoccurrence when negative.

(56) a. It took place today that it rained (= it did)
      b. It didn't take place today that it rained (= it didn't)
      c. It began to rain (= it did)
      d. It didn't begin to rain (= it didn't)

Appraisals like *take place* make a simple predication about the comple-ment event occurring, and as we mentioned earlier, they take a *that* com-plementizer, although no other type of Occurrence complement does. Appraisals like *begin* have been called *aspectuals* because they describe a temporal aspect of an event, its initiation, duration, or cessation (cf. New-meyer 1975). These predicates occur only with a subject-to-subject raising construction, where the complement is extraposed and its subject is raised to become the subject of the higher clause, taking on the same grammatical relation as the extraposed complement had had.

The cognitive-physical reactions taking a Predetermined Occurrence complement, like *watch* and *hear*, have been called perception verbs because they describe a direct perception of an event (cf. Rogers 1974). These reac-tions fall into the category of Karttunen's *if-verbs* (1971 a, c), since they imply the truth of their complements when they are affirmative, but make no implication when they are negative. In form, they are peculiar in that they take a null complementizer with a nonfinite verb:

(57) a. Wendy watched him swim away (= he did)
      b. Wendy didn't watch him swim away (≠ he did)
      c. Wendy heard him swim away (= he did)
      d. Wendy didn't hear him swim away (≠ he did)

There are several cognitive-physical predicates that take a Predeter-mined Action complement. Some are *implicative* predicates like *remember* and *manage*, which when affirmative imply the performance of the action described in their complement but when negative imply its falsity:

(58) a. Jerry remembered to call (= he did)
      b. Jerry didn't remember to call (= he didn't)
      c. Jerry managed to call (= he did)
      d. Jerry managed to call (= he didn't)

These implicatives all take self-directed type complements.

Some cognitive-physical predicates like *force* and *be necessary* are *if verbs*, which when affirmative imply the performance of the act described in their complement, but when negative have no implications:

(59) a. Sue forced him to leave (= he did)
      b. Sue didn't force him to leave (= he may not)
      c. It was necessary for him to leave (= he did)
      d. It wasn't necessary for him to leave (= he may not)

Appraisals like *be necessary* take not only the predictable *for-to* complementizer, but as mentioned earlier, they also take a *that* complementizer with a present subjunctive mood:

(60) It is necessary that he leave

The Predetermined complements of cognitive-physical predicates are evidenced in every type of Information Modality and the combination has important consequences for meaning and complement form. It is these that have been referred to as *necessitative* constructions.

Now let us look at the Determined complements of cognitive-physical predicates, which also have a distribution in each type of Information Modality and influence complement meanings and forms. They express someone's cognitive or physical reaction to, or appraisal of, the expectation expressed in the complement. Many of these predicates belong to the class of predicates that Horn (1975) called *midscalars* because they were interpreted as expressing a modality between necessary and possible, and because they underwent Neg-Raising. Their complements tend to be the least insulated against movement, deletion, and extraction.

Many higher predicates take a Determined Truth complement, like *decide, explain, believe, seem,* and *be likely.* Because many of these predicates provide cognitive testimony about the truth of the complement, they have been associated with meanings and forms called "evidential", "inferential", or "presumptive". These predicates fall into the category that Thompson and Hooper (1973), and Hooper (1975) called *assertives,* because they asserted the truth of their complements by expressing an expectation of its truth, and because many of their complements could undergo syntactic variations involving fronting, parenthetical formation, tag-questioning, and others. All of these take a *that* complementizer, though they may have other surface realizations as well:

(61) a. They decided that John is happy
      b. They believe that John is happy
      c. It is likely that John is happy

The higher predicate *doubt* appears to take a Determined Truth complement, but like *claim*, there is a negative interpretation of its complement. People usually interpret it as equivalent to *think not*, and unlike *claim*, *pretend*, and *wish*, the negative is supported by the interpretation of *any* as "none". *Doubt* can take either the predictable *that* complementizer or an *if* or *whether* complementizer, but it still has a Negative Determined Truth meaning and not the usual Indeterminate meaning of these complementizers:

(62) a. She thought that he had not finished any (= none)
      b. She doubted that he had finished any (= none)
      c. She doubted if/whether he had finished any (*or not)

As far as I can tell, all these sentences have the same meaning.

The higher predicate *expect* and a subject-raised version of *be likely* are two of the few examples of cognitive-physical predicates taking a Determined Future Truth complement:

(63) a. They expect that John will be happy soon
      b. John is likely to be happy soon

The only cognitive-physical predicates that I know of in English that can take a Determined Occurrence complement are the reaction *wait* and the appraisals *be about to* and *tend*. However, there are numerous cognitive-physical predicates taking complements with a Determined Action Modality, like *pressure, help, decide, intend, be important*. Cognitive predicates taking a Self-Directed Determined Action complement, like *decide* and *intend* have been associated with meanings and forms called "intentional" or "commissive" (cf. Austin 1968). Physical predicates taking an Other-Directed Determined Action complement like *pressure* and *help* have been associated with meanings and forms called "jussive" for commands, or "precative" for polite requests.

The cognitive-physical predicates that take an Undetermined complement describe a cognitive or physical reaction to, or evaluation of, the possibility of the complement. There are a few predicates that take an Undetermined Truth complement, like *consider* and *speculate*, but few that take an Undetermined Future Truth Modality, like *look for*. There are some like *capable* and *ready* that can take an Undetermined Occurrence Modality, and there are a number that can take an Undetermined Action Modality, like *try, be able, have a chance, allow, enable,* and *be acceptable*.

The combination of a cognitive-physical predicate with an Undetermined Truth complement, whether affirmative or negative, has been associated with what linguists call a "dubitative" meaning or form, which is supposed to express a lack of assurance. The combination of a cognitive-physical predicate with an Other-Directed Undetermined Action complement has been associated with a "permissive" meaning or form, and with a Self-Directed Undetermined Action complement, there is an association with a "potential" meaning or form, expressing a positive consideration of what is possible.

Finally, there are cognitive-physical predicates that can take an Indeterminate complement, and these describe a cognitive or physical reaction to or appraisal of the question in the complement. Several take either a Truth or an Action complement, like *wonder, question, know, decide, be questionable*, and *be unclear*, but few take an Indeterminate Future Truth complement like *foresee* and *predict* or an Indeterminate Occurrence complement, like *watch* and *hear*:

(64)   a.   They wondered whether she had finished
     b.   They wondered to finish
     c.   It was unclear whether she had finished
     d.   It was unclear whether to finish

While all Indeterminate complements occur with either an *if*, a *whether*, or a *whether-to* complementizer, the higher predicates *possible, permit*, and *be able* appear to take, in addition to their Undetermined Truth or Action complements, an Indeterminate Truth or Action complement with a *for-to* complementizer:

(65)   a.   It is possible for her to have gone *or not*
     b.   We permitted her to go *or not*
     c.   She was able to go *or not*

Thus we have covered the meanings resulting from combinations of the three semantic classes of higher predicates with the different types of complement modalities, and we have seen the effect of these meaning combinations on complement form. Now let us look at the contributions made by the noun phrases that these higher predicates take and their nominal roles.

The Nominal Roles of the Matrix NP's

The noun phrases in a higher sentence can have a variety of nominal roles, just as those in a simple sentence can. They can have the primary roles of subject, direct object, indirect object, and benefactor, or the secondary roles of noun modifiers, and objects of prepositions. A noun complement can assume any of these roles except those of indirect object or benefactor, which have to be animate. In this section we will examine the relations between the complement and the primary nominal roles in the sentence.

The most frequent role of the complement is as an object of the higher predicate. We called higher predicates taking object complements "reactions" because they described a reaction to the complement. The subject of a reaction predicate is usually animate and often human. In the following sentences, Willy's linguistic, emotive, and cognitive-physical reactions to his own leaving are described (It is intended that "he" be interpreted as "Willy"):

(66) a. Willy said that he left early
      b. Willy hoped to leave early
      c. Willy decided to leave early
      d. Willy promised Sue to leave early

The nominal roles in the higher sentences consist of the subject as "Willy" and the direct object as the complement; in (d), "Sue" is the indirect object. In each of these sentences, the subject of the complement is understood as identical to the subject of the higher sentence: the one doing the leaving is Willy. In Korean, the subject of the complement could be deleted in each of these cases. In English, it could be deleted only if the complement had a *for-to* (or a gerund) complementizer, as in (b), (c), and (d).

When higher predicates like *decide* and *promise* take an Action Modality complement, they require the subject of their complement to be identical to the subject of the higher sentence: NPa decide [NPa VP]; NPa promise NPb [NPa VP]. This constraint was identified by Perlmutter (1971) as the "like-subject' constraint, and it has been called here a "self-directed" constraint.

In the following sentences with object complements, the subject of the complement is understood to be different from the subject of the higher sentence, so that Sue is the one doing the leaving:

(67)   a. Willy said that Sue left early
        b. Willy hoped for Sue to leave early

(67.1)a. Willy persuaded Sue that she left early
      b. Willy persuaded Sue to leave early

(67.2)a. Willy suggested to Sue that she leave early
      b. Willy suggested to Sue to leave early

(67.3)a. Willy recommended to Sue that she leave early
      b. Willy recommended to Sue to leave early

In the higher sentences above, the nominal roles consist of the subject as "Willy", the direct object as the complement, and in (67.1) through (67.3), the indirect object as "Sue". In each complement, the subject is understood to be different from the subject of the higher sentence: the one doing the leaving is Sue, not Willy. In (67.1) through (67.3), the complement subject is interpreted as identical to the indirect object. In Korean, if the subject of the complement is identical to a noun phrase in the higher sentence, as in (67.1) through (67.3), it could be deleted. In English, the subject of the complement can be deleted only if it is both identical to a noun phrase in the higher sentence and contained within a *for-to* (or a gerund) complement, as in the (b) sentences in (67.1) through (67.3).

When higher predicates like *persuade*, *recommend*, and *suggest* take an Action Modality complement, they require their complement subject to be different from the subject of the higher sentence: NPa persuade NPb [NPb VP]; NPa recommend (to NPb) [NPb VP]; NPa suggest (to NPb) [NPb VP]. This constraint could be included with Perlmutter's (1971) "unlike-subject" constraint, and it has been called here an "other-directed" constraint.

The rule for deleting complement subjects has been called Equi NP Deletion, and it has been described as applying obligatorily if the subject of the complement is identical to another noun phrase in the higher sentence. Since complementizers have usually been previously treated, à la Rosenbaum, as optional variants, it was not recognized that, in English, Equi applies only if there is a *for-to* (or a gerund) complementizer. Having shown that most infinitives and required indentity constraints can be predicted on the basis of complement modality, with the rest lexically specified, we can allow Equi to apply without exception to all identical complement subjects within infinitives (and gerunds). Thus, what has been called the "control problem" is really a constraint on Action Modality complements and not on Equi.

Having dealt with object embedded complements, now let us turn to the more problematic nominal relations in higher sentences with subject complements. We called higher predicates taking subject complements "appraisals" because they described an appraisal of the complement. Although the complement plays the part of the subject, there is still an animate major participant, either explicit or implied, to whom the appraisal is attributed (the director) or for whom the appraisal is directed (the receiver). This animate participant can have the syntactic role of a direct or indirect object, or benefactor, or it can be an implied person, either the speaker or a nonreferential indefinite "someone", as shown in the following sentences:

(68) a. It pleased *Bob* that he played well
       b. It behooved *Bob* to play well

(69) a. It was apparent *to Bob* that he'd played well
       b. It was important *to Bob* to play well
       c. It was unclear *to Bob* whether to play well

(70) a. That he played well was exciting *for Bob*
       b. To play well was easy *for Bob*

(71) a. It was true (*for/to whom?*) that Bob played well
       b. It was rumored (*by whom?*) that Bob played well

Each of these sentences is intended to be about Bob's playing well, so that the "he" should be interpreted as "Bob". When the subject of the complement is identical to one of the noun phrases in the higher sentence, as in (68) through (70), Korean allows it to be deleted. In English, it can be deleted only if there is both the identity and a *for-to* (or gerund) complementizer, as in the (b) sentences in (68) through (70). In the higher sentences in (71), there is no animate participant mentioned, but there is one implied, which could either be interpreted as the speaker, as is more likely with (71a), or as a nonreferential "someone", as is more likely with (71b).

When higher predicates like *behoove*, *be easy*, and *be unclear* take an Action Modality complement, they require the subject of their complement to be identical to a noun phrase in the higher sentence, but since the complement is the subject, this constraint cannot be called a like-subject or an unlike-subject constraint. With *behoove*, the constraint appears to be an other-directed constraint comparable to *persuade*, except that there is no higher subject: [NPa VP] behoove NPa. With *be easy* and *be unclear*, the constraint appears to be a self-directed constraint comparable to constructions with *decide* and *promise*, except for the lack of a higher subject: [NPa VP] be easy (for NPa); [NPa VP] be unclear (to NPa).

Equi deletes the subject of the complement on identity with the (prepositional) object in the matrix. The prepositional phrase can be deleted if its object is an indefinite noun phrase ((for someone) to swim is easy (for someone)), or if it is identical with a noun phrase in the immediate context, which could be the speaker ((For me) To swim is easy (for me)), or in extended discourse, the topic of the discourse:

As the two-mile race began, Sheila dove effortlessly into the water. (For her) To swim was easy (for her), but it was unclear (to her) whether (for her) to put out all of her energy right away.

When higher predicates like *be important* take an Action Modality complement, they can have an explicit or an implied noun phrase in the higher sentence, one which is assumed to be present in deep structure, and their complement subject can be like or unlike that noun phrase: [NPa/b VP] be important (to/for NPa). If it is like that noun phrase, then the construction is interpreted as self-directed, and the complement subject is deleted. If it is unlike that noun phrase, then the construction is interpreted as other-directed, and the complement subject cannot be deleted:

(72) a. It was important *to/for me* that Bob play well
      b. It was important *to/for me* for Bob to play well

(72.1)a. It was important *to/for Bob* that he play well
      b. it was important *to/for Bob* (for him) to play well

(72.2)a. It was important *to/for me* that I play well
      b. It was important *to/for me* (for me) to play well
      c. It was important (*to/for me*) (for me) to play well

(72.3)   It is always important (*to/for someone*) (for someone) to play well

In (72.1) through (72.3), the complement subject is identical to a noun phrase in the higher sentence and, when the complementizer is *for-to*, as in (71.1b), (72.2,b), (72.2,c) and (72.3), Equi applies to delete the subject of the complement. In (72a) and (72b), the complement subject is different from the noun phrase in the higher sentence and cannot be deleted. In (72.2c), the prepositional object has been deleted because it is identical to the noun phrase in the immediate context, namely the speaker, and in (72.3), it has been deleted because it is an indefinite, nonreferential noun phrase.

Thus the nominal roles of the higher sentence influence the meanings and forms of the complement. Now let us turn to another way in which the higher sentence influences the complement.

Higher Sentence Polarity and the Complement

When the higher sentence is negated, the complement and its Evaluation Modality can be affected in a variety of ways, depending on the type of higher predicate. All higher predicates can take what's called *external* or *broad-scope negation* (BSN). This type of negation is interpreted as negating the entire construction, and is equivalent to saying "It is not the case that S". There is an implied contradiction of a previous assertion or expectation about it being the case, and a special contradiction intonation contour is used (cf. Lieberman and Sag 1974):

(73) a. I didn't regret that he left; I don't even know who you're talking about
     b. We didn't force him to leave; he left of his own accord
     c. I didn't predict that he'd leave; I predicted he wouldn't leave
     d. She didn't say that he had left; she said he might have left

In each example above, the entire construction is negated, as though one were saying "It is not the case that...." In order for the hearer to know why it is not the case, an explanation is necessary. In the first example, the initial sentence is said not to be the case, and the explanation is that neither the higher predicate nor the complement is the case. In the second example, the initial sentence is said not to be the case because the higher predicate is not the case. In the third example, it is the complement proposition that is not the case, and in the fourth example, it is the Evaluation Modality of the complement that is not the case. In each of these sentences, there is a negative applying to the meanings of the entire affirmative sentence with its particular affirmative higher predicate and complement proposition, and its particular evaluation meanings. The explanatory sentence then picks out the part of the affirmative sentence that is the cause for the contradiction.

While all higher predicates can take *external* or *broad-scope negation*, (BSN) only a few can take *internal* or *narrow-scope negation* (NSN). Narrow-scope negation can affect one or more parts of the sentence; it consists of three types, depending on which parts are affected.

Narrow-Scope Negation I

One type of narrow-scope negation affects only the polarity of the higher predicate, what we will call *Narrow-Scope Negation I* (NSN I). This type of negation occurs with a class of higher predicates identified by the Kiparskys (1970) as *factives*. These predicates take complements whose propositions are interpreted as true, regardless of whether the higher predicate is affirmative or negative, so that the truth of the complement is said to be presupposed:[9]

(74) Predetermined Truth
   a. Helen regrets/doesn't regret that Joe left (= he left)
   b. Helen knows/doesn't know that Joe left (= he left)
   c. Helen discovered/didn't discover that Joe had left (= he left)

(75) a. Predetermined Future Truth
   a. Helen foresaw/didn't foresee that Joe'd leave (= he left)
   b. Helen anticipated/didn't anticipate that Joe'd leave (= he left)

These factive higher predicates would have to be specified as taking a Predetermined Truth or Future Truth meaning, regardless of whether the higher predicate is affirmative or negative, because there are no alternatives to the truth or future truth of the complement proposition, respectively.

Another type of construction that can undergo NSN I occurs with predicates that take an Indeterminate complement, both the Committed types like *know* and the Uncommitted types like *wonder*:

(76) a. I know/wondered whether he had left or not
   b. I didn't know/wonder whether he had left or not

(77) a. I know/wondered whether to leave or not
   b. I didn't know/wonder whether to leave or not

With both affirmative and negative higher sentences, the Indeterminate complements express the availability of equal alternatives, as shown by coocurrence with "or not". The negative has no effect on the polarity or the modality of the complement. It affects only the polarity of the higher sentence. With Committed higher predicates, the negative cancels the expression of knowledge or expectation about the complement proposition, making these predicates like the Uncommitted predicates, but the complement is unaffected.

Thus NSN I, which affects the polarity of the higher sentence but not that of the complement, can occur not only with factives but also with non-factives. Factives then can be seen as higher predicates that take Predetermined Truth complements and undergo NSN I.

Narrow-Scope Negation II

A second type of narrow-scope negation, Narrow-Scope Negation II (NSN II), affects the polarity of both the higher predicate and the complement proposition, but not the Evaluation Modality of the complement. One type of construction that takes this negation is a class of predicates that Karttunen (1971 a, c) called *implicatives*. These higher predicates are

described as implying the truth of their complement proposition when affirmative but implying its falsity when negative. Although Karttunen considered
only infinitive complementizers, the same construction occurs with *that*
clauses as well:

Predetermined Truth
(78) a. He happened to leave/It happened that he left
          (= His leaving is Predetermined)
          (*but he didn't/*may not have)
     b. He didn't happen to leave/It didn't happen that he left
          (= His not leaving is Predetermined)
          (*but he didn't/*may not have)
     b. It isn't true that he left
          (= His not leaving is Predetermined)
          (*but he did/*but he may have)

Predetermined Occurrence
(80) a. He began to leave
          (= His leaving is Predetermined)
          (*but he wasn't leaving/
          *but he may not have been leaving)
     b. He didn't begin to leave
          (= His not leaving is Predetermined)
          (*but he was leaving/
          *but maybe he was leaving/
          *but maybe he was leaving)

Predetermined Action
(81) a. He managed to leave
          (= His leaving is Predetermined)
          (*but he didn't/*may not have)
     b. He didn't manage to leave
          (= His not leaving is Predetermined)
          (*but he did/*but he may have)

In these sentences, the negation of the higher predicate is intepreted as
affecting the polarity of both the higher predicate and the complement proposition, but not the Evaluation meaning of the complement: if he didn't
happen, begin, or manage to leave, then the evaluation expressed is that he
didn't leave, with no other alternatives available. These higher predicates

all take a complement with a Predetermined Evaluation meaning, whether affirmative or negative.

One can find the same type of negation applying to higher predicates that take complements with a Determined Evaluation meaning. In these cases, the affirmative higher prediate takes a complement whose proposition is expected to be the case, but with alternatives available. When the higher predicate is negative, it takes a complement whose proposition is expected to be negative but still allows alternatives. The negative affects both the polarity of the higher predicate and the polarity of complement, but it does not affect the Evaluation Modality of the complement:

Determined Future Truth

(82) a. I believe that he left
          (= His leaving is Determined)
          (but he *didn't/*isn't expected to have/ may not have)

      b. I don't believe that he left
          (= His not leaving is Determined)
          (but he *did/*is expected to have/may not have)

Determined Future Truth

(83) a. I expect that he'll leave
          (= His leaving is Determined)
          (but he *won't/*isn't expected to/may not)

      b. I don't expect that he'll leave
          (= His not leaving is Determined)
          (but he *won't/*isn't expected to/may not)

Determined Action

(84) a. I intend to leave
          (= My leaving is determined)
          (but I *won't/*don't expect to/may not)

      b. I don't intend to leave
          (= My not leaving is Determined)
          (but I *will/*expect to/may not)

In these sentences, the affirmative higher predicate is followed by a complement whose proposition is expected to be the case, but with alternatives available: thus there is an affirmative belief, expectation, or intention, and the leaving is expected to be the case.[10] When the higher predicate is negated, giving a negative belief, expectation, or intention, its complement proposition is also interpreted as negated: thus the leaving is expected not to be the case.

This pattern of negation also occurs with certain higher predicates that take an Undetermined Evaluation meaning. Again the negation affects the higher predicate and the complement proposition, but not the Evaluation Modality of the complement:

Undetermined Future Truth
(85) a. I want her to run
          (= Her running is Undetermined)
          (but she won't/may not)
      b. I don't want her to run
          (= Her not running is Undetermined)
          (but she will/may)

Undetermined Occurrence
(86) a. I like for her to run
          (= Her running is Undetermined)
          (but she won't/may not)
      b. I don't like for her to run
          (= Her not running is Undetermined)
          (but she will/may)

When the higher predicate is affirmative, the complement proposition is interpreted as possibly being the case, but with no expectations. When the higher predicate is negated, the negative affects the polarity of the higher predicate, giving a negative interpretation of the wanting or liking, and it affects the polarity of the complement proposition, giving a negative interpretation of the possibility of her running, but it does not affect the Undetermined Evaluation Modality of the complement.

Regardless of whether the affirmative higher predicate has a Predetermined, Determined, or Undetermined complement, if it takes a Narrow-Scope Negation II (NSN II), the negation will affect the polarity of the higher predicate and the polarity of the complement proposition, but not the Evaluation Modality of the complement.

In previous analyses, this type of negation has been treated variously, depending on the Evaluation Modality of the complement. When it occurs with predicates that take a Predetermined Evaluation, it has been used as a defining feature of a class of verbs that Karttunen (1971a,c) called implicatives, and with a Determined or Undetermined Evaluation, it has been used as a defining feature for a class of verbs that Horn (1975; 1978) called midscalar and that he and others analyzed as undergoing negative raising or negative transportation, a rule that was supposed to raise the negative out of the lower clause and into a higher clause.

In the present analysis, both types of negation are treated in the same way, regardless of the Evaluation Modality of the complement. The negative is held as originating in the higher sentence, and it is interpreted as negating both the higher predicate and the complement proposition (Ransom 1986).

This approach allows for a more unified approach, and accounts for why verbs like *happen* and *turn out*, which take Predetermined complements, and *want* and *like to*, which take Undetermined complements, were exceptions to Horn's claim because they underwent negative raising but were not midscalar predicates. If we treat negative raising as a type of Narrow-Scope Negation which affects both the higher predicate and the complement (NSN II), then we can treat the negation of *happen* in the same way as we treat the negation of *likely*, and the negation of *manage* in the same way as that of *believe* and *want*.

In most of these cases where Narrow-Scope Negation II affects the higher predicate and the complement proposition, but not the Evaluation Modality of the complement, it seems that there is an equivalence relation between the negated higher predicate with an affirmative complement proposition and an affirmative higher predicate with a negated complement proposition:

(87) a.   It isn't true that she smoked (= It is true that she didn't smoke)
b.   She didn't happen to smoke (= She happened not to smoke)
c.   I don't believe that she smoked (= I believe that she didn't smoke)
d.   I don't want her to smoke (= I want her not to smoke)

A negative attitude about her smoking in each case seems equivalent to a positive attitude about her not smoking.

However, there is a group of higher predicates which does not show a similar equivalence:

(88) a.   She didn't manage to smoke (≠ She managed not to smoke) (= She didn't manage, and she didn't smoke)
b.   She didn't begin to smoke (≠ She began not to smoke) (= She didn't begin, and she didn't smoke)
c.   It didn't take place that she smoked (≠ It took place that she didn't smoke)

(= It didn't take place, and she didn't smoke)

Part of the reason for the lack of equivalence is that these higher predicates do not readily take negative complements.[11] If a negative is used, it must be interpreted as a positive event, like avoiding smoking, or else it is prohibited, since one cannot describe an aspect of a nonoccurrence or predicate an occurrence of a nonoccurrence.

Narrow-Scope Negation III

A third type of negation, Narrow-Scope Negation III (NSN III), affects not only the higher predicate and the complement proposition, but also the Evaluation meaning of the complement:

Predetermined Truth
(89) a. It was certain that he left
           (= His leaving is Predetermined)
           (*but he didn't/*but he may not have)
      b. It was not certain that he left
           (= His not leaving is Undetermined)
           (but he may have/but it's likely he did)

Predetermined Action
(90) a. It had been necessary for him to leave
           (= His leaving is Predetermined)
           (?but he hadn't/?but he may not have)
      b. It had not been necessary for him to leave
           (= His not leaving is Undetermined)
           (but he may have/but it's likely he did)

The affirmative sentences in (89a) and (90a) imply that she left and thus are interpreted as having a Predetermined Evaluation; the negative sentences imply not that she didn't leave, but that she may not have left. That is, under negation, the complement proposition is no longer treated as necessarily the case, but as possibly not the case.

This type of negation has been dealt with in modal logic. For epistemic necessity, as exemplified in (90) above, logicians give the following definition:

(91) a. "It is necessary that p" implies p
      b. "It is not necessary that p" implies "it is possible not p"

Saying that something is not necessary is equivalent to saying that it is possible for it not to be the case. A parallel definition is given for deontic necessity:

(92) a. "It is obligatory that p" implies p
      b. "It is not obligatory that p" implies "it is permitted not p"

Saying that something is not obligatory is equivalent to saying that it is permitted not to be the case. This type of Narrow-Scope Negation, NSN III, applies to a small, unpredictable set of higher predicates. It applies to Karttunen's (1971a,c) if-verbs, like *force*, which in the affirmative take Predetermined complements that imply the truth of the proposition, but when negative take a negative Undetermined complement that does not imply the truth of the proposition. Not being forced to do something is equivalent to being permitted not to.

Thus NSN III affects the polarity of the higher predicate, the polarity of the complement, and the modality of the complement, shifting it from Predetermined to Undetermined.

There is a slightly different variation of NSN III, one that we will call NSN IIIB, to distinguish it from the previous one, which we will call NSN IIIA. NSN IIIB applies to a small, unpredictable set of higher predicates that, in the affirmative, take an Undetermined complement. Like NSN IIIA, NSN IIIB negates the higher predicate and the complement, but unlike NSN IIIA, it shifts the Evaluation Modality from Undetermined to Predetermined instead of the reverse:

(93) a. She is able to leave
          (= Her leaving is Undetermined)
          (but she may not/but she's not likely to)
      b. She isn't able to leave
          (= Her not leaving is Predetermined)
          (*but she did/*but she may)

(94) a. She permitted him to leave
          (= His leaving was Undetermined)
          (but he may not/but he's not likely to)
      b. She didn't permit him to leave
          (= His not leaving was Predetermined)
          (?but he did/?but he may)

In the affirmative, the leaving is treated as possible and as having alternatives available, but in the negative, the leaving is treated as not possible and as having no alternatives available, even if in the real world there are alternatives.

This type of negation, NSN IIIB, affects Karttunen's only-if verbs, which, if affirmative, express no implications about the truth of the complement, and thus take an affirmative Undetermined evaluation, but if negative, they imply that their complement propositon is negative, and thus take a negative Predetermined Evaluation.

This type of negation has also been dealt with in modal logic. One of the definitions of epistemic possibility is the following:

(95) a. "possible S" implies "not necessary S"
      b. "not possible S" implies "necessary not S"

Saying that something is not possible is equivalent to saying that it is necessary for it not to be the case. A parallel definition is used for deontic possibility:

(96) a. "permitted S" implies "not obligatory S"
      b. "not permitted S" implies "obligatory not S"

Saying that something is not permitted is equivalent to saying it is obligatory for it not to be the case.

Both Narrow-Scope Negation IIIA and IIIB apply to a small, unpredictable set of higher predicates, the former to certain ones taking Predetermined complements, the latter to certain ones taking Undetermined complements. Both have in common that they affect the polarity of the higher predicate and the polarity of their complements, and they cause the Evaluation Modality of the complement to shift, either from Predetermined to Undetermined, or from Undetermined to Predetermined.

Thus there are three types of narrow-scope negation that affect higher predicates. One that affects only the polarity of the higher predicate and not the complement, NSN I; one that affects only the polarity of the higher predicate and the polarity of its complement, but not the Evaluation Modality of the complement, NSN II; and finally, one that affects the polarity of the higher predicate, the polarity of the complement, and the Evaluation Modality of the complement, NSN III A and III B.

Lexical Negatives

The negation that we have been discussing so far has resulted from the negative *not*. There are also negative sentences that do not have a *not* but instead have a lexical higher predicate with an implied *not*, as with *dislike*, *deny*, *doubt*, *refuse*, and *forbid*. Let us examine the ways that these lexical negatives affect the complement meanings.

There are negative higher predicates which are interpreted as having

Narrow-Scope Negation I: *dislike, detest, hate, be unknown, be unclear*. In each of these, it is the higher predicate that is negated, and there is no effect on the polarity of the complement or its modality:

(97) a. I dislike that he said that
          (His saying that is Predetermined)
      b. It is unknown whether he said that
          (His saying that is Indeterminate)

There are also negative higher predicates that are interpreted as having Narrow-Scope Negation II: *deny, doubt, refuse*, and *forbid*. In these cases, the negation affects both the polarity of the higher predicate and the polarity of the complement, but the modality of the complement stays the same:

(98) a. I deny that he left
          (His not leaving is Determined)
      b. I doubt that he left
          (His not leaving is Determined)
      c. I refuse to leave
          (My not leaving is Determined)
      d. I forbid you to leave
          (Your not leaving is Determined)

There are a few negative higher predicates that are interpreted as having Narrow-Scope Negation III: *uncertain, unnecessary, impossible*, and *impermissible* (cf. Na 1981). In these cases, the negation affects the polarity of the higher predicate, the polarity of the complement, and the modality of the complement in the same way that *not* does, causing it to shift from affirmative Predetermined to negative Undetermined, or affirmative Undetermined to negative Predetermined:

(99) a. It is uncertain that she left
          (Her not leaving is Undetermined)
      b. It is impossible for her to leave
          (Her not leaving is Predetermined)

There do not seem to be any negative higher predicates that are interpreted as taking Broad-Scope Negation.

Negative Polarity "Any"

Now let us look at the way the negated complements resulting from Narrow-Scope Negation II and III, interact with the negative polarity item *any*. This expression is used in Standard English as a negative form of the indefinite pronoun *some* with the interpretation "none". It occurs with this meaning only when the sentence that it is in is interpreted as negative in meaning, as shown in the examples below:

(100) a.   He ate some/any (that he could find) ($\neq$ none)
        b.   He didn't eat *some/any (= none)

In cases where the higher predicate is negated but the polarity of the complement is unaffected, the pronoun *any* cannot be used with the meaning of "none", as shown in (101)-(102), but in cases where the polarity of the complement is affected, as with NSN II and III, the pronoun *any* can be used with the meaning of "none", as shown in the sentences in (103)-(104):

NSN I: Negation of Higher Predicate Only
(101) a.   He regrets that he *ate any* (= some, $\neq$ none)
        b.   He doesn't regret that he *ate any* (= some, $\neq$ none)

(102) a.   He knows whether she *ate any* (= some, $\neq$ none)
        b.   He doesn't know whether she *ate any* (= some, $\neq$ none)

NSN II: Negation of Higher Predicate and Complement
(103) a.   It *isn't* true that she *ate any* (= none)
        b.   It *is false* that she ate *any* (= none)
        c.   She *didn't* manage to eat *any* (= none)
        d.   I *don't* believe that she ate *any* (= none)
        e.   It *doubt* that she ate *any* (= none)
        f.   I *don't* want her to eat *any* (= none)

NSN III: Negation of Higher Predicate and Complement with Evaluation Shift
(104) a.   It *isn't* certain that she ate *any* (= none)
        b.   It *was unnecessary* to eat *any* (= none)
        c.   She *wasn't* able to eat *any* (= none)
        d.   She *forbid* him to eat *any* (= none)

While cooccurrence with the Negative Polarity *any* is regular, cooccurrence with the more variable polarity items, like *until Sunday* and *lift a finger to help* is not regular, but the restrictions on these are not well understood as yet.

In summary, it seems that higher predicate negation affects the higher predicates and their complements in four different ways. There is broad-scope negation (BSN), which negates the entire construction, contradicting previous presuppositions or expectations and resulting in no conclusion. This type occurs with all higher predicates and would not have to be specified in the lexicon as having any restriction on cooccurrence.

Then there are the three narrow-scope negations, one which affects only the polarity of the higher predicate (NSN I), one that affects the polarity of both the higher predicate and the complement (NSN II), and one that affects the polarity of the higher predicate, the polarity of the complement, and the Evaluation Modality of the complement (NSN III A and III B). These three types of narrow-scope negation occur with a small number of unpredictable verbs, each of which would have to be specified in the lexicon for the particular type of negation it took.

Higher Sentence Modality and the Complement

Just as the polarity of the higher sentence can have varying effects on the complement, so too can its modality, whether it has the modality of a question, an imperative, or some other modality represented by a modal. There seem to be two types of effects, what will be called Narrow-Scope Modality I (NSM I) and Narrow-Scope Modality II (NSM II).

Narrow-Scope Modality I

In most cases, the modality of the higher sentence affects only the higher sentence and not the complement:

(105) a.   Did Joe persuade Mary that she won?
            (≠ Did Mary win?)
       b.   If Joe persuaded Mary that she won, she'll go out ot eat
            (≠ If she won, she'll go out to eat)
       c.   Joe may persuade Mary that she won
            (≠ Mary have won)
       d.   Joe must persuade Mary to win
            (≠ Mary must win)
       e.   Pesuade Mary that she will win!
            (≠ Mary, win!)

In each of these sentences, it is the persuasion and not the winning that is questionable, conditional, considered possible, or necessitated. Since this type of higher sentence modality affects only the higher sentence, it is analogous to Narrow-Scope Negation I and will be called Narrow-Scope Modality I (NSM I).

Narrow-Scope Modality II

A second type of effect is one in which the modality of the higher sentence affects the modality of both the higher sentence and the complement. This happens with a small class of higher predicates:

(106) a. Did Jo manage to win? (= Did Jo win?)
     b. If Jo managed to win, she'll go out to eat
     c. Jo may manage to win (= Jo may win)
     d. Jo must manage to win (= Jo must win)
     e. Manage to win! (= Win!)

(107) a. Is it true that Jo won? (= Did Jo win?)
     b. If it's true that Jo won, she'll go out to eat
         (= If Jo won, she'll go out to eat)
     c. It may be true that Jo won (= Jo may have won)
     d. It must be true that Jo won (= Jo must have won)

(108) a. Did you think to water the plants?
         (= Did you water the plants?)
     b. If you thought to water the plants, I'll reward you
         (= If you watered the plants, I'll reward you)
     c. She may have thought to water the plants
         (= She may have watered the plants)
     d. She should have thought to water the plants
         (= She should have watered the plants)

In each case, the modality of the higher predicate affects both the higher predicate and the complement. Both are treated as questioned, conditioned, or considered as possible or necessitated. This type of modality transference occurs with a subset of the higher predicates that take Narrow-Scope Negation II, and it is comparable to narrow-Scope Negation II, since the modality, like the negative, of the higher sentence affects both the higher sentence and the complement. Consequently, this type of modality is called Narrow-Scope Modality II (NSM II).

There does not seem to be a modality construction comparable to Narrow-Scope Negation III, where the negative affects the polarity of both the higher sentence and the complement as well as the modality of the complement. Nor does there seem to be one corresponding to Broad-Scope Negation, where the negative affects the entire construction.

However, there are a few higher predicates which differ somewhat from the types of higher predicate modality we've discussed so far. There are some higher predicates that are affected by questioning, and to some extent by conditionals, but not by other types of modalities:

(109) a. Did you say that he left?
       (= Did he leave?)
   b. If you say that he left, Jo will be glad
       (?= If he left, Jo will be glad)
   c. You may have said that she left
       (≠ She may have left)
   d. You must've said that she left
       (≠ She must've left)
   e. Say Mary left!
       (≠ Mary left/Mary, leave!)

(110) a. Did you say for Mary to leave?
       (= Should Mary leave?)
   b. If you say for Mary to leave, I'll reward you
       (≠ If Mary leaves, I'll reward you)
   c. He may have said for Mary to leave
       (≠ Mary may have left)
   d. He must have said for Mary to leave
       (≠ Mary must have left)
   e. Say for Mary to leave!
       (≠ Mary, leave!)

(11) a. Do you suppose that she left?
       (= Did she leave?)
   b. If you suppose that she left, John will be glad
       (?= If she left, John will be glad)
   c. He may have supposed that Mary left
       (≠ Mary may have left)
   d. He must've supposed that Mary left
       (≠ Mary must've left)
   e. Suppose Mary left!
       (≠ Mary, leave!)

(112) a. Do you think she left?
       (= Did she leave?)
   b. If you think she left, John will be glad
       (?= If she left, John will be glad)
   c. He may have thought she left
       (≠ She may have left)

    d. He must have thought she left
        (≠ She must have left)

In these examples, the question modality, and to some extent the conditional, affect the complement, but the modal evaluations and the imperative do not.

The higher predicates that allow their complement to be affected by their modality could be described either by the use of special lexical markings to signal the transference with questions and conditionals, or one could rely on pragmatic inferences based on the assumption that higher predicates like *say*, *suppose*, and *think* contribute little to the construction other than evidential qualification: You don't usually ask someone if they said, supposed, or thought something without being interested in what they were asserting to be the case.

Thus the modality of a higher predicate typically affects only the higher predicate, but with a small set of higher predicates, it affects both the higher predicate and the complement; and in a still smaller set of higher predicates, just the question modality, and to some extent the conditional modality, affect the complement.

Summary

In this chapter, we have shown how the meanings and forms of complement constructions are affected not only by the complement modalities but also by the meanings of the higher sentence: its personal and temporal deixis, the type of higher predicate it contains, the types of nominal roles of its noun phrases, and the types of polarity and modality it takes. Examples of different types of higher predicates are given in Tables 20-22. Having examined complement modalities individually, in combination, and in relation to the higher sentence, now let us turn to ways that these modalities can be represented in a grammar and the implications they have for linguistics.

TABLE 20
Linguistic Higher Predicate Types

	TRUTH	FUTURE TRUTH	OCCURRENCE	ACTION
	LINGUISTIC REACTIONS			
PREDET	acknowledge			
	admit			
	concede			
	inform			

DETER:	advise	predict	advise
	agree	prophesy	agree
	announce		ask
	affirm		beseech
	assure		bid
	assert		command
	claim		choose
	confess		demand
	charge		defy
	confirm		direct
	contend		forbid
	deny		offer
	declare		order
	guarantee		promise
	grant		propose
	insist		pledge
	promise		recommend
	reassure		refuse
	repeat		require
	say		say
	submit		suggest
	suggest		swear
	swear		tell
	state		urge
	tell		vow
	vow		volunteer
	warn		warn
UNDET:	pray	pray	authorize
			permit
INDET:	ask	predict	ask

LINGUISTIC APPRAISALS

PREDET:		predictable	
DETER:	rumored		advisable
	said		
UNDET:			permissible
INDET:			

TABLE 21
Cognitive-Physical Higher Predicate Types

	TRUTH	FUTURE TRUTH	OCCURRENCE	ACTION
	COGNITIVE-PHYSICAL REACTIONS			
PREDET:	aware	anticipate	cause	begin
	comprehend	foresee	feel	cause
	discover	foreshadow	hear	compel
	forget	forewarn	make	condescend
	grasp	preindicate	notice	entice
	know	portend	observe	force
	learn		overhear	get
	notice		perceive	know
	prove		see	make
	realize		show	manage
	remember		watch	oblige
	understand			
DETER:	allege	expect	wait	aim
	answer			bribe
	assume			beckon
	believe			cause
	comment			coax
	convince			commission
	concluede			compel
	decide			conspire
	deduce			contrive
	determine			convince
	disclose			decide
	doubt			determine
	dream			entice
	emphasize			force
	estimate			get
	explain			goad
	feel			help
	find out			hesitate
	guess			impel
	hear			intend
	hold			influence

	imagine			inspire
	indicate			make
	infer			oblige
	maintain			persuade
	mean			plan
	mention			remind
	persuade			resolve
	presume			scream
	pretend			see fit
	reveal			signal
	report			tempt
	scream			threaten
	see			write
	sense			
	show			
	signal			
	suppose			
	suspect			
	think			
UNDET:	conjecture	look	capable	able
	speculate		ready	allow
	consider			attempt
				empower
				enable
				endeavor
				entitle
				have permission
				have time
				have the right
				let
				ready
				try
				venture
INDET:	conjecture	anticipate	watch	conjecture
	inquire	foresee		inquire
	question			question
	wonder			wonder

COGNITIVE-PHYSICAL APPRAISALS

PREDET:	apparent	certain (sr)	begin	crucial
	clear	sure (sr)	continue	essential
	certain		cease	impossible
	correct		come about	necessary
	dawn on		come to pass	obligatory
	evident		develop	vital
	false		happen	
	fitting		keep	
	happen		occur	
	obvious		persist	
	occur to		take place	
	strike		transpire	
	sure		start	
	true			
	turn out			
DETER:	appear	likely (sr)	about	best
	likely		tend	important
	probable			urgent
	seem			
	strike			
UNDET:	possible		possible	difficult
	uncertain			easy
				hard
				simple
INDET:	questionable			questionable
	uncertain			uncertain
	unclear			unclear
	unknown			unknown

TABLE 22
Emotive Higher Predicates

	TRUTH	FUTURE TRUTH	OCCURRENCE	ACTION

EMOTIVE REACTIONS

PREDET:	alarmed
	amazed

amused
annoyed
appreciate
bothered
deplore
detest
dislike
enjoy
fascinated
glad
happy
hate
like
love
lucky
mad
nauseated
proud
regret
sad
tolerate

DETER:	afraid		
	fear		

UNDET:	concerned	afraid	abhor	desire
	hope	anxious	adore	prefer
	worried	desire	dislike	want
		eager	enjoy	willing
		hope	hate	wish
		prefer	like	
		want	love	
		wish		

INDET:	concerned
	disturb
	worried

EMOTIVE APPRAISALS

PREDET:	alarm,-ing
	amaze,-ing

amuse,-ing
annoy,-ing
bother,-some
clever
dumb
exilarate,-ing
fascinate,-ing
foolish
funny
great
important
instructive
interest,-ing
nice
odd
please,-ing
puzzle,-ing
right
significant
smart
stupid
surprise,-ing
sad
tragic
wonderful

DETER:				
UNDET:	hopeful	desirable	amazing	desirable
		preferable	amusing	preferable
			annoying	
			bothersome	
			delightful	
			exciting	
			fun	
			interesting	
			nice	
			satisfying	
INDET:	disturb,-ing			
	worrisome			

NOTES

1) The meanings of the complement constructions also consist of the meanings of the lexical content, the meanings associated with discourse relations (topic, focus, and rhetorical pattern), and the meanings associated with the speaker's intentions or emotional overtones, often represented by the suprasegmentals.

2) It is unfortunate that we do not have a term that will describe the semantic relation that I am calling here the "major participant", that is a word that can refer to a syntactic subject or object, or to an implied participant. One suggestion is the use of the term "director" to mean the one responsible for the actual or possible direction of the reaction or evaluation. Then instead of a like-subject or self-directed constraint, one could talk about a like-director constraint, and instead of an unlike-subject or other-directed constraint, one could talk about an unlike-director constraint and, for cases where the participant that the complement subject must be identical to is the "receiver" rather than the director, we could talk about an unlike-director, like-receiver constraint.

Regardless of whether we come up with satisfactory terms to characterize these identity constraints, it is clear that they must be specified in the lexicon for each higher predicate taking an Action complement. The means of doing this will be discussed in the next chapter.

3) Noonan (to appear) suggested that these complements tend to have nonfinite forms because their time reference is predictable and forms representing them would be redundant. However, the meanings of the higher predicate do not always specify the time reference that their complement will take: some do, as with the complements of *watch* and *command*, but others like the complement of *see* could have either a free choice of time if the complement has a Truth Modality or the same time as the higher sentence if the complement has an Occurrence Modality. Both time reference and nonfinite forms are predictable from modality.

Givón (1980) made the claim that nonfinite reduced forms were correlated with the semantic influence that an agent in the higher sentence had over the complement: the greater the influence (semantic dependence or binding of the complement relative to the higher sentence), the greater the reduction of complement form (syntactic dependence or binding of the complement relative to the higher sentence). This generalization cannot capture the syntactic reduction that occurs in many languages with the perception verbs, which take an Occurrence Modality complement and exhibit no influence. The cooccurrence of finite and nonfinite complements is better predicted on the basis of complement modality, and the restrictions on time reference and subject identity are also directly related to complement modality.

4) Some analyses treat extraposed complements as basic rather than transposed word order. Such an analysis requires extra rules to interpret the complement as the subject of the higher predicate as well as an optional rule to prepose the complement to subject position with some predicates. Such an analysis is not considered here.

5) The constraint on extraction from clause-initial subject complements was dealt with by Ross's Sentential Subject Constraint (1967). However, the constraint appears to apply not to items extracted from a clause, but to items placed in front of a clause-initial subject complement but within the same clause, whether adverbs, inverted auxiliary verbs or question words:

a.   Surely, it is true that she likes Bach
      *Surely, that she likes Bach is true
b.   Is it true that she likes Bach?
      *Is that she likes Bach true?

   c.   Who is it true that she likes?
        *Who is that she likes true?

Thus the Sentential Subject Constraint needs to be revised to the Sentential Subject Precedence Constraint.

   6) In some American Indian languages like Navajo, commands are expressed by future predictions or desires.

   7) Although the predicates *be said* and *be rumored* look like passive forms, they are thought to be separate from any object-embedding active forms. First of all, *be rumored* does not take a passive agent:

   a.   *It was rumored by someone/John that you were leaving

Also, there is no active form that *be rumored* could have come from:

   b.   *He rumored that you were leaving

Both *be said* and *be rumored* take Subject-raising:

   c.   You were said to be leaving
   d.   You were rumored to be leaving

but the active form of *say* cannot:

   e.   *Someone said you to be leaving

Thus it is thought that there is an object-embedding *say* which can take an active or passive form but cannot take subject-raising, and then there is a subject-embedding *be said* and *be rumored* which can take subject raising.

   8) There are no linguistic predicates taking complements with an Occurrence Modality, but if there were, they would describe someone's linguistic reaction to the occurrence of a simultaneous event and would resemble constructions like "talk his ear off", "read him to sleep", "sing the sun in flight", or "bid him farewell". They are not inconceivable and might be found in other languages. In the Bible, one finds statements like "He commanded the waves to part", which could be thought of as either a linguistic causative with an Occurrence complement or as an Action complement with a personification of the waves. Also, there do not appear to be many linguistic predicates that take a Predetermined complement. One finds a few that take Predetermined Truth, like *inform* and *admit*, which describe a linguistic reaction that communicates the absolute truth of a proposition, but people are more likely to trust what someone does than what they say. One finds a few predicates that take Predetermined Future Truth, like *prophesy*, which describe a linguistic reaction that communicates the absolute future truth of a proposition, but only fortune tellers and their clients would be likely to hold with such predictions.

   9) Although the truth of factive complements is said to be presupposed regardless of the truth value of the higher predicate, it is still possible to deny the truth, as shown by the contrast between (a) and (b) below:

   a.   I regret/don't regret that he left (= he left)
   b.   I don't regret that he left because he didn't leave

While in (a), the complement is interpreted as true, in (b) it is not. The lack of contradiction in (b) has been attributed to broad-scope negation (It is not the case that S), which is capable of cancelling all presuppositions.

10) There is another interpretation of the negation in these sentences as broad-scope negation, where there is no belief or intention at all. This interpretation, like that which cancels presuppositions with factives, also cancels expectations.

11) This constraint on negation applies to all complements required to have the same time reference as the higher predicate, namely, to all Occurrence complements and to a few Action complements, as discussed in Chapter II.

CHAPTER VI

The Representation of Modality and Its Implications

In the preceding chapters, we have seen evidence from English and other languages for the existence of two sets of complement modalities, the four Information Modalities called Truth, Future Truth, Occurrence, and Action, and the four Evaluation Modalities called Predetermined, Determined, Undetermined, and Indeterminate. Each of these eight modalities was shown to be characterized by certain basic meanings, cooccurrence restrictions, and in some languages, by forms.

The two sets of four modalities were shown to combine to provide sixteen possible combinations of complement meanings, many of which are characterized in languages by particular forms. Furthermore, their interaction with the meanings of higher sentences and with certain discourse functions were shown to make up familiar sentence types and speech acts, thereby influencing complement meanings, and in some languages, complement forms.

In this chapter, we will examine ways that these complement modalities can be represented in a grammar and the kinds of implications these modalities have for various areas of linguistic studies.

The Representation of Modality

Any description of language will have to represent the meanings associated with each modality, their cooccurrence restrictions, and their lexical, syntactic, and suprasegmental forms. First let us examine some of the ways that linguists have tried to represent the modality meanings.

In earlier versions of generative-transformational theory (Chomsky 1965; Katz and Fodor 1964), the semantic description of a sentence was accounted for by semantic interpretation rules. These rules made use of the meanings of lexical items, as specified in the lexicon, and their grammatical relations in a sentence, as specified by the phrase structure rules. Consequently, most attempts to account for modality meanings in complement constructions focused on finding lexical forms to which the modality meanings could be linked.

Some analyses tried to attach modality meanings to the meanings of the higher predicate; this will be called the higher predicate analysis. Others tried to attach these meanings to forms used within the complement, like complementizers, modals, or mood; this will be called the complement form analysis. Still another type of analysis, a variation of which will be argued for here, treated modality as a type of grammatical relation which, like the notion "subject", had to be represented in the deep structure. They tried to attach certain modality meanings to abstract markers associated with sentences in the phrase structure. This is a type of nonlexical analysis that will be called the phrase structure analysis.

The Higher Predicate Analysis

First let us examine the various attempts to use the lexical meanings of the higher predicate to represent the modalities and their restrictions.

Linguists working on speech acts within a generative semantics framework examined higher predicates like *declare, command, promise*, and *permit*, which describe modalities and speech acts explicitly (cf. Ross 1970, Lakoff 1971, R. Lakoff 1968, McCawley 1968, Sadock 1969, and Searle 1970, 1979). These linguists tried to account for the similarities between independent and dependent declaratives and commands by hypothesizing abstract semantic predicates or features meaning declare (DECLARE or [+declarative]) and command (IMPERE or [+ imperative]) as part of the deep structure representation of both sentence types, and as part of the lexical representation of higher predicates like *say* and *command*:

(1) a. You win = I DECLARE TO YOU [YOU WIN]
     b. I say that you win = I DECLARE TO YOU [YOU WIN]

(2) a. Win! = I IMPERE YOU [YOU WIN]
     b. I command you to win = I IMPERE YOU [YOU WIN]

The sentences in (1) are about the truth of the proposition "you win", which has a Truth Modality, while the sentences in (2) are about your performance of the action of winning, which has an Action Modality. These differences in meaning were captured by the abstract linguistic predicates *DECLARE* and *IMPERE* or by features like [+declarative] and [+imperative].

Because the meanings of these abstract predicates or features consist of a combination of linguistic meanings and Determined Truth or Determined Action meanings, they can only be used to represent constructions with these meanings. Any variations in the linguistic meaning or the complement modality meaning would require a different abstract semantic predicate or feature. Thus a linguistic predicate with a slightly different meaning from a command but with the same Determined Action complement as a command would have to be represented with an entirely different abstract semantic predicate or feature, as with *promise*. A linguistic predicate like *declare*, but one that takes a Determined Future Truth complement, would also require a separate abstract predicate or feature, as with *predict*. Also, a linguistic predicate like *tell*, which can take a Determined Truth or Action as well as an Indeterminate Truth or Action complement, would have to be treated as four separate verbs with four separate abstract predicates or features. Nonlinguistic higher predicates like *persuade* and *decide*, which cannot be used performatively, could not be represented by this approach, even though they can have the same types of complement modalities:

(3) a. I told/persuaded them that you'd won
         (Determined Truth complements)
     b. I told/persuaded them to win
         (Determined Action complements)
     c. I promised/decided that you'd won
         (Determined Truth complements)
     d. I promised/decided to win
         (Determined Action complements)

A final negative consequence of this approach occurs with constructions that do not have higher predicates governing them but have Truth or Action Modality meanings. This happens with noun clauses used as objects of prepositions, as appositives, or as predicate nouns, as well as adjective and adverb clauses (Ransom 1981 and 1984):

(4) a. They solved the problem of *whether to go*
         (Indetermined Action complement)
     b. The opportunity *to go* finally came
         (Undetermined Action complement)
     c. The reason *that he goes* is *that it's fun*
         (Predetermined Truth complements)
     d. I saw the book *that you read/for you to read*
     e. I bought the book *because you read it/in order for you to read it*

Each example contains an embedded sentence with a Truth or an Action Modality, but none of them could be construed as having a higher predicate, whether real or abstract like *DECLARE* and *IMPERE*, which could account for their meanings and restrictions.

G. Lakoff (1970) tried to represent the meanings of the nonlinguistic higher predicates *persuade that* and *persuade to* by hypothesizing the abstract semantic predicates *CAUSE TO BELIEVE* for the former, and *CAUSE TO INTEND* for the latter. The abstract predicate *BELIEVE* appears to represent the Determined Truth meaning of the complement, as does the complement of the real verb comparable to it, and *INTEND* the Determined Action meaning, just as the complement of the real verb *intend* does, but these semantic predicates cannot represent other combinations of Information and Evaluation Modalities, like Determined Future Truth (*predict*) or Predetermined Action (*force*).

Another problem with this analyis is that *persuade* has to be treated as two separate predicates, rather than as one predicate taking two types of complements, and consequently, it is in conflict with evidence from conjunction reduction and gapping that these are the same predicates:

(5)   He persuaded her that it was raining and to take her umbrella

Still another problem is that the Truth/Action contrasts in these two complements cannot be related to other Truth/Action contrasts, like those between *signal that/to*, *remember that/to*, and *decide that/to*, as well as those occurring in other types of sentences, as mentioned above.

R. Lakoff (1968), in analyzing Latin, dealt with sentences embedded under both linguistic and nonlinguistic higher predicates, and with simple sentences, as well as adjective and adverb clauses. She hypothesized a number of abstract semantic predicates which were to be found in the base component (presumably expanded by the phrase structure rule for Verb, though there is not much detail about how this would be done): *imper* for imperative meanings, *vel* for optative meanings, *poss* for potential meanings, *vol* for the meaning of purpose clauses, etc. These abstract predicates were not given lexical representation, but rather were treated as parallel to lexical items, so that they were to be interpreted by the same semantic interpretation rules as real verbs, and they were to govern the same syntactic constraints as real verbs of the same class; finally these abstract verbs were to be deleted or given no surface representation.

This analysis cannot show meaning relations between constructions that have different higher predicates but take the same complement modalities, as for example the fact that the abstract predicates that Lakoff calls [Imper] (commands), [Hort] (requests), [Oport] (obligation), and [Lic] (permission) all take an Action Modality complement, differing either in the type of Evaluation Modality their complement can take (Determined vs. Undetermined) or in the semantic class of the higher predicate (linguistic vs. nonlinguistic).

Like the previous higher predicate analyses, R. Lakoff's cannot show the similarities and differences with constructions that have the same higher predicates but take different complement modalities, like *tell that*, *tell whether*, *tell to*, and *tell whether to*, which would have to be treated as four separate verbs.

Finally, her analysis would require a separate abstract higher predicate for every variation in meaning that results from the meaning of the higher predicate, the meaning of the Information Modality, the meaning of the Evaluation Modality, or different combinations of these. There would have to be a separate abstract predicate for *warn that*, *warn to*, *warn whether*, and *warn whether to*; for *decide that*, *decide to*, *decide whether*, and *decide whether to*; as well as for *believe*, *guess*, and *imagine*, and so on.

In another type of higher predicate analysis, Givón (1980) presented a scalar analysis of complement constructions based on the influence that occurs between the agent in the higher sentence and the complement proposition. This type of influence is typically seen with Action complements which require their complements to be interpreted as controllable by a self- or other-directed agent. At the top of Givón's influence scale are higher predicates like *manage* and *force*, which take a Predetermined Action Modality complement. Lower on the influence scale were higher predicates like *command* and *pressure*, which take a Determined Action Modality, and still lower were higher predicates like *permit* and *be able*, with Undetermined Action Modality complements.

This top part of the scale deals only with Action complements and the scale corresponds to the degrees of alternatives in the Evaluation Modalities. Unlike the speech act analyses, this analysis can show the relationship between constructions in which either linguistic or nonlinguistic higher predicates take an Action complement with the same Evaluation Modality, as with *command*, *pressure*, *tell to*, *decide to*, and *intend to*, all of which take Determined Action complements. However, it cannot show the relationship between constructions in which the same higher predicate can take more than one type of complement modality, as with *tell to* and *tell that* or *decide to* and *decide that*, which all take either a Determined Truth or a Determined Action complement.

The lower part of the influence scale covers higher predicates that take

Truth, Future Truth, and Occurrence complements with all types of Evaluation Modalities, making for rather heterogeneous levels. The next rung on the scale consists of the emotive verbs that Givón felt expressed some influence through an emotional commitment to the complement proposition, like *hope*, which takes an Undetermined Truth or Future Truth Modality complement and *want*, which takes an Undetermined Future Truth or Action Modality. Presumably, emotive higher predicates, like *regret*, which takes a Predetermined Truth complement, and like *be concerned whether*, would also fit on this level, but perhaps *be concerned whether to* would belong higher on the scale with the Action complements.

The lowest rung on the influence scale, with no influence, consists of what Givón called epistemic verbs, like *know that*, which takes a Predetermined Truth complement, and *say that*, which takes a Determined Truth complement. When these same higher predicates take an Action complement, they are placed higher on the scale. One might guess that *wonder whether* would fit on this lower level with the epistemic verbs, but *wonder whether to* might be placed higher on the scale with the Action complements.

When these emotive and epistemic verbs take a Truth, Future Truth, or Occurrence complement rather than an Action complement, there are no constraints on the controllability of the complement predicate and thus no direct influence of a higher agent. The emotive higher predicates can express an indirect influence only if the complement can be interpeted as a controllable act like *stop smoking*. When you hope or want to stop smoking it is more likely that you will. However, in such cases the epistemic verbs also can express influence: if you know or say that you will quit smoking, you are more likely to do so. The possibility of influence with these two types of predicates rests not with their being emotive or epistemic but rather with the content of their complements. If either the emotive or the epistemic verbs have a complement with an uncontrollable predicate like *be tall*, neither can express any influence. Regardless of whether one hopes or wants to be tall, or knows or says they will be tall, they can have no influence over being tall.

Givón's analysis can deal only with object complements, since only they have higher agents that can influence the complement. It cannot show the similar relationships between the subject complements of *behoove* and *be necessary*, which take Action complements and express influence, and *seem* and *be true*, which take Truth complements and do not, since none of these have a higher agent. Nor can Givón's analysis deal with other types of constructions which have the same modality meanings but no higher agent, such as the Truth-Action distinction between simple sentence declaratives and commands, and adjective and adverb clauses (The book that you read/for you to read; He arrived early because he had a good seat/in order to get a good seat).

Furthermore, because this analysis associates the reduction of complement forms with influence, this analysis cannot deal with perception verbs, which have reduced complement forms but no influence, and it cannot deal with the generalization that in English, all complement constructions with nonfinite "null" complementizers, as with *watch*, *make*, and *let*, require the complement to have the same time reference as the higher sentence.

In all of these higher predicate analyses, the higher predicate was treated as the repository of all modality meanings. Consequently, there was no way to compare the similarities and differences in meaning found in the complement modalities, much less those found in constructions not governed by a higher predicate.

The Complement Form Analysis

While the higher predicate analyses placed the burden of the meaning on forms outside the complement, there were also complement analyses which placed the burden on forms inside the complement: on complementizers, modals, or mood forms. The biggest advantage to most complement form analyses over the higher predicate analyses was that the meanings of the complement modalities were freed from the meanings of the higher predicate, so that verbs like *tell* could be treated as one verb taking more than one type of complement rather than as four separate verbs, and the modalities of sentence types other than subject and object complements governed by higher predicates could be accounted for.

Bresnan's analysis (1970, 1972) used complementizers as the source of the semantic and syntactic constraints. Higher predicates were subcategorized by abstract complementizers to signal which type of complement they would take: *know* was specified as taking both [___that] and [___wh].

One problem with this analysis is that, as Grimshaw (1979) points out, the form of the complementizer does not always signal the semantic type of the complement: *wh* could represent an interrogative or an exclamative type of sentence, and since these have different meanings and cooccur with different types of higher predicates, they need to be kept distinct. Furthermore, the meanings of the individual modalities and the systematic ways they can be combined cannot be represented, like the meaning relationships between *say that* and *say to*, both of which have the same Determined evaluation but a Truth-Action contrast, versus *pray that* and *pray to*, both of which have an Undetermined evaluation but a Truth-Future Truth contrast.

Finally, this type of analysis can deal only with subject and object complements which have higher predicates for subcategorizing the complementizers. It cannot deal with the same types of modalities found in other types of sentences which have no higher predicates to subcategorize them, like those embedded as noun modifiers or as objects of prepositions, or in simple sentences, which in some languages can occur with complementizers (cf. Latin, Russian, and Korean), or in adjective and adverb clauses, which can also have complementizers.

Langendoen (1968, 1970) and Postal (1970) independently proposed the use of modals as the source of certain complement modalities. They hypothesized that infinitives contained underlying modals which had to be deleted, or in the case of the "can't seem" constructions pointed out by Langendoen, had to be raised into the higher sentence. These modals carried the modality meanings which Langendoen and Postal held responsible for certain semantic and syntactic constraints.

This approach, unlike that using complementizers, could acount for modality meanings in all types of simple and embedded sentences since it would not require a higher predicate. The major drawback to it is that the modals cannot provide a one-to-one representation of the modality meanings. In English, each modal represents more than one combination of Information and Evaluation meanings (*may* = Undetermined or Indeterminate Truth, Future Truth, or Action), and different combinations of modality meanings can have more than one modal to represent them (Undetermined and Indeterminate Action can be represented by both *may* and *can*, despite prescriptive efforts):

(6) a. Wilma says that Winston *may* be right
     b. Wilma says that Winston *may or may not* be right
     c. Wilma says that Winston *may* be hired
     d. Wilma says that Winston *may or may not* be hired
     e. Wilma says that Winston *may* leave if he wishes
     f. Wilma says that Winston *may* leave or not, as he wishes

(7) a. Wilma says that Winston *may/can* leave if he wishes
     b. Wilma says that Winston *may/can* leave or not, as he wishes

Furthermore, there are sixteen combinations of modality meanings possible, but there are a small number of modals, and even though they are used ambiguously to represent the Information Modality meanings, they still do not represent all of the sixteen meanings. Which modals could be said to underlie the Predetermined and Determined Occurrence complements of *watch*, *begin*, and *tend*?

Finally, since the modals are ambiguous as to the Information Modality they represent, they cannot account for the systematic similarities and differences in their possible combinations. Consequently, they cannot represent the relationships between *remember that* with its Predetermined Truth meaning and *remember to* with its Predetermined Action meaning, or *remember whether* with its Indeterminate Truth meaning and *remember whether to* with its Indeterminate Action meaning.

One last attempt to represent modality meanings with forms inside the complement was Jacobs' analysis of mood (Jacobs 1981). He distinguished between two basic mood forms, indicative and hypothetical, which he postulated as underlying simple and embedded sentences.

The indicative mood was associated with tensed (finite) complement forms and with meanings typically associated with declarative, interrogative, and exclamative sentence types. These meanings include the meanings of the Predetermined, Determined, Undetermined, and Indeterminate Truth Modality. However, because of Jacobs' reliance on finite complement forms to distinguish this mood, he would also have to include the meanings of the Future Truth and Occurrence complements that take finite complements (Predetermined, Determined, and Indeterminate Future Truth: *foresee that/ whether* and *predict that/whether*; and Predetermined and Indeterminate Occurrence: *take place that* and *watch whether*).

The hypothetical mood was associated with tenseless (nonfinite) complements, excluding those derived from raising, a construction which Jacobs and others have mistakenly identified with indicative complements (cf. *require*). The meanings of the hypothetical mood were called "hypothetical" or "irrealis". They included meanings found in what Jacobs called "imperative complements", which correspond to Action complements taking a future time reference and having a linguistic higher predicate. They also had to include meanings found in other infinitive complements like those of *hope to*, with its Undetermined Future Truth meaning, and that of *hate to*, with its Undetermined Occurrence meaning. Because of the reliance on nonfinite forms to distinguish mood, the analysis would have to treat as having a hypothetical mood those nonfinite complements with a Predetermined Modality, whether coupled with Truth (*be pleased to*), Occurrence (*watch*), or Action (*force* or *manage*). Although these complements have nonfinite forms, they clearly do not have hypothetical or irrealis meanings.

Although this analysis could deal with all types of sentences, simple and dependent, it could not characterize the sixteen different modality meanings or their combinations, and it could not account for the systematic relationships between the modalities and their forms.

All of these lexical analyses of complement meaning, whether they use higher predicates or complement forms as the source of the complement meaning, are inadequate to account for the meanings and constraints that we have described here. They cannot account for the four Information Modalities or the four Evaluation Modalities, independently or in their sixteen combinations with each other, and they cannot account for their combinations with the meanings of the higher predicates, or their combinations with certain discourse meanings.

One final objection to using one particular lexical form to represent modality meanings is that across languages, and especially in English, one finds modality represented by a variety of forms, combinations of the meanings of higher predicates, sentence adverbs, complementizers, modals, and mood: "Certainly, I believe that we should go". To choose one of these forms would be to ignore the versatility that languages have in representing modality meanings.

Nonlexical Analyses

Now let us look at approaches which do not attempt to use lexical forms *per se* to represent the meaning.

Grimshaw's analysis (1979) achieves some generality by representing modality meanings with the use of semantic selectional restrictions on higher predicates, rather than using the meanings of the individual predicates themselves. Working within the Extended Standard Theory, which relied on syntactic markers to trigger semantic interpretation, she tried to show that for each higher predicate, the lexicon had to contain not only subcategorizational restrictions on its syntactic configurations, but also semantic selectional restrictions in order to account for complement selection. The semantic selectional restrictions associated with each higher predicate were expressed as "semantic frames" consisting of specifications of the semantic types which the predicate selected: *know* would have the semantic frames [___P] to specify that it could take a propositional *that* clause and [___Q] to specify that it could take an interrogative *wh* clause.

This analysis represented the modality meanings as distinct from the meanings of the higher predicate, so that it would be able to treat *tell* as one higher predicate capable of taking a variety of complement types. However, because the modality meanings were represented as selectional restrictions associated with a higher predicate, this analysis could only apply to constructions involving higher predicates with subject and object complements, and could not apply to other types of complements, to simple sentences, or to adjective and adverb clauses. Also, it could not represent the individual modalities or show the systematic ways in which they could be combined with each other, with the meanings of higher predicates, or with other discourse meanings.

Another type of nonlexical approach is one by Katz and Postal (1964), who treated the modality meanings not as part of lexical forms or even as part of the lexicon at all, but rather as abstract markers associated with either a simple or an embedded sentence by the phrase structure rules. The abstract marker *I* would occur with simple sentence imperatives as well as embedded sentences signifying a command. Similarly, the abstract marker *Q* would be used for simple and embedded questions:

(8)   You fut leave --› You will leave
        Q You fut leave --› Will you leave
        I You fut leave --› Leave!

(9)   He Pres say [You fut leave] --›
            He says that you will leave
        He pres ask [Q you fut leave] --›
            He asks whether you will leave
        He pres say [I you fut leave] --›
            He says for you to leave

This approach could be applied to sentences without higher predicates, like complements not used as subjects or objects, and adjective and adverb clauses. Furthermore, it could represent the modality meanings as separate from the meanings of the higher predicate. The drawbacks to this approach were that the use of markers like *I* combined the linguistic and modality meanings with the discourse meanings. The use of a single abstract marker made it impossible to describe all the possible meanings of the modalities and their combinations.

The Phrase Structure Analysis

What is needed is a nonlexical approach which, like that of Katz and Postal's, can represent the modality meanings of complements as a part of the complement, separate from the higher sentence, and as a property of the sentence rather than a property of a lexical form. Unlike that of Katz and Postal's, it should be able to represent these modality meanings as consisting of a combination of one of the four Information Modalities and one of the four Evaluation Modalities, yielding sixteen possible combinations. Finally, since these modality meanings determine to a large extent the propositional content of the complement and the segmental and nonsegmental constrasts that accompany the modalities, these meanings need to be available to lexical insertion rules, which means they cannot be represented in the lexicon, but must be represented in the phrase structure rules, as with the Katz and Postal approach.

Such an approach could represent the Information and Evaluation Modalities by a phrase structure node such as MODAL, MOOD, or even COMP, which is realized by lexical items. However, we have seen the drawbacks to choosing any one of these. What is proposed here is that the modalities be represented by a phrase structure node that is an expansion of the sentence node, in a way comparable to Katz and Postal's analysis, and also to an analysis by Fillmore (1968), which couples all sentences with a modality marker. A Sentence node (S) would be expanded into a Propositional Modality node (PM) and a Propositional Content node (PC):

(10)   S --> PM PC

This approach would resemble the Katz and Postal approach, except that instead of using a unitary abstract marker like Q or I to represent the Propositional Modality, two separate sets of modality markers would be used: markers for the four Information Modalities (IM) and markers for the four Evaluation Modalities (EM), which would allow these modalities to be combined into the sixteen possible combinations. The Propositional Content could be expanded into the typical Noun Phrase and Verb Phrase:

(11)   PM --> IM EM
       PC --> NP VP

The Information Modality node could then be expanded into a choice of Truth, Future Truth, Occurrence, or Action nodes; and the Evaluation Modality node could be expanded into a choice of Predetermined, Determined, Undetermined, and Indeterminate nodes:

(12) IM --> <Truth, Future Truth, Occurrence, Action>
      EM--> <Predetermined, Determined, Undetermined, Indetermi-
      nate>

In order to account for the polarity of the sentence, there would also have
to be a Polarity node (P), which could accompany the modality nodes and
could be expanded into a choice of Affirmative or Negative:

(13) S   --> P PM PC
      P   --> <Affirmative, Negative>

In order to account for the notion *immediate context* and the speech participants, as well as the speech time and location, a simple and direct approach
would be to have an abstract higher sentence containing only the identity of
the speaker, the audience, the time reference, and the location:

(14) SPEAKER <a> UTTERS <S...> TO AUDIENCE <b> AT
      TIME <t> IN LOCATION <l>

This type of higher sentence could probably be used as the single root for
multiple conjoined sentences in a discourse episode by one person to one
audience at one contiguous span of time and place, whether it be a speech,
a conversation, or some other form of connected discourse.

Unlike previous analyses of abstract higher sentences, this analysis
would not be used to represent the modality of the sentence below it as
declarative or imperative. Rather, the modality of the sentence below it
would be represented by the modality nodes attached to the lower sentence,
as exemplified by the following diagram:

(15)

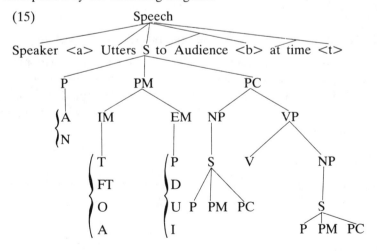

This analysis could be adapted to the Extended Standard Theory by treating the modality symbols as abstract categorial symbols which are expanded by the phrase structure rules into terminal symbols. Perhaps these symbols could have features attached to them so that they could be available to the redundancy rules, the lexical insertion rules, the transformational rules, and the semantic interpretation rules in order to account for the restrictions and interpretations associated with the modalities.

Another alternative is to think of these symbols as carrying information that does not need further interpretation, whether in the form of formal logic notation, as in the semantic analyses of Montague Grammar, or in the form of natural language expressions, as in the semantic analyses of Wierzbika (1980).

Regardless of the method used to represent these meanings, any linguistic description needs to be able to treat modality as separate from lexical items, as properties of sentences, and as consisting of the four Information and the four Evaluation Modalities, which combine with each other to provide sixteen combinations that affect the meanings and forms of the sentence.

The Representation of Meaning Restrictions

Now let us look at the ways that the restrictions on modality meanings can be accounted for. Certain meaning restrictions are predictable on the basis of the Information Modality of the complement and some on the basis of its Evaluation modality. Other meaning restrictions are not predictable on the basis of the complement modalities but are dependent on the particular higher predicate that the complement occurs with.

Meaning Restrictions Predictable from the Information Modalities

The Information Modalities have restrictions on their propositional content that may affect their subject, predicate, or time reference. Only the Truth Modality has no constraint on the type of subject, predicate, or time reference. That makes it the only one that allows a predicate with a permanent state or a time reference that precedes the time of the higher predicate. There would not need to be any restrictions on propositional content with this type of modality:

(16) a.   Wendy knows that she is a Leo/is tall is being teased/is leaving
      b.   Wendy knows that Harry left/is leaving/Will leave

The Future Truth Modality has a constraint on the time reference of the complement: it must be interpreted as future to the time of the higher predicate, and this holds true for the aspects of the verb:

(17) a. Wendy predicts that Harry will leave soon/*yesterday
      b. Wendy is eager for Harry to leave soon/*yesterday
      c. Wendy is eager for Harry to have left before noon/*yesterday
      d. Wendy is eager for Harry to be leaving soon/*yesterday)

Future Truth Modality complements will have to be marked as taking a time reference that follows the time of the higher predicate.

Another constraint on the Future Truth complement is that it must have a predicate that can be interpreted as coming true at a future time, so that it must be capable of change, like acts, events, or temporary states, but not permanent states:

(18) a. Wendy predicts that Harry will be tall soon/*be a Leo soon
      b. Wendy is eager for Harry to be tall/*be a Leo

The Occurrence Modality requires the complement predicate to be interpreted as an event. Consequently, predicates describing acts and events are acceptable, but temporary or permanent states are not unless they can be interpreted as events:

(19) a. Wendy watched Harry leave/*like the movie/*be tall
      b. It took place that Harry left/*liked the movie/*was tall

Also, the Occurrence Modality usually requires the complement predicate to have the same time reference as the higher predicate:

(20) a. At 3PM, Wendy watched Harry leave
          (= at 3PM/*2PM/*4PM)
      b. At 3PM, it took place that Harry left
          (= at 3PM/*2PM/*4PM)
      c. At 3PM, Wendy tends to leave
          (= at 3PM/*2PM/*4PM)

Finally, the Action Modality has a number of constraints. First of all, the complement subject must be interpreted as an agent and the complement predicate as a controllable act. Consequently, the complement can contain predicates describing controllable acts like leaving or playing chess, but not uncontrollable acts or events like having a heart attack or being taken by surprise, or uncontrollable states like being tall or having a headache:

(21) a. Wendy decided to leave/*be tall/*be taken by surprise
      b. Wendy urged Harry to leave/*be tall/*be taken by surprise

Unless one can force a controllable interpretation onto being tall (like wearing shoes) or onto being taken by surprise (like pretending to be surprised), then the Action complements are unacceptable.

Another constraint on Action complements is that the time reference must be interpreted as nonpast, so that it cannot occur before the time of the higher predicate. Usually the time reference must be future to the higher predicate, but certain higher predicates require a contemporaneous time reference:

(22) a. At 3PM, Wendy decided to leave (= after the decision/*while deciding/*before deciding
      b. At 3PM, (Wendy urged Harold to leave
           (= after the urging/*while urging/*before urging)
      c. At 3PM, Wendy forced Harold to leave
           (= at the same time as the forcing/*before the forcing/?after the forcing)

The preceding constraints shape the meanings of the Information Modalities by specifying the kinds of propositional content that occurs with each. Because they affect the content of their proposition, they determine which lexical items can be chosen by the lexical insertion rules. Consequently, it is necessary to make these constraints explicitly available to the lexical insertion rules if one wants to avoid generating a profusion of garbage. This could be done by a set of redundancy rules that apply after the phrase structure rules and before the lexical insertion rules and the transformational rules:

(23)   I. Base Component Rules
             PS Rules
             Redundancy Rules
          II. Lexical Insertion Rules
          III. Transformational Rules

Meaning Restrictions Predictable from the Evaluation Modalities

Now let us turn to the constraints on the Evaluation Modalities. These involve restrictions on the alternatives that an expression can offer when it occurs with a particular Evaluation Modality.

Predetermined complements, which make an absolute claim that allows no alternatives, cannot be accompanied by expressions that offer alternatives to the complement proposition. Thus expressions like *but it is not the case*, which negates the alternative presented, *but it isn't expected to be the case*, which negates the expectation of the alternative presented, *but maybe not*, which offers a possible alternative, and *or not* which offers equal alternatives, would be incompatible, and expressions like *any* would have to be interpreted with the holistic meaning of all, with no alternatives:

(24   a. We know that he left, *but he didn't/
          *but it isn't expected that he did/
          *but maybe he didn't/*or not
      b. We forced him to leave, *but he didn't/
          *but it isn't expected that he did/
          *but maybe he didn't/*or not

(25) a. We know that he ate *any* he found
      b. We forced him to eat *any* he found

Determined complements, which express an expectation about one alternative but allow for the possibility of alternatives, cannot ocur with expressions like *but it is not the case*, which negate the expected alternative, those like *but is isn't expected to be the case*, which negate the expectation, and those like *or not*, which allow equal possibilities, would be incompatible, but those like *but maybe not* would be compatible, and expressions like *any* would be interpreted with the holistic meaning of an expectation of all, but with alternatives available:

(26) a. I have decided that he left, *but he didn't
          *but it isn't expected that he did/
          *but maybe he didn't/*or not
      b. I have decided to leave, *but I won't/
          *but it isn't expected that I will/
          *but maybe I won't/*or not

(27) a. We decide that he ate *any* he found
      b. We decided to eat *any* we found

With Undetermined complements, which make no claim but allow for the possibility of alternatives, expressions like *but it is not the case*, which negate the alternative presented, and *or not*, which offer equal alternatives, are incompatible, but expressions like *but it isn't expected to be the case*, which negate any claims, and *but maybe not*, which offer alternatives, are compatible, and expressions like *any* are interpreted with the holistic meaning possibly all, but with many alternatives:

(28) a. We hope that he left, *but he didn't/
          but it isn't expected that he did/
          *but maybe he didn't/*or not

      b. We are willing to leave, *but he won't/
          but it isn't expected that we will/
          *but maybe we won't/*or not

(29) a. We hope that he ate *any* he found
      b. We are willing to eat *any* we find

With Indeterminate complements, which make no claims but which offer equal alternatives, the only compatible expression among those above is *or not*, and expressions like *any* are interpreted with the partitive "free choice" meaning of some, one, or none, where alternatives are equally available:

(30) a. We wonder whether he left, *but he didn't/
          ?but it isn't expected that he did/
          ?but maybe he didn't/or not

      b. We wonder whether to leave, *but we didn't/
          ?but it isn't expected that we will/
          ?but maybe we will/or not

(31) a. We wonder whether he ate *any* he found
      b. We wonder whether to eat *any* we find

These constraints require that each Evaluation Modality have associated with it an explicit description of the levels of alternatives available to it. Since conjoined expressions like *but it is not the case* are sentences with their own Polarity and Evaluation Modalities, it would be possible to match the explicitly stated levels of alternatives available with each proposition.

Certain expressions like *any* would have to have two interpretations, one partitive "free choice" interpretation compatible with the equal alternatives of the Indeterminate Modality, and one holistic interpretation compatible with the various levels of restricted alternatives found in the Predetermined, Determined, and Undetermined ranges. When expressions like *any* occur in a sentence, its interpretation would have to be matched with the level of alternatives found in the modality of that sentence.

All of these constraints on the Information and Evaluation Modalities hold true not only for complements, as shown here, but also for other types of sentences as well (cf. Ransom 1981 and 1982). Although the constraints have been exemplified largely with data from English, the same semantic constraints will be found in other languages.

Meaning Restrictions Governed by Higher Predicates

Now that we have discussed ways of representing the predictable restrictions on modality meanings, we are left with ways of representing those complement meanings that are not predictable solely on the basis of the modalities alone. Many of these meanings are governed by a combination of particular higher predicates with certain complement modalities. These meanings consist of certain time reference restrictions on the complement and restrictions on the identity of the complement subject.

First let us look at the restrictions on the time reference of complements embedded under certain higher predicates. There are a small number of higher predicates that require their complements to have the same time reference as they have. While this restriction is predictable for Occurrence Modality complements, it is not predictable for Action Modality complements. Almost all Action complements require a future time reference, as in (32) below, but those embedded under a small number of unpredictable predicates like *force* and *manage* require the same time reference as their higher sentence, as in (33) below:

(32)   a.   At 3, we commanded them to leave
             (= *before 3/*at 3/*after 3*)
             (= after we commanded them)
       b.   At 3, we remembered to leave
             (= *before 3/*at 3/*after 3*)
             (= after we remembered)
       c.   At 3, it is necessary that they leave
             (= *before 3/*at 3/*after 3*)
             (= after saying it is necessary)

(33)   a.   At 3, we forced them to leave
             (= *before 3/*at 3/*after 3)
             (= same time as we forced them)
       b.   At 3, we managed to leave
             (= *before 3/*at 3/*after 3)
             (= same time as we managed)
       c.   At 3, we were able to leave

(= *before 3/*at 3/*after 3)
(= same time as we were able)

If all higher predicates like *force* and *manage* are specified in the lexicon as taking Action complements with the same time reference, then all the other higher predicates taking Action complements could be treated as taking a predictable future time, which could be specified by the redundancy rules. Or else, both of these types of higher predicates could be specified in the lexicon as taking Action complements with a time reference that is either future to or the same as the time reference of the higher sentence. If we allow the time of the higher sentence to be represented by the variable tm, then we can specify the complement time reference for predicates like *force*, *manage*, and *be able* as tm, and the complement time reference for predicates like *command*, *remember*, and *necessary* could be specified as $tm+1$:

(34) a. command:___[Determined Action [NP VP $tm+1$]]
     b. force:___[Predetermined Action [NP VP tm]]

Now let us look at the restrictions on complement subject identity, which are governed by certain higher predicates taking Action Modality complements, what Perlmutter (1971) called the Like and Unlike Subject Constraint and what Postal (1970) called the "control problem".[1] As we saw in Chapter II, all Action Modality complements require their subject to be interpreted as an animate agent who is either self-directed (Like-Subject) or other-directed (Unlike-Subject). Which one it is depends on the higher predicate.

First let's look at cases of higher predicates that require their complement subject to be different from another noun phrase in the higher sentence:

(35) *Warren recommended/beckoned [for Harold/(*Warren) to leave]*

This type of identity restriction is described by Perlmutter's Unlike-Subject constraint and is what has been called here an other-directed construction.

There are other higher predicates that require their complement subject to be identical to the subject of the higher sentence:

(36) *Warren* managed/decided/intended/was able
      [(*for Warren/*Harold) to leave]

This identity requirement is described by the Like-Subject constraint and what has been called here a self-directed construction.

There are other cases which cannot be captured by either the Like-Subject or the Unlike-Subject constraint. One such type involves the requirement that the complement subject must be different from one noun phrase and identical to another, as in the following sentences:

(37) Warren told/forced/persuaded/permitted*Harold* [(for *Harold/*
Warren) to leave]

Although the Unlike Subject constraint and the other-directed analysis can describe the lack of identity between the complement subject and the subject of the higher sentence, neither they nor the Like-Subject constraint can describe the required identity between the complement subject and the indirect object of the higher sentence.

Another identity relation that cannot be captured by Perlmutter's constraints is one found in the following sentences:

(38) a. [(*for Warren/*Bill*) To leave] was easy for *Warren*
b. [(*for Warren/*Bill*) To leave] was important to *Warren*
c. It behooves *Harold* [(for *Harold/*Warren) [to leave]

In each of these sentences, the complement subject is required to be identical to either a prepositional object or a direct object. Neither of these restrictions could be described by the Like-Subject and Unlike-Subject constraints. Although the terms self-directed, as applied to (38a and b), and other-directed, as applied to (38c), can apply to both subject and object complements, they cannot specify exactly the array of nominal roles and their identity relations.

In order to deal with the constraints on complement subject identity, the following selectional restrictions are proposed for higher predicates in the lexicon. These selectional restrictions specify the types of complement modalities that each higher predicate can take, the types of nominal roles its noun phrases can take, and the identity relations among the noun phrases, as shown in the following examples:

(39) a. know: NPa____[Predet Truth: S]
[Indet Truth: S]
[Predet Act: NPa VP]
[Indet Act: NPa VP]
b. manage: NPa____Predet Act: NPa VP (tm)]
c. tell: NPa____NPb [Det Truth: S]
[Indet Truth: S]
[Det Act: NPb VP]
[Indet Act: NPb VP]
d. force: NPa____NPb [Predet Act: NPb VP (tm)]

    e. beckon: NPa____[Det Act: NPb VP]
    f. easy: [Undet Act: NPa VP (tm)]__for NPa
    g. unclear: [Indet Truth: S]____to NPa
                 [Indet Act: NPa VP]____to NPa
    h. behoove: [Det Act: NPa VP]____NPa
    i. necessary: [Predet Act: NPa VP]___to NPa
                 [Predet Act: NPa VP]___to NPb

In expressions like "It is unclear whether to leave" or "It is necessary to leave", although there is no explicit complement subject, there is an implied one, which can be either the speaker or a nonreferential pronoun like "one". It is assumed that there is also an implied prepositional phrase, as in (f), (g), and (i), which the complement subject is identical to.

These selectional restrictions can also be applied to the two exceptional higher predicates *claim* and *pretend*, both of which would have the same restrictions shown in (40) below:

  (40) a. claim: NPa____[Det Truth: S]
                   [Det Truth: (for-to) NPa VP]
        b. pretend: NPa____[Predet Truth: S]
                   [Predet Truth: (for-to) NPa VP]

Both *claim and pretend* can take regular Truth complements, as shown by the first selectional restriction, and they can take an exceptional type of Truth complement that takes a *for-to* complementizer and has an identity constraint on the complement subject.

There is one more restriction on complement meaning that is governed primarily by the higher predicate, but in some cases by a combination of the higher predicate and certain complement modalities. This restriction results from the way negation and modality in the higher sentence interact with the higher predicate.

All higher predicates appear to undergo what's called broad-scope negation which affects the entire construction. Only a few unpredictable higher predicates take a narrow-scope type of negation or modality. Those that do need to be specially marked for which type they take, whether narrow-Scope I, which affects only the higher predicate and not the complement, Narrow-Scope II, which affects both the higher predicate and the complement, and Narrow-Scope III, which applies only with negation and which affects the polarity of the higher predicate and the complement and causes the modality of the complement to shift:

(41) a. regret: NPa____[Predet Truth S] <NS I>
      b. decide: NPa____[Det Truth: S] <NS III>
                   [Det Action: NPa VP] <NS III>
                   [Indet Truth: S] <NS I>
                   [Indet Action: NPa VP] <NS I>
      c. believe: NPa____[Det Truth: S] <NS II>
      d. certain: [Predet Truth: S]____ <NS III>
      e. possible: [Undet Truth: S]   <NS III>

The selectional restrictions presented here would be sufficient to represent all of the time and identity restrictions and the restrictions on higher predicate negation and modality, all of which are governed by a combination of the higher predicate and its complement modalities.

The Representation of Complement Forms

So far we have examined the restrictions on meaning associated with the modalities. Now let us look at some examples of the restrictions on complement forms in English and other languages. Some are predictable on the basis of the modalities, and others are governed by certain higher predicates.

Form Restrictions Predictable from Modality

Higher predicates will be lexically specified for the types of Information and Evaluation Modalities they take. Higher predicates like *regret*, *believe*, *predict*, *watch*, *command*, *be willing* and *be true* will be specified as taking only one set of Modalities (but (c) and (d) can take Indeterminate too):

(42) a. regret: NPa____[Predet Truth: S]
      b. believe: NPa____[Det Truth: S]
      c. predict: NPa____[Det Future Truth: S]
      d. watch: NPa____[Predet Occurrence: S]
      e. command: NPa____[Det Action: NPb VP]
      f. be willing: NPa____[Undet Action: NPa VP]
      g. be true: NPa____[Predetermined Truth: S]

Higher predicates like *remember*, *decide*, *tell*, *hope*, *like*, *prefer*, *wonder* and *happen* will be specified as taking more than one set of modalities:

(43) a. remember:...[Predetermined/Indeterminate;Truth/
               Action]...

     b. decide:...[Determined/Indeterminate; Truth/Action]...
     c. tell:...[Determined/Indeterminate;Truth/Action]...
     d. hope:...[Undetermined; Truth/Future Truth]...
     e. like:...[Predetermined Truth; Undetermined Occurrence]...
     f. prefer:...[Undetermined Future Truth; Determined Action]...
     g. wonder:...[Indeterminate; Truth/Action]...
     h. happen: [Predetermined; Truth/Occurrence]...

Sentence Adverbs and Modals will all be specified in the lexicon for the types of modalities they can represent:

(44) a. absolutely: [Predetermined Truth]
      b. possibly: [Undetermined Truth]
      c. predictably: [Determined Future Truth]
      d. intentionally: [Determined Action]
      e. willingly: [Undetermined Action]

(45) a. must: [Predetermined; Truth/Action]
      b. will: [Predetermined; Future Truth/Action]
      c. may: [Undetermined; Truth/Future Truth/Action]
      d. can: [Undetermined; Occurrence/Action]

Complementizers also will be lexically specified for the types of modalities they represent:

(46) that: [Predetermined/Determined/Undetermined; Truth]
          [Predetermined/Determined; Future Truth]
          [Determined; Action]

(47) for-to: [Predetermined/Determined/Undetermined; Action]
           [Undetermined; Occurrence/Truth]

(48) whether/if: [Indeterminate Truth/Future Truth/Occurrence]

(49) whether (for NP) to: [Indeterminate Action]

For Korean, the complementizers will be specified as follows:

(50) a. *kes*: [Predetermined; Truth/Action]
      b. *ko*: [Determined; Truth/Action]
      c. *ki*: [Undetermined; Truth/Action]
      d. *ci*: [Indeterminate: Truth/Action]

Basque complementizers in certain dialects will be specified as below:

(51) a. *-elako*: [Predetermined; Truth/Future Truth]

    b. *-ela*:   [Determined/Undetermined; Truth/Future Truth]
    c. *-en*:   [Indeterminate; Truth/Action]
    d. *-teko*:   [Predetermined/Determined/Undetermined; Action]

There will be a similar specification in the lexicon for mood forms in English:

(52) Indicative Mood Forms: [Predetermined/ Determined/Undetermined/Indeterminate; Truth], [Predetermined/Determined; Future Truth]

Since the subjunctive mood forms do not occur generally, they will have to be specified with the higher predicates they occur with:

(53) a. recommend: [Determined; Action] [*that*+Present Subjunctive]

      b. wish: [Negative Predetermined; Truth] [Past Subjunctive]

Perhaps even the intonation contours in English should be specified in the lexicon:

(54) a. rising-falling: 2-3-1 [Predetermined/Determined/Undetermined/Indeterminate]

      b. rising-partial falling: 2-3-2 [Undetermined/Indeterminate]

      c. falling-rising: 2-1-3 [Indeterminate]

The specifications given above can account for the case of complement forms that are predictable on the basis of modality.

Form Restrictions Governed by the Higher Predicate

    Now let us look at the forms which are not predictable solely on the basis of modality but rather are governed by particular higher predicates. We have already discussed the exceptional character of the present and past subjunctive. There are also *that* and *for-to* complementizers that occur with certain higher predicates and cannot be predicted on the basis of a general rule:

(55) a. take place: [Predetermined Occurrence: **that** + indicative S]__

      b. watch: NPa____[Predetermined Occurrence: null complementizer S]

      c. pretend: NPa____[Negative Predetermined Truth: S/*for-to* NPa VP]

      d. claim: NPa____[Negative Undetermined Truth: S/*for-to* NPa VP]

While these cases involve individual idiosyncracies of higher predicates, there are also cases that involve small groups of predicates that can be isolated by type. These types could be specified by lexical redundancy rules:

(56) a.   Subject-embedding emotive predicates taking a Predetermined Truth complement can optionally take a *for-to* complementizer

b.   Subject-embedding predicates taking a Predetermined/Determined Action complement can optionally take a *that* + Subjunctive complement

There are certain syntactic variations in word order and grammatical relations that interact with the modalities or with particular higher predicates or types of higher predicates.

There is a rule called Equi NP Deletion which deletes complement subjects that are identical to a noun phrase in the higher sentence. While in languages like Korean, this rule applies in all types of complements, finite or nonfinite, in English, it applies only to *for-to* complementizers and gerunds. We have seen that certain higher predicates taking Action Modality complements require that their complement subjects be identical to one of the noun phrases in the higher sentence, either the director or, in the few cases where there is one, the receiver, and since all Action Modality complements can take *for-to* complementizers, one finds that many Action Modality complements undergo the Equi rule:

(57) a.   *We* managed/decided/tried [to leave]/[*for *us* to leave]

b.   We forced/told/permitted *Margo* [to leave]/[*for *her* to leave]

c.   [*For *us* to leave]/[To leave] was easy/hard/difficult for *us*

d.   It behooved *us* [to leave]/[*for *us* to leave]

e.   It was necessary/essential/important to *us* [to leave]/[*for *us* to leave]

We mentioned the peculiar cases of *pretend* and *claim* which, when they take a *for-to* complementizer, require their complement subject to be identical to the subject of the higher sentence. In these cases, Equi also applies:

(58) a.   *We* pretended [to be angry]/[*for *us* to be angry]

b.   *We* claimed [to be angry]/[*for *us* to be angry]

Finally there are higher predicates that take complements with no identity constraints on their complement subjects, but if the subjects happen to be identical to a noun phrase in the higher sentence, then they undergo Equi.

(59) a. *We* hoped [to win]/[*for *us* to win]
    b. [To win]/[*for *us* to win] is fun for *us*
    c. It amazed *me* [to win]/[*for *me* to win]

Thus Equi can be treated as a general rule which in English applies obligatorily to complements with *for-to* complementizers and gerunds to delete a complement subject that is identical to a noun phrase in the higher sentence.

We pointed out in Chapter V that topicalization, a rule that typically applies to definite noun phrase objects, is more likely to apply to object *that* complements which are Predetermined, and one would expect it to be less acceptable the lower on the Evaluation Scale the complement is:

(60) a. That he left, we regret
    b. That he left, we realize
    c. ?That he left, we believe
    d. *That he left, we hope
    e. *Whether he left, we wonder

    f. That he'll leave, we foresee
    g. ?That he'll leave, we predict
    h. *That he'll leave, we expect

    i. That he leave, we insist
    j. *That he leave, we recommend

Certain rules like Complement Deletion, Parenthetical Formation, Complement Tag Question Formation, WH Movement of complement subjects, and NP Raising tend to occur with particular higher predicates, especially but not exclusively those taking Determined Modality complements:

(61) a. I believe/*regret/*hope he left
    b. He left, I believe/*regret/*hope
    c. I believe/*regret/*hope that he left, didn't he?
    d. Who do you believe/*regret/*hope left?
    e. I believe/*regret/*hope him to have left

(62) a. It seems/happens/*amazed me/is possibe he left
    b. He left, it seems/happens/*is possible/*amazed me
    c. It seems/*happens/*amazed me/*is possible that he left, didn't he?
    d. Who does it seem/happen/*amaze him (Who *is it possible) left?
    e. He seems/happens/*amazed me/*is possible to have left

(63) a. I expect/predict/*foresee she will win
      b. She will win, I expect/predict/*foresee
      c. I expect/*predict/*foresee that she will win, won't she?
      d. Who does she expect/predict/*foresee will win?
      e. I expect/*predict/*foresee her to win

None of these rules apply generally, but rather they are dependent on the particular higher predicate. Since certain predicates tend to take sets of rules, these rules could all be triggered by a feature associated with these higher predicates, like their lack of insulation from movement, deletion, and insertion. Thus a feature like [-insulation] could capture the generalization that certain higher predicates can take all of these rules. Those higher predicates that allow only some of these rules to apply would have to be specified for each rule that they could take.

Summary

Thus we have examined the kinds of meanings, cooccurrence restrictions, and forms that must be accounted for by a description of complements. We have seen the dependency relations between the modality meanings and their cooccurrence restrictions, and we have seen how these meanings interact with complement forms, whether segmental, such as modals, moods, complementizers, etc., or nonsegmental, such as through word order, grammatical relations, or the suprasegmentals of stress, pitch, and juncture. If one is to account for all these interrelations, it seems inevitable that the deep structure must make the modality meanings available to the lexical insertion rules and that the lexicon must make use of the modality meanings for certain selectional restrictions.

The modality meanings, or categorial symbols standing for them, can be generated by the phrase structure rules. Certain cooccurrence restrictions can be accounted for by redundancy rules applying to the modality meanings or categorial symbols, and the lexical insertion rules can make use of modality features associated with lexical forms to generate compatible meanings and forms. Finally, those transformational rules which have particular conditions on their application, like Equi applying only to *for-to* and gerund complementizers, can make use of the forms provided by the lexical insertion rules, or the features, like [-insulated], or the selectional restrictions on rules associates with particular higher predicates.

Although most of what has been said has concentrated on English data, the few cxamples from other languages should be sufficient to show that similar meanings, cooccurrence restrictions, and formal representations occur in other languages. The differences between languages occur in the particular forms used to represent the modalities rather than in the basic meanings themselves.

Also, this study has concentrated on subject and object complements, with only suggestions about the ways that the same meanings, cooccurrence restrictions, and forms function in other types of clauses. Simple, compound, and complex sentence, adjective and adverb clauses as well as other types of noun clauses, need to be studied for the kinds of modality meanings they can represent and the types of forms that are used with them. Although some of the forms seem to be the same, it is surprising that more are not and that languages are not more economical in their use of the same forms to represent the same meanings regardless of the type of sentence used.

We have examined the consequence that this analysis has for the description of language. Now let us look at the consequences that it has for other areas of linguistic study.

Implications of Modality for Linguistics

In studying the history of certain language changes, like modals, mood, complementizers, and other modality bearing forms, it should be easier to describe patterns of meaning-form shifts if one distinguishes between the meanings of the Information and Evaluation meanings and their interactions with polarity meanings, the meanings of higher predicates, and the meanings of discourse purposes.

Using a modular treatment of meanings, rather than the conglomerate approaches described earlier, makes it easier to describe shifts related to modality meanings. For example, as the leveling of inflections in Old English obscured the mood forms, certain higher predicates changed into modal auxiliaries, and these changes in modality forms were accompanied by changes in modality meanings. The higher predicate *magan* changed into the modal auxiliary form *may*, and it retained its Undetermined meaning while changing from a self-directed ability meaning representing Undetermined Action (to have the physical power to do something; He has the strength to ride: *he maeg ridan*, prevalent about 800-1600) to an other-directed permission meaning, also representing Undetermined Action, (*You may go now*, prevalent about 1300 to date), and also to a possibility or eventuality meaning, representing Undetermined Truth and Future Truth (*I may be mistaken/go*, prevalent about 1100 to date) (Traugott 1972: 198).

In comparing language systems, for theoretical or teaching purposes, the modality systems are usually the most problematic because the same types of forms are not always used to represent the modality meanings and because the meanings may consist of different combinations of the Information and Evaluation meanings, the polarity meanings, the meanings of higher predicates, and other conventional meanings. Being able to analyze various types of forms, whether modals, mood complementizers or some other type, as consisting of different combinations of these modality and other meanings would give a clearer basis for comparison. Thus in comparing English and Korean complementizer systems, we can show how the Korean system tends to be based on Evaluation meanings (*kes* is for Predetermined complements, *ko* for Determined, *ki* for Undetermined, and *ci* for Indeterminate) while the English system is based on a combination of Information and Evaluation meanings (*that* for Predetermined, Determined, and Undetermined Truth; *for-to* for Predetermined, Determined, and Undetermined Action; and *whether* for Indeterminate Truth and *whether (for NP) to* for Indeterminate Action).

In studying language acquisition, whether first or second, one could analyze developments or errors in the use of particular forms to represent particular combinations of modality meanings. When do children, or second language learners, first learn to use complementizers, modals, mood, etc., and what errors can be expected? Do children, or second language learners, learn one type of meaning before another? Are certain combinations of meaning more difficult for them to learn than others? Being able to analyze the meanings into their separate components should make it easier to describe which meanings are developing, which are not, and which forms are being associated with which meanings.

In studying language aphasia, it is possible that modality meanings or their forms could be affected. In trying to assist someone in regaining these meanings and forms, it would be helpful to be able to identify which of the modality meanings were missing, and whether they were missing in all of the forms or in only some of them. It would also be helpful to be able to use modality meanings associated with one set of forms to create new connections when other modality meanings or their forms are lost. In studying language in the brain, it would be important to find out how we store and process modality meanings and their related forms.

In studying or teaching sign language, it would seem important to be able to identify ways that the modality meanings and forms in speech correspond to sign language.

In working with computer languages, one would think that the modality meanings of natural language would also play an important part, and being able to break them down into a small number of systematically combinable parts would be far simpler than trying to account for all the possible combinations separately.

In studying the philosophy of language, one needs to be able to distinguish the types of modality meanings that occur in natural language and the ways that their properties resemble or differ from the properties of the modalities of classical logic. The analysis for natural language suggests that logic may have to become more multivalued, representing not only necessary and possible, but other alternatives as well. Furthermore, the separation of epistemic and deontic logics may need to be reconsidered and other causes for their differences provided, as Aristotle proposed.

In areas like sociolinguistics, psychology, or literature, where human personalities and their interactions are studied, the use of modality meanings plays an important part. One could analyze personality types according to which Evaluation Modality range they use. Those that use the Predetermined range would be offering no alternatives, making use of power over others by knowledge or authority, and could be considered by some as aggressive and perhaps impolite. Those using the Determined range would be offering few alternatives, presenting strong or weak claims or pressure, and would be considered assertive. Those using the Undetermined range would be offering more alternatives, presenting no claims or pressure but only positive considerations, and they would be considered polite, perhaps cooperative, but not particularly assertive. Those using the Indeterminate range would be offering equal alternatives, presenting no claims, pressure, or even positive considerations, and they could be considered extremely polite, even wimpy.

In any area involving language, one will find that the modality meanings play an important part, so that it is essential to be able to analyze the kinds of meaning combinations that they occur in and to be able to identify the kinds of forms that they occur with.

Conclusion

We have now looked at the parts that make up the tapestry of complement constructions. We have seen how a multiplicity of sentence meanings and forms can be accounted for by breaking down sentence meaning into a small set of modules and showing how these modules combine to express certain meanings and how complement forms are related to them and their combinations. We have found support for Jespersen's belief that "the main general classifications expressed by grammatical forms will always be found to have some logical foundation" (Jespersen 1965-81)

NOTES

1) Perlmutter's analysis is the first attempt at a semantic approach to constraints on complement subject identity. There have been a variety of syntactic analyses (cf. Rosenbaum (1967), Postal (1970), and Chomsky and Lasnik (1977)).

Rosenbaum had proposed a "minimal distance principle", which was designed to recover uniquely the identity of a deleted complement subject. While this analysis worked for sentences like "Mary wanted to leave" and "Mary told John to leave", it failed for "Mary promised John to leave", where the distance was not minimal, and it failed for "Mary wrote John about leaving", where the deleted NP is not uniquely recoverable.

Postal introduced the term "control problem" to cover the question of which NP determined the deletion of the complement subject. He hypothesized underlying modals to account for which NP was deleted, making use of their deontic (Action) meaning, since coreference usually occurs only with Action complements. He used the unlike-subject, or other-directed modals "should" and "ought" for constructions with unlike-subjects or other-directed constructions, and the like-subject or self-directed modals "will" and "would" for like-subject or self-directed constructions. This attempt to capture the meaning and form relations between modals and complement modalities has been criticized at the beginning of this chapter.

Chomsky and Lasnik treat restrictions on complement subject identity and deletion in a variety of ways. Cases like *manage*, where a complement subject is required to be identical with a matrix NP are treated as having "obligatory control". Since their complement subjects cannot be realized by lexical or pronominal forms, they are assigned a PRO marker. "Rules of control" make use of the properties of the matrix verbs to assign an index representing the proper identity of the complement subject.

Structures with *whether to* complements, where complement subjects are prohibited, are also treated as having "obligatory control" and are also assigned a PRO marker. In these cases, if there is no matrix verb for the "rules of control" to refer to in assigning an index, then an arbitrary index is assigned, as with constructions like "It is unclear whether to leave".

Chomsky and Lasnik distinguish cases of obligatory control with verbs like *manage* and constructions like *whether to* from cases of optional identity, as with verbs like *want*. With optional identity constructions, if the complement subject happens to be identical to a matrix NP, it is represented by a reflexive (PRO-self), which would signal Equi and result in deletion, leaving a trace "t" as distinct from the "PRO" of obligatory control.

This analysis cannot deal with the identity constraints that do not result in deletion, as with the unlike-subject or other-directed constraint on verbs like *beckon for* and *demand that*. Thus, it does not allow a unified treatment of identity restrictions associated with self-directed and other-directed Action complements, some of which result in deletion and some of which do not.

A far simpler analysis is possible when complement modalities are taken into consideration (cf. Ransom 1984b). All matrix predicates have to be specified for the types of complement modalities they can take, and when they take an Action Modality complement, they also have to have specified the identity constraints on the complement subject, whether self-directed or other-directed, or either. Since Action complements can all take infinitive complementizers, Equi can be used to apply to any infinitive complement whose subject is identical with a matrix NP regardless of whether the subject is obligatorily or optionally identical. Thus Equi can apply generally to *for-to* and gerund complements with identical complement subjects, and there is no need for a separate treatment of complement subject identity depending on whether it is obligatory or optional.

A construction like *whether to*, which takes an Action complement, can be treated as having a *whether for-to* complementizer. With higher predicates like *tell*, the complement subject has to be interpreted as other-directed, and with those like *decide*, self-directed. Higher predicates like *be unclear* have an optional "to NP" to which the complement subject must be identical. When the prepositional phrase is omitted, it can be interpreted to be either the person in the immediate context, usually the speaker, or an indefinite person, as can be seen by the reflexives: "It was unclear whether to excuse myself/herself/oneself".

Complement subject identity constraints need to be treated as related to modality, and restrictions on complement subject deletion need to be treated as resulting from either identity or indefiniteness.

REFERENCES

Allwood, Jens, Lars-Gunnar Andersson and Osten Dahl. 1979. *Logic in Linguistics*. Cambridge University Press.

Austin, John L. 1968. *How to Do Things with Words*. J.O. Urmson (ed). Oxford University Press.

Bach, E. and Harms, R. (eds.) 1968. *Universals in Linguistic Theory*. Holt, Rinehart and Winston.

Baker, 1968. *Indirect Questions in English*. Unpublished dissertation, University of Illinois at Urbana-Champaign.

Bierwisch, M. and Heidolph, K.E. 1970. *Progress in Linguistics*. The Hague: Mouton.

Bolinger, D. 1982. "Nondeclaratives from an Intonational Standpoint". In *papers from the Parasession* on Nondeclaratives. Chicago Linguistic Society.

Bresnan, Joan B. 1970. "On Complementizers: Toward a Syntactic Theory of Complement Types". *Foundations of Languages*. 6.3: 297-321.

-----. 1972. *A Theory of Complementation in English Syntax*. Unpublished dissertation, MIT.

Chomsky, Noam. 1965. *Aspects of the Theory of Syntax*. MIT Press.

Chomsky, Noam. and Lasnik, H. 1977. "Filters and Control". *Linguistic Inquiry* 8:3.

Cole, P. (ed). 1978. *Syntax and Semantics 9*. Academic Press.

Cole, P. and Morgan, J. (eds). 1975. *Syntax and Semantics 3*. Academic Press.

Comrie, Bernard. 1981. *Language Universals and Linguistic Typology*. University of Chicago Press.

Costa, Rachel. 1972. "Sequence of Tenses in *That*-Clauses". In *Papers from the Eighth Regional Meeting* of the Chicago Linguistic Society.

Davidson, D. and Harman, G. (eds). 1972. *A Semantics of Natural Language*. Reidel Press.

Dembetembe, N.C. 1976. *The Syntax of Sentential Complements in Shona*. Unpublished dissertation, University of London.

Edmonds, J. 1970. *Root and Structure Preserving Transformations*. Indiana University Linguistics Club.

Fillmore, Charles. 1968. "The case for case", In: Bach and Harms 1968: 1-90.

Givón, Talmy. 1971. "Dependent Modals, Performatives and Factivity: Bantu Subjunctives and What Not". *Studies in African linguistics* 2.1: 61-81.

-----. 1975. "Cause and Control: on the Semantics of Interpersonal Communication". In: Kimball 1975: 59-90.

-----. 1976. "Definiteness and Referentiality". In: Greenberg 1976.

-----. 1980. "The Binding Hierarchy and the Typology of Complements". *Studies in Language* 4.3: 333-377.

Greenberg, J. 1976. *Universals of Human Language.*

Grice, H. Paul. 1975. "Logic and Coversation". In Cole and Morgan 1975: 41-58.

Grimshaw, Jane. 1979. "Complement Selection and the Lexicon". *Linguistic Inquiry.* 10.2: 279-326.

Halliday, M.A.K. 1976. "Intonation and Meaning". In Kress 1976.

Hooper, Joan. 1975. "On Assertive Predicates". In: Kimball 1975: 91-124.

Hooper, Joan, and Sandra Thompson. 1973. "On the Applicability of Root Transformations". *Linguistic Inquiry* 4.4: 465-498.

Horn, Laurence R. 1972. *On the Semantic Properties of Logical Operators in English.* Unpublished dissertation, University of california at Los Angeles.

-----. 1975. "Neg-raising Predicates: Toward an Explanation". *Papers from the Eleventh Regional Meeting of the Chicago Linguistic Society.* 279-294.

-----. 1978. "Remarks on Neg-Raising". In: Cole 1978: 129-220.

Hutchinson, J.P. 1976. *Aspects of Kanuri Syntax.* Unpublished dissertation, Indiana University.

Jacobs, Roderick A. 1981. "On Being Hypothetical". *Papers from the Seventeenth Regional Meeting of the Chicago Linguistic Society*: 99-107.

Jacobs, R. and Rosenbaum, P. (eds). 1970. *Readings in Transformational Grammar.* Ginn.

Jacobovits L. and Steinberg D. (eds). 1971. *Semantics: an Interdisciplinary Reader in Philosophy, Linguistics and Psychology.* Cambridge University Press. 232-296.

Jespersen, Otto. 1965. *The Philosophy of Language.* Norton Press.

Karttunen, Lauri. 1971a. "The Logic of English Predicate Complement Constructions," Indiana Linguistics Club.

-----. 1971b. "Some Observations on Factivity". *Papers in Linguistics* 4: 55-69.

-----. 1971c. "Implicative Verbs". *Language.* 47.2: 340-358.

Karttunen, Lauri. 1977. "The Syntax and Semantics of Questions". In *Linguistic and Philosophy* 1.1: 3-44.

Karttunen, Lauri, and Stanley Peters. 1976. "What Indirect Questions Conventionally Implicate." *Papers from the Twelfth Regional meeting of the Chicago Linguistic Society*.

Katz, J., and Fodor, J. 1964. *The Structure of Language*. Prentice-Hall.

-----. 1964. "The Structure of a Semantic Theory". In: Katz and Fodor 1964: 479-518.

Katz, J., and Postal, P. 1964. *An Integrated Theory of Linguistic Descriptions*. MIT Press.

Keenan, E., and R. Hull. 1973. "Logical Syntax of Direct and Indirect Questions". In: *You Take the High Node and I'll Take the Low Node*. Chicago Linguistic Society.

Kimball, J. (ed). 1975. *Syntax and Semantics 4*. Academic Press.

Kiparsky, Paul, and Carol Kiparsky. 1970. "Fact". In: Bierwisch and Heidolph. 1970. 143-173.

Kress, G.R. 1976. *Halliday: System and Function in Language*. Oxford University Press.

Lakoff, George. 1970. *Irregularity in Syntax*. Holt, Rinehart, and Winston.

-----. 1971. "On Generative Semantics". In: Jacobovits and Steinberg 1971: 232-296.

Lakoff, Robin. 1968. *Abstract Syntax and Latin Complementation*. MIT Press.

Lakoff, Robin. 1970. "Tense and its Relation to Participants" in *Language*: 46.4.

Langendoen, D. Terence. 1968. "Modal Auxiliaries in Infinitive Clauses in English". *Ohio State Working Papers in Linguistics* 3: 114-121.

-----. 1970. "The 'Can't Seem To' Construction". *Linguistic Inquiry* 1.1: 25-36.

Lees, Roberts B. 1960. *The Grammar of English Nominalizations*. Indiana University Press.

Lieberman, Mark, and Ivan Sag. 1974. "Prosodic Form and Discourse Function". *Papers from the Tenth Regional Meeting of the Chicago Linguistic Society*: 416-427.

Lightfoot, David W. 1979. *Principles of Diachronic Syntax*. Cambridge University Press.

Lord, Carol. 1976. "Evidence for Syntactic Reanalysis: from Verb to Complementizer in Kwa". *Papers from the Parasession on Diachronic Syntax*.

Chicago Linguistic Society: 179-191.

Lyons. 1978. *Semantics*. 2. Cambridge University Press.

Maxwell, E.R. 1971. "Aspects of Lithuanian Complementation". *Papers in Linguistics* 4.1: 169-196.

McCawley, James D. 1968a. "Lexical Insertion in a Transformational Grammar without Deep Structure". *Papers from the Fourth Regional Meeting of the Chicago Linguistics Society*: 71-89.

McCawley, James D. 1968b. "The Role of Semantics in a Grammar". In: Bach and Harms 1968: 125-170.

Morgan, Jerry L. 1973. *Presupposition and the Representation of Meaning: Prolegomena*. Unpublished dissertation, University of Chicago.

Na, Young-hee. 1981. "A Constraint on the Lexicalization of negation", *Papers from the Seventeenth Regional Meeting of the Chicago Linguistic Society*. 239-248.

Newmeyer, Frederick J. 1975. "English Aspectual Verbs". The Hague Mouton.

Noonan, Michael. "Complementation". To appear in T. Shopen.

Perlmutter, David. 1970. "The Two Verbs 'Begin'". In: Jacobs and Rosembaum 1970: 107-119.

-----. 1971. *Deep and Surface Constraints in Syntax*. Holt, Rinehart and Winston.

Perlmutter, David, and Paul M. Postal. 1974. Lectures on Relational Grammar. LSA Summer Institute.

Postal, Paul M. 1970. "On Coreferential Complement Subject Deletion". *Linguistic Inquiry* 1.4: 439-500.

Postal, Paul. 1974. *On Raising: One Rule of English Grammar and its Theoretical Implications*. MIT Press.

Ransom, Evelyn N. 1974. *A Semantic and Syntactic Analysis of Noun Complementation Constructions in English*. Unpublished dissertation, University of Illinois at Urbana-Champaign.

-----. 1977. "On the Representation of Modality". *Linguistics and Philosophy* 1.3: 357-379.

Ransom, Evelyn N. 1980. "A Crosslinguistic Analysis of Complement Meanings and Forms". Paper presented at the LSA Winter Meeting.

-----. 1981. "A Crosslinguistic Analysis of Modality". Paper presented at SUNY at Buffalo.

-----. 1982. "The Meanings and Forms of a Type of Nondeclarative Sentence". *Papers from the Parasession on Nondeclaratives*, Chicago Linguistic Society: 168-177.

-----. 1984. *Sentential Modality: Its Meanings and Forms*. (In preparation).

-----. 1984b. "Complement Subjects: Their Identity and Deletion Constraints". (In preparation).

-----. 1986. "Higher Sentence Negation and Complement Meaning". *ESCOL 86*. (To appear).

Riddle, Elizabeth. 1975. "Some Pragmatic Conditions on Complementizer Choice". In *Papers from the Eleventh Regional Meeting of the Chicago Linguistic Society*: 467-474.

-----. 1978. *Sequence of Tenses in English*. Unpublished dissertation, University of Illinois at Urbana-Champaign.

Rogers, A. 1974. *Physical Perception Verbs in English*. Unpublished dissertation, University of California at Los Angeles.

Rosenbaum, Peter S. 1967. *The Grammar of English predicate Complement Constructions*. MIT Press.

Rosenberg, M. 1975. *Counterfactives: A Pragmatic Analysis of Presupposition*. Unpublished doctoral dissertation, University of Illinois at Urbana-Champaign.

Ross, John R. 1967. *Constraints on Variables in Syntax*. Dissertation, MIT, Indiana University Linguistics Club.

-----. 1969. "Auxilliaries as Main Verbs". In: Todd 1969.

-----. 1970. "On Declarative Sentences". In: Jacobs and Rosenbaum 1970.

Ross, John R. 1972. "Act". In: Davidson and Harman 1972.

Sadock, Jerrold. 1969. "Hypersentences". *Papers in Linguistics* 1.2: 283-270.

-----. 1974. *Toward a Linguistic Theory of Speech Acts*. Academic Press.

Schmerling, S. 1978. "Synonymy Judgments as Syntactic Evidence". In: Cole 1978.

Searle, John R. 1970. *Speech Acts*. Cambridge University Press.

-----. 1979. *Expression and Meaning: Studies in the Theory of Speech Acts*. Cambridge University Press.

Shopen, T. et al. (eds). *Language Typology and Syntactic Fieldwork* (To appear).

Steele, Susan. 1975. "Is it Possible?". *Stanford Working Papers on Language Universals* 18.

Takahara, Kumiko. 1972. "The Japanese Modal System". *Linguistics* 81: 92-105.

Todd (ed). 1969. *Studies in Philosophical Linguistics* (Series 1) Great Expectations Press.

Traugott, E. 1972. *A History of English Syntax*. Holt, Rinehart and Winston.
Wales, M.L. 1981. "Parataxis: A Penthouse Next Door?" *Glossa*. 15.1: 53-82.
Wierzbicka, Anna. 1980. *Lingua Mentalis: the Semantics of Natural Language*. Academic Press.
Young, Robert W., and William Morgan. 1980. *The Navajo Language: A Grammar and Colloquial Dictionary*. University of New Mexico Press.

In the TYPOLOGICAL STUDIES IN LANGUAGE (TSL) series the following volumes have been published thus far, and will be published during 1986:

1. HOPPER, Paul (ed.): *TENSE-ASPECT: BETWEEN SEMANTICS & PRAGMA-TICS.* Amsterdam, 1982.

2. HAIMAN, John & Pam MUNRO (eds.): *PROCEEDINGS OF A SYMPOSIUM ON SWITCH REFERENCE, Winnipeg, May 1981.* Amsterdam, 1983.

3. GIVÓN, T. (ed.): *TOPIC CONTINUITY IN DISCOURSE: A QUANTITATIVE CROSS-LANGUAGE STUDY.* Amsterdam, 1983.

4. CHISHOLM, William, Louis T. MILIC & John GREPPIN (eds.): *INTER-ROGATIVITY: A COLLOQUIUM ON THE GRAMMAR, TYPOLOGY AND PRAGMATICS OF QUESTIONS IN SEVEN DIVERSE LANGUAGES, Cleveland, Ohio, October 5th 1981 - May 3rd 1982.* Amsterdam, 1984.

5. RUTHERFORD, William E. (ed.): *LANGUAGE UNIVERSALS AND SECOND LANGUAGE ACQUISITION.* Amsterdam, 1984.

6. HAIMAN, John (ed.): *ICONICITY IN SYNTAX. Proceedings of a Symposium on Iconicity in Syntax, Stanford, June 24-6, 1983.* Amsterdam, 1985.

7. CRAIG, Colette (ed.): *NOUN CLASSES AND CATEGORIZATION. Proceedings of a Symposium on Categorization and Noun Classification, Eugene, Ore. October 1983.* Amsterdam, 1986.

8. SLOBIN, Dan I. & Karl ZIMMER (eds.): *STUDIES IN TURKISH LINGUISTICS.* Amsterdam, 1986. n.y.p.

9. BYBEE, Joan L.: *Morphology. A Study of the Relation between Meaning and Form.* Amsterdam, 1985.

10. RANSOM, Evelyn: *Complementation: its Meanings and Forms.* Amsterdam, 1986.

11. TOMLIN, Russ (ed.): *GROUNDING AND COHERENCE IN DISCOURSE.* Outcome of a Symposium on -, Eugene, Ore, June 1984. Amsterdam, 1986. n.y.p.

12. NEDJALKOV, Vladimir P. (ed.): *TYPOLOGY OF RESULTATIVE CONSTRUCTIONS.* Translated from the original Russian edition publ. by "Nauka", Leningrad, 1983, English translation edited by Bernard Comrie. Amsterdam, 1986. n.y.p.